Five Plus Five Makes Fifteen

· A MEMOIR ·
Barb Gonie

Blessings!
Barb Gonie

◆ FriesenPress

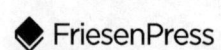

Suite 300 - 990 Fort St
Victoria, BC, V8V 3K2
Canada

www.friesenpress.com

Copyright © 2018 by Barb Gonie
First Edition — 2018

All rights reserved.

No part of this publication may be reproduced in any form, or by any means, electronic or mechanical, including photocopying, recording, or any information browsing, storage, or retrieval system, without permission in writing from FriesenPress.

ISBN
978-1-5255-2066-2 (Hardcover)
978-1-5255-2067-9 (Paperback)
978-1-5255-2068-6 (eBook)

1. BIOGRAPHY & AUTOBIOGRAPHY, PERSONAL MEMOIRS

Distributed to the trade by The Ingram Book Company

Five Plus Five Makes Fifteen

Table of Contents

ix	Preface
1	Chapter 1: Meet my Family: My Thirteen Siblings
5	Chapter 2: My Mom (Evelyn Ruth Hellekson)
8	Chapter 3: Grandma Hellekson
11	Chapter 4: My Dad (Joe Burge)
14	Chapter 5: Grandpa (George Burge)
17	Chapter 6: Grandma (Joanna Burge)
19	Chapter 7: Uncle Leonard Burge
21	Chapter 8: Moving On
23	Chapter 9: Home, Sweet Home
25	Chapter 10: First Twins (Nioma And Nelson)
28	Chapter 11: Great Grandma (Sarah Timmoth)
32	Chapter 12: Moving To Grandpa's
37	Chapter 13: My Brother Lloyd
41	Chapter 14: Welcome To My World (Barbara)
44	Chapter 15: My Sister Judy
47	Chapter 16: Big Moves For All
50	Chapter 17: Twin Boys (Grant and Graham)
52	Chapter 18: Time Away From Home
57	Chapter 19: A Rough Ride
60	Chapter 20: Another Work Day
63	Chapter 21: Mom's Love For Poetry
64	Chapter 22: Grandpa Burge's Homestead Is Sold
68	Chapter 23: Back To The Meadow Quarter
76	Chapter 24: Fun Chores

79	Chapter 25: The More The Merrier
83	Chapter 26: My Family Faces Death
86	Chapter 27: The Third Set Of Twins (George And Leonard)
89	Chapter 28: The Fourth Set Of Twins (Lillian and Lewis)
91	Chapter 29: Another Baby (Debra)
93	Chapter 30: A Tough Year
97	Chapter 31: We Welcomed Each Season (Fall)
103	Chapter 32: Winter
105	Chapter 33: Spring
107	Chapter 34: Summer
109	Chapter 35: More Twins (Lance and Laura)
111	Chapter 36: Hair Day
112	Chapter 37: Moving From the Meadow
116	Chapter 38: Homemade Entertainment
119	Chapter 39: Prayer of Gratitude
125	Chapter 40: Grandpa Hellekson
128	Chapter 41: Grandma Ruth Visits
131	Chapter 42: Life Improves
135	Chapter 43: Boogie Bus
138	Chapter 44: I Take The Wheel
141	Chapter 45: Leaving The Nest
143	Chapter 46: The Last Sibling (Josephine)
147	Chapter 47: Fishing Day
150	Chapter 48: Instilling Faith
155	Chapter 49: School Days
162	Chapter 50: Mom Said Goodbye To Grandma
174	Chapter 51: Our School House Home
177	Chapter 52: Nioma Becomes A Mother
180	Chapter 53: I'm A Bride!
185	Chapter 54: Moulding Together
189	Chapter 55: Granddad Gonie:
191	Chapter 56: It's Just Me!
196	Chapter 57: New Life With A Family (Dan, Joe, Angie, Bart)

200	Chapter 58: Time for Frills
205	Chapter 59: My Last Baby Boy
207	Chapter 60: Sunday Is For Rest
213	Chapter 61: Our Kids Grow Together
217	Chapter 62: An Unforgettable Trip
220	Chapter 63: I Fear For Lloyd's Health
222	Chapter 64: Sickness Strikes (Cattle)
225	Chapter 65: Fishing Day — The Next Generation
233	Chapter 66: Problems At The Lake
235	Chapter 67: Facing My Trials
238	Chapter 68: Changes Come
242	Chapter 69: My Family Is Split
247	Chapter 70: Mom Meets Albert
250	Chapter 71: Dan
258	Chapter 72: We Have A Son in-law
262	Chapter 73: Lloyd's Siblings
265	Chapter 74: Life Continues
267	Chapter 75: We Lose A Brother-In-law (Paul)
270	Chapter 76: Time For Changes
274	Chapter 77: Losing a Sibling (Lloyd Burge)
276	Chapter 78: The Open Road
280	Chapter 79: My Grandson's Accident
295	Chapter 80: Family Fun
298	Chapter 81: Reaching Out to In-Laws
302	Chapter 82: Looking Forward To A Celebration
305	Chapter 83: My Sisters And Brothers

Preface

The following words are glimpses of my memories as I learned to laugh, pray, and work with my siblings. I had six sisters and eight brothers; one brother died at birth. Eighteen years separate my oldest and youngest sisters. Each of my siblings shared a variety of different talents, and characteristics.

I started my journey in life in the small town of Pierceland, Saskatchewan, where the country schools were part of the landscape. The school in my area was called Black Raven, S.D., number 5122. Some other schools in the area were Deer Haven, Chocolate Valley, Glenvale, Mudie Lake, Northern Pine, Smoky Hill, and Venusberg.

Life in the Forties was much different from the life that we know in the third millennium. Today's amenities of power and indoor plumbing, as well as living in a large house with only a child or two were not the norm. I acquired wisdom as I faced hardships, joys, and rewards in my large family.

I never considered myself poor, deprived, or different from any other family; I just lived in a fuller house. Five sets of twins and five single births was the norm for me. I don't remember the hardship with another birth. I just remember that another place was set at our table, and another body needed to squeeze into a full bed. I enjoyed my childhood. I had many people to help with the chores, and we had enough players for a ball team too. I am thankful for each unique sibling who walked along the road of life with me. I was never alone, and I started a new adventure each day into the wondrous unknown world.

I flourished from my school years to my first job, and then on to marriage. I didn't know many of life's pleasures, but I dreamed of becoming rich and living in a big mansion. The world had much to offer, and I had my own ideas for a better future: a job and a career.

I matured and married a local farmer. We raised our four children in the same area that we both grew up in.

My dreams changed, but I learned that I was "rich" with my many siblings, a good husband, and children to help me know how to love. I found a fulfilling life a radius of 32 kilometers from the place where I was born. I discovered that: "Our big family may not have had it all together, but together we had it all."

Chapter 1:
Meet my Family: My Thirteen Siblings

Some siblings

The children of Joseph and Evelyn Burge:

Nioma Irene was born in Edson, Alberta on Nov. 23, 1943.
Nelson Joseph was born in Edson, Alberta on Nov. 23, 1943.
Lloyd Raymond was born in Cold Lake, Alberta on Feb. 5, 1946.
Barbara Ann was born in Pierceland, Saskatchewan on Dec. 12, 1947.
Judy Evelyn was born in Pierceland, Saskatchewan on Feb. 18, 1949.
Graham Harold was born in Pierceland, Saskatchewan on Oct. 1, 1950.
Grant Malcolm was born in Pierceland, Saskatchewan on Oct. 1, 1950.
Leonard was born in Goodsoil, Saskatchewan on Jan. 28, 1953.
George Earl was born in Goodsoil, Saskatchewan on Jan. 28, 1953.
Lillian Rose was born in Goodsoil, Saskatchewan on Feb. 24, 1954.
Lewis Robert was born in Goodsoil, Saskatchewan on Feb. 24, 1954.
Debra Mary was born in Goodsoil, Saskatchewan on Oct. 25, 1956.
Laura Kathleen was born in Goodsoil, Saskatchewan on April 9, 1958.
Lance James was born in Goodsoil, Saskatchewan on April 9, 1958.
Josephine Elizabeth was born in Goodsoil, Saskatchewan on Feb. 23, 1961.

Take my hand, and I will lead you back in time to my childhood and my family, known as the "Twin Family."

My parents are Evelyn and Joseph Burge. Ten of my siblings are twins; yes, my mother gave birth to five sets of twins and five single births, making us a large family. (One twin brother died shortly after birth.) I will always wonder how my parents survived in a small house with fourteen bodies under foot. I know from raising my own family that kids are not happy every day. How were my parents able to cope with sick kids, crabby kids, and the other trials that life often holds?

There were no aunties, uncles, in-laws, or grandparents living nearby. Mom and Dad both were raised away from their parents: Mom with her grandparents and a sister; and Dad with his dad and a brother. Was this the reason for Mom and Dad's determination to keep us together as a family? I married, and we had four children within five years. I know how hard it is to keep every child happy, and *I* never had to wonder what I had in the house to cook for meals. Wow, Mom: You were blessed with good health for yourself and your children.

I had a good childhood and felt that my family had everything: three meals a day, a horse to ride, and both Mom and Dad lived with us to make a complete family.

My friend, Pat Thomas, lived with her granny because her parents were divorced. Her granny was a great person, but Pat never saw her dad. I thought that was heartbreaking. I recall going with my dad in the cutter (a small, one-horse, closed-in sleigh with an opening in front for the reins to pull through for the driver) when he trapped muskrats on the small lake. There was a little stove in the closed-in area. We took a lunch to eat. Dad placed my sandwich on the stove and toasted it. The smell of those burnt crumbs lasted a long time. It's a good memory.

The muskrat traps were checked on the way along the lake and on the way back too. Dad skinned the rats, put the hides into a gunny sack, and left the carcass in the bush for a hungry coyote or a fox to eat. The hides were taken home to be stretched and dried. The stretcher was made from a board with a curbed top where the skinned rats head were placed. The fur side was placed onto the board, and the skin side was scraped until all the fat and flesh of the rat was gone. After a few days, the hide was dry and taken off the board. Dad took the fur into Pierceland to be sold. The fur was sold at McClellan's, the local store. This store operated for about seventy years, passed down to the son, who operated it in the same way that his dad had. The store was later sold, but it still stands in its original spot.

Now back to Pat: I felt bad for Pat because she never saw her dad, and I vowed that I would never allow my family to be separated when I matured and chose to marry. How hard it was for me to understand how Pat's dad never was a part of her life. Everybody needs a dad as part of their family. My family lived together in a small house where we learned to love and support each other.

I liked Pat's Scottish granny. She was a short lady with a round face and a good sense of humour. Sometimes she sat on the bed near us and told us stories of Scotland; she talked funny. Granny allowed Pat and me to talk or play cards into the night and then sleep in until noon. Granny cooked us macaroni with tomatoes when we got up. Mom never allowed us to sleep in. I can understand why. She needed to have everyone together at the table so that breakfast would be over, and she could start the many jobs that waited her attention. Mom had to run her household like a business with everything done on time and in a routine. Mom taught her kids how to be organized and to keep a schedule. My meals were on time when I raised my family too.

Chapter 2:
My Mom (Evelyn Ruth Hellekson)

My mom, Evelyn Ruth Hellekson, was born on October 29, 1924 in Edson, Alberta to Harry and Ruth (Timmoth) Hellekson.

Mom's hair was short, dark, and without any curl. She never liked her hair and wished she had curly hair like her sister, Irene. Mom is a determined woman — a hard worker, and a leader who can keep everyone busy. Her small, short frame didn't stop her from any jobs. Mom organized the inside chores and then went outdoors to get Dad moving as she worked beside him at most jobs. I often thought of Mom as an army sergeant. She ruled us all and kept us in line. I know that each of her children are better citizens because she forced us to take responsibility and get the job done before we ran off to play; work came first.

Mom never had the chance to get close to her mother, as my grandma moved away when Mom was five years old, and she didn't return for many visits. I can only imagine the hurt that Grandma carried to her grave, as a mother longs to be with her children, but will do what is best for everyone involved. Grandma made the choice to stay out of her girl's life and allowed her daughter's dad and grandma to take charge. Did Grandma make the best choice? I think so.

My paternal grandmother, Grandma Hellekson, was the caregiver for Mom and her sister Irene for about ten years. A recent visit with my cousin Sarah helped me to see that love had turned to hate for Mom's parents; they didn't want to be in the same room with each other.

My cousin Sarah cared for Mom's mother, Grandma Ruth, in her last years. Grandma Ruth told Sarah that she and Grandpa Harry were on a wagon ride during the fall hunting season. They stopped for a rest and a lunch. Grandpa went to put a dark horse blanket on his horse. It was in the fall of the year, and a hunter was out hunting for the winter's meat supply. The hunter thought that the horse was a moose and shot.

Mom recalls a man running from the bushes and screaming; he had shot Grandpa Hellekson and came to get help. Grandpa was shot in the hip. He was taken to the railroad track where they flagged down the train, and he was transported to Edson, Alberta. The doctor in Edson had worked on many gunshot wounds in the war. Grandpa spent three months in the hospital as his injuries healed. What pain he must have suffered. I'm surprise that he didn't get an infection. Mom's father, Grandpa Harry, was a hard man to live with. He was a short, stubborn man who demanded his way when doing things. His short brown hair was well groomed; he thought that all men should look their best at all times because life was to be enjoyed. He loved to dance and go on different outings without any thoughts of the work that needed to be done the following day. He often stated, "I'll worry about tomorrow when it comes." Grandpa had a care-free spirit.

Grandma Ruth needed help with the chores when Grandpa was in the hospital. She hired a young bachelor man, "Blondie," who lived in the area. I guess he did all the chores. A relationship developed between him and Grandma, and she became pregnant. She felt that she had shamed the family and was no longer welcome in that area. She left with Blondie, the hired hand.

Mom's father returned from the hospital a few months later. Her mother took Irene, Mom's sister, and went to her own mother's home. Mom was left with Grandma Hellekson and felt that her mother had chosen Irene over her. But eventually, her father went and brought Irene back to live with him and my mom. Mom was five years old and missed her mother. "I cried myself to sleep for many nights, I was mad at everyone," Mom said to me.

My mom always felt that everybody noticed Irene; she had curly hair and was pretty. Irene loved all the remarks about her hair. Mom was the quiet one and never seemed to have any attention. Mom said, "I was big and fat with straight hair. Why would anyone talk to me?" Mom felt that she could not measure up to Auntie Irene, and these feelings remained with her.

Mom remembers that she and Aunty Irene received beautiful dolls for Christmas that first year. It was many years later that Mom learned the dolls she and her sister had received at Christmas time had been sent to them by their mother. No one bothered to tell the girls who had sent the precious gift. Santa Claus must have delivered them.

The girls lived with their dad and Grandma Hellekson for ten years. Mom remembered her daddy coming home from the hospital. Mom said, "I ran to my daddy when he came home from the hospital. He had spent about three months there, and I missed him. Daddy stretched out his arms to hold me." Mom also told me that the hired man slipped out the back window at the same time. Oh, the things we recall.

Mom's mother and "Blondie" moved to British Columbia. They were married, and together they had a set of twins (Alva and Eric), two sons (Jack and Dean), and a daughter (Darlene Stahl). Eric died at an early age. There was also a tragic accident when Jack was about ten years old. Grandma Ruth had a gun in the house, and she kept it loaded as she was taught to always be prepared. Grandma and Blondie went to town and left the kids alone. Alva and Jack were playing house, and Jack took down the gun. The gun went off, and Alva was shot. She died in the hospital shortly after. Jack carried this event to an early grave — a suicide death when he was in his late fifties. Jack married Doreen, and together they had a daughter, Juanita. Mom wasn't close to her step-family due to the large distance; Mom didn't have the means or the money to travel. Years later, Mom was united with her mother, and her step-family, but this relationship was never warm.

Chapter 3:
Grandma Hellekson

Mom said her paternal grandmother, Grandma Hellekson, who raised her, was a gentle and caring person. She was small — about five feet tall, and she had a twenty-inch waist. She liked her jewellery and pretty dresses. Her appearance was important to her. She always put on a clean apron before serving her company. Grandma was a good cook, and many people had a good meal at her house. Grandma made pies and cookies to serve to everyone, but there was only one cookie or one piece of pie — no more — for each person.

I liked Grandma Hellekson. She was a sweet lady, who came to visit Mom and her family when I was growing up.

As a young girl, Grandma Hellekson lived on a ranch in South Dakota along the White River. Grandma moved to Camrose, Alberta, when she married Grandpa. This lady was a horse lady. She drove her team, Babe and Lass, and she also rode horses. Grandma's parents were Anna Marie (Amundson) and Nels Anderson from South Dakota. The family had lived across the White River by the Oglala Indian Reserve. Grandma knew both of the chiefs from the reserves — White Blanket and Strange Horse, who had been in the battle of the "Little Big Horn".

Mom's young life, growing up without her mother, had much pain. Mom's father worked with his brothers on the farm, and they shared the income from the farming. It seems to me that the brothers didn't always see eye to eye; one always thinking he did more work than the other boys.

Here is a painful incident that Mom recalled with tears: Grandpa and his brothers had a dispute over the crop. Grandpa was told that he wouldn't get his share of the crop because he hadn't helped with the seeding in the springtime. Without a crop share, Grandpa needed to go to work away from the farm. Grandpa took his girls to stay with their maternal grandmother, Grandma Timmoth. Grandma Hellekson was full of tension, and his girls didn't need to be there. Mom was thirteen years old, and Aunty Irene was three years younger. I can just feel the heartbreak that Grandma Hellekson had when her boys were fighting, and then when her grandchildren were uprooted from her home; it would have been so devastating. The girls were "plucked" away from her loving arms because her son needed to leave and find work. Mom's heart was filled with sadness.

Mom was a teenager, and a hole was left in her heart as she longed for Grandma Hellekson, the mother figure who she had come to love. Grandma remained a big part of Mom's life after she married and had her kids. Mom recalls the move to Grandma Timmoth's. The weeks were long and not much fun. But on Sunday, Grandma attended church, and Mom could expect a visit from her daddy. What a brightness he brought to this household when he came to visit his girls and have supper with Grandma.

Grandpa worked away from the farm for about a year. When he returned to his farm, the girls were settled in at Grandma Timmoth's and were managing fine. There was no need to move them again.

Mom knew that each grandma was of a different nature and had different demands. Grandma Hellekson was warm and gentle and enjoyed having fun like picnics and dancing. Grandma Hellekson said, "Life is to be enjoyed."

Grandma Timmoth was strict and firm. She kept the girls busy through the teen years and didn't think that fun was important. Their days were filled with useful work. Grandma often stated, "We all must earn our keep, and work was the best way to keep kids out of trouble. There's no need to have pretty dresses and jewellery to work."

Mom was sixteen when she left Grandmas Timmoth's to go to high school in Edson. Her daddy found Mom work after school to pay for her room and board. Mom worked for a senior couple, who had a spinster daughter who was a school teacher. The man was bed-ridden and the woman was legally blind. After school, the daughter helped Mom care for her parents.

Mom learned how to cook, clean, and be organized. All things had to be put back in the right spot for the blind lady so that she could open a drawer and find what she needed without feeling around for a long time. This lady would tell Mom, "Go to the drawer by the china cabinet, and on the right-hand side of the drawer is my nail file." What a start Mom had to the working world!

Today Mom is in her nineties, and her drawers are still well organized. I remember Mom insisted that we keep our dresser drawers clean. She would come into our rooms and dump everything out on to the bed, and we needed to put things back in an orderly fashion. I soon learned to keep my drawers neat and tidy.

Later Mom worked at the Edson bakery; another great opportunity to learn how to cook in large quantities.

Mom finished grade eleven before moving on to work. Her father found a job for her at the logging camp. Grandpa said, "I'm working as the barn boss at the logging camp. Evelyn, you should come to work here because you could make better money working at a 50-man camp."

Mom's life took a new twist. There was no more school. Mom said, "It was hard to leave school and the bakery job I loved, but I didn't think I could disappoint Daddy." Mom followed her dad's advice and went to the logging camp to work.

Mom worked near her daddy for the winter months, but in the spring, Grandpa returned to his farm. Mom stayed at the camp to work. Mom often ponders, "How different my life could have been if I had stayed working at the bakery."

Chapter 4:
My Dad (Joe Burge)

Burge coat of arms

My dad, Joseph Raymond Burge, was born on March 19, 1915 in St. Peter's Bay, Prince Edward Island. The son of George Burge, he was the oldest child in his family. I can see why Dad caught Mom's eye. Dad was tall and slim with dark hair and blue eyes. I'm told that he resembled his mother's side of the family.

As a child, Dad was a determined kid and often found a way to entertain himself. He attended school and loved to learn. He became self-taught man in many things. I do remember Dad cooking, but when it came to helping Mom change, bath, or dress the kids, Dad didn't offer any help. I also recall Dad tossing things around. He had a temper that he often didn't control and trouble found him. I can assume he acted before he had thought.

Dad read everything he got his hands on — especially sports articles. (I recall the Joe Lewis fights that held his attention on the radio. The battery on the radio was saved for listening to news and his sports.) Dad had big dreams of become rich, and this dream never did leave him. He liked to gamble, buy tickets, and enter his name in all contests. I remember that he won a corncob whistle that was yellow and resembled a cob of corn. This big win arrived in the mail. His comment was, "Now that was a corny prize to win." Dad also won a snow mobile in 1963.

My dad moved with his father, Grandpa Burge, from the Eston, Saskatchewan area to Pierceland, Saskatchewan. Dad drove a team of four horses to his new home, and his brother Leonard and his father each drove a team of two horses for our neighbours, Robert and Hazel Little. All the family's possessions were loaded in the wagons. One wagon had grain loaded, and the others had their possessions for their new life in Pierceland.

It was later in the fall when Robert and Hazel Little arrived in Pierceland by car. There was 15 centimetres of snow for their model "A" Ford car to drive through. This was one of the first cars in the Pierceland area. The Littles filed for a homestead about five kilometres east from Grandpa Burge's homestead. It was situated on the trail to the town of Pierceland, Saskatchewan.

Grandpa Burge filed for a homestead about 5 kilometres west of Pierceland. After a year of living on the homestead, a title would be issued for 5 dollars. The Quarter of SW-6-26-62-W3 became Grandpa's homestead quarter. There were very few roads in this area because it was only beginning to open to settlers. A railroad grade was started to connect Saskatchewan and Alberta. The railroad grade was never finished, and no train came to this area. I was told that the horses got sick with swamp fever and many died. That was the end of the work on the railroad grade, although the railroad grade became the travelled road to Pierceland, Saskatchewan.

A local family, the Lillicos, owned a saw mill near the Beaver River about five kilometres south of Pierceland. Grandpa and Dad found work at the Lillico mill, as Grandpa had worked with an axe falling trees in earlier years and had knowledge of the bush. With this work they were able to buy lumber and shingles to build a two-storey house on Grandpa Burge's homestead. It was a structure about 6 by 7 metres. (Bill Gonie Jr. now lives there.)

The Burges and Littles were not the only families making Pierceland their home. In 1933, many homesteads became available in Northern Saskatchewan, including in the Pierceland area, and many settlers moved north to seek a better living for their families.

I found a story about the Depression in our pioneer's book:

1929: Dried out.

1930: Frozen out.

1931: Dried out.

1932: Hailed out.

1933: Grasshoppers ate us out.

1934: Dried out.

1935: Rusted out.

1936: Dried out.

1937: Blown out.

1938: Moved out. Pierceland, here we come!

Chapter 5:
Grandpa (George Burge)

As a young lad of about fourteen, Grandpa George Burge went to Maine and became an accomplished axe man. Later, Grandpa returned to Prince Edward Island. It was there that he met his future wife, Joanna Gorman.

He was a small man with blue eyes and a soft voice. Mom told me that Grandpa Burge was a very determined man and wasn't afraid to tackle any job. He liked to work, and he picked rocks by the moonlight. Grandpa said, "The day just doesn't have enough hours."

George Burge was born into the family of Thomas Burdge Sr., who originated from England. It was about 1900, when the spelling changed from Burdge on Thomas' certificate of immigration to "Burge."

Legend has it that a large family of "Burdges" landed on the North Shores of P.E.I. in the 1800's. It is believed that the father of this family had served in the British Navy and had visited P.E.I. in 1790. The Burdge families were Anglican, but since there was no Anglican Church in that area, they settled at (Five Houses) and attended the Roman Catholic Church at St. Peters Bay.

The family had left Somersetshire because of inheritance laws. All properties went to the eldest son; this son was not married. When he died, the property was given to the next of kin. The income from the property in Somersetshire was received by the P.E.I. Burdges. Some of the family needed to return to England to finalize the claim. Failing that, the estate would automatically revert to the British Chancery. Some of the Burdge sons set sail for England. No word was ever received of them. It is known that they did *not* arrive in England; it was assumed that they died at sea. That ended all hope of any inheritance for the Burge family.

The memories I have of Grandpa Burge are few, but very vivid. Grandpa Burge had curly, grey hair. He did not like his curls and tried to straighten them by soaking them with water, but soon the curls bounced back.

This small frame of a man could hold his temper. If he became angry, his words of frustration were, "Oh sugar" or "Jumping Moses." I never did hear him swear. Grandpa always walked with a limp. (Mom said that he had broken his hip when he was a young lad working in the bush.)

I remember Grandpa's small, twisted fingers wrapped around his black rosary beads. He prayed, as he limped along to Sunday mass to give thanks for the week's blessings. He walked to church a long way ahead of Grandma; maybe she was to slow for him. His thinking was, "Mass was a good way to give thanks for last week's blessings and a good way to ask for blessings before starting the new week."

I remember staying at Grandpa Burge's; we shared tea and some store-bought biscuits from his pantry by the stove. I saw Grandpa kneel by his bed on the cold floor to say his night prayers. (I lie in my warm bed.)

My friend Chris also remembers Grandpa kneeling by the bed to pray. How was I to know that Chris and I would become lifelong friends? We went to school together, made our first communion together, and then we both married farmers. Now we live 2 kilometres apart. We don't visit a lot, but we have a relationship that withstands the trials of life, and each of us knows that the other is there when needed. We are able to pick up from wherever we left off.

When my parents lived with Grandpa Burge at one point in their marriage, Grandpa helped Mom. He carried in the drinking water and emptied the slop pail, and in the winter time, he kept the snow shovelled to the clothes line. Mom could walk along the shovelled line to hang the sheets and overalls outdoors without walking in snow to her knees. Grandpa said to Mom, "Your children are busy and you need to put your energy toward caring for them. I have always been a chore boy."

Mrs. Little told Mom that Grandpa said, "Evelyn was a good wife and mother." Grandpa never told Mom this. What a boost Mom would have had hearing that come from her father-in-law. I'll try to give praise more often, and thank the people who are there to make my life easier; often I take others for granted and carry on in a quiet way.

Most of the memories Mom has of Grandpa are good. Mom said, "You know that everybody has some faults. Your Grandpa Burge would remind me often that Joe and his family was living at *his* place. That hurt, but I couldn't do a thing to change it."

I know how important it is for women to have a place that to call their own. A house is a woman's castle. Women like to hang curtains, pictures, and articles that make their home unique. I wouldn't want anybody telling me I couldn't change the décor of my home. I am queen in my home.

Mom begged Dad for a place to call *their* own. In the summer of 1950, Dad and Mom leased a quarter of land about 1.5 kilometres south of Grandpa's homestead and left the comfort of his two-storey house.

Chapter 6:
Grandma (Joanna Burge)

Dad's mother, Joanna (Gorman) Burge, was born in P.E.I. I recall Mom telling me that Joanna was a tall, slim lady. She took after her dad's side of the family, who were tall people. Dad said, "Grandpa Gorman was a tall man; he just stepped over a gate rather than stopping to open it." Two of Dad's sons, George and Lewis, are over six feet, like the Gorman side of his family. How sad it is that I don't know any more of my great-grandparents.

Grandpa George and Joanna Gorman met, and they soon were married. This marriage brought forth three children: Joseph Raymond, Leonard, and Mary. Joanna and George Burge lived on a small potato farm with their three children. Times were hard when the potato crop failed. Grandpa thought it was best to go west where there was more work. This was in the twenties — about 1922 — and they ventured in search of a better life. They took Mary and Leonard with them. Joe, my dad was attending school, and stayed behind with the Gorman grandparents (his maternal grandparents). Grandpa George and Joanna moved to Eston, Saskatchewan. Grandpa worked at anything he could while in the west. About a year later, Dad's parent returned to P.E.I. to get him and take him with them to Eston. I'm not sure why Grandpa chose Eston to live in. Times were hard, and soon their marriage ended. Grandma Joanna left with their only daughter, Mary, and went to Calgary, Alberta.

Prince Edward Island was left behind as a memory for many years. Dad never recalled any details, and he didn't speak of his former dwelling. I don't recall Dad ever speaking of his mother; maybe he didn't have any memory of her either, as he was young when he and his brother moved away from their mother and sister.

Grandpa raised his two sons alone. Dad was about twelve years old, and Leonard was about ten years old when this family was split. Dad and Uncle Leonard learned to work; they both could cook and care for their own needs. Grandpa Burge must have been concerned about how he would raise his boys and keep them out of trouble. As a parent, I know that he would have been. Dad didn't keep in touch with his mother and his sister, who lived in Calgary Alberta.

Chapter 7:
Uncle Leonard Burge

Dad's brother, Leonard, was muscular with a shorter and fuller build than Dad. He had blue eyes too, but his hair was blond. I remember Uncle Leonard as a soft-spoken man, who had time to talk to everyone. He was different from Dad. I was a teenager the first time I met him, but he soon became my special uncle with a big smile.

George Little, a son of the family that Dad and Grandpa had helped moved to Pierceland, was going back to Eston to visit his family. He asked Nioma and me to go along. This was the first trip that I remembered taking. We ate at the café, and we had ice cream too. It was great!

Uncle Leonard Burge entered the forces as a young lad. Dad had dreams of also joining the forces, but Dad had a heart condition that prevented that from happening. When Uncle Leonard came home from the forces, he returned to Eston, Saskatchewan. He met Aunt Amy who became the love of his life. They were married and raised six children: Gary, Lynn, Pat, Jim, Beth, and Tom. I only met these cousins a few times, and I was never close to them. Uncle Leonard and Aunt Amy passed away, and my family lost touch with our Burge cousins.

I remember Uncle Leonard's blue eyes that seemed to dance when he laughed. He was so different from my dad, and expressed more emotion. I was hurt when my Uncle Leonard passed away, and only my brother Lance attended the funeral. Lance was working in the area and about the same age as our cousin Tom. He arrived at Uncle Len's to visit Tom and was shocked at seeing the hearse in front of their house. Lance recalled how hard it was to be the only Burge cousin at the service. Nobody had called Mom or any one of us to tell us about the funeral. Mom was disappointed, but it is what it is.

Chapter 8:
Moving On

As a young lad, Dad got itchy feet and wanted to make more money than what he was making at the sawmill in Pierceland, Saskatchewan. He felt that with his logging experience he could make better money in a bigger area. Dad went with a group of men to Edson, Alberta. Dad found work at the logging camp, where Mom worked as a cook's helper.

Mom recalls when she first met Dad. She said, "Joe was sick for a few days and stayed in camp. One afternoon, Joe came to the kitchen and helped me peel potatoes for supper. The camp was feeding fifty men, three meals a day."

Mom was drawn to Dad's big blue eyes, dark hair, and his will to help her in the kitchen. It wasn't long before Mom and Dad enjoyed one another's company. Sparks began to fly. It was a short courtship, and Mom and Dad were engaged on Valentine's Day, February 14, 1943. A few short months later, on April 4, 1943, they were married in Edson, Alberta. Mom never had any of the frills or fringes that most bride do. It was a simple ceremony, and nobody rejoiced or congratulated this young couple. Mom said that there was the minister and a couple to sign the certificate. Mom's sister, Irene, and her daddy were not at the wedding. How hard that must have been for Mom as the wedding day is often the most precious day for a woman to remember.

Dad hadn't seen his mother for years, so he took his new bride

Evelyn to Calgary to meet her. The road from Edson, Alberta to Calgary, Alberta must have been quite a long way. I think the couple rode the train because I don't think they owned a vehicle. The distance from Edson to Calgary is about 447 kilometres

Was that a hard visit for Dad and Mom? It must have been painful to recall, as that visit was not spoken of. Mom said that she and Dad lived in Calgary for a short time and rented a small place. Dad worked for a large company, Imperial Oil. Dad soon got bored and didn't think that he was moving up fast enough, so he quit his job.

Mom and Dad went back to Edson, Alberta. Not long after, Dad got word that Grandma was sick. His mother was diagnosed with a brain tumour. Grandma deteriorated quickly from this disease. She knew that she was a grandparent, however, she never saw the twins. Grandma Gorman Burge died in January 1944 in Calgary, Alberta. Mom didn't say if Dad was able to attend his mother's funeral or if he heard about her death in time.

I feel sad that I don't know anything more about Dad's mother, my grandmother.

I will make time for my kids, grandkids, and great-grand kids and be sure that they all will have a chance to get to know who I am and what is important in my life.

I hope I am given many years to show my family about my values that I hold dear and to teach them how to love, appreciate, and give thanks for a peaceful world where food is plentiful. I am blessed to live in Canada where peace is important, and peace is kept. I will always give thanks and be willing to share with others who do not have the same opportunities, as I feel that I am my brother's keeper.

Chapter 9:
Home, Sweet Home

Mom and Dad rented their first house in Edson, Alberta when the returned from Calgary. It consisted of one room. There was no electricity, plumbing, or any other fringes. The wood and water was carried into the house, as it was needed. Mom and Dad shaped their simple life, and they managed to buy the bare necessities like a stove, table, and a bed. Mom said, "We bought used furniture for fifty dollars. Today, my grandchild moves into a house with everything new." I told Mom that many couples today put goods on credit cards, and then they are stressed out when the bill comes because they cannot pay the large amount.

As a married couple, Mom and Dad found whatever jobs were available. One of Dad's jobs in Edson was nailing grain elevator doors and floors for the fall harvest. This job lasted for the summer months. Mom worked at a hotel where she changed beds and did laundry and dishes. Mom said, "There was a washing machine at the hotel. I've washed mountains of clothes in my lifetime and many on a scrub board!"

Mom and Dad had other challenges to be worked out too. Dad was raised in a Catholic, Irish family. I know that the Catholic religion has many rules to follow. My Irish Grandpa loved his faith, and he taught his boys to follow the church, as they were growing up. This was a different faith from the Baptist faith in which Mom's grandparents had raised her. When different faiths come together, an open mind and listening ears are needed. Was it Mom's determination to keep her family together that made Mom promise to raise the kids in the Catholic faith?

Whatever it was, my parents joined together and raised a Christian family of fourteen children. This may be seen as a blessing after we became adults, but how difficult it must have been when the babies kept coming, often two at a time. In Genesis 1:28, we read: *"Be fertile and multiply; fill the earth and subdue it."* I guess I can say that my parents followed the bible in whatever faith they practiced.

It wasn't too long before Mom was pregnant. There were no ultra sound machines back then, and she had no idea that she was carrying two babies. Mom never dreamed that in her life she would deliver five sets of twins; maybe that was a good thing because that thought would be too much for anyone woman to handle. How can I say or feel what Mom felt, as I never gave birth to twins?

Mom worked hard with very little frills. I am amazed that she has not become a bitter old lady. Mom enjoys each day at the lodge where she lives today. She is full of joy when her kids take time to visit her. Mom is proud of her large family. We take turns at visiting her and also taking her to her appointments. I am thankful for the many sacrifices that Mom made for me.

Chapter 10:
First Twins (Nioma And Nelson)

On November 23, 1943, Mom and Dad started their family.

They became the proud parents of premature twins, Nioma and Nelson. How were my parents to know that this was only the start of many more sets of twins? Perhaps it's the unplanned events that are the most rewarding.

Premature twins are always critical; now think back to 1943, when there wasn't much known about how to save premature babies, and there were no special machines in the smaller hospitals. It was by God's grace that their lives were spared.

The future looked bright to this young couple who dreamt of a perfect life with a perfect family — a boy and a girl. The days moved along, and Mom learned more each day about the twins and what a critical state they were in.

Mom told me, "I only ever had that one doll to play with as I grew up. I was not raised with babies around me either. How would I manage two babies?"

Mom cared for her babies, and wanted the best for them, as every mother does. I'm sure Mom didn't have a lot of confidence.

Nioma weighed 3.1 pounds and Nelson weighed 3.7 pounds. "Miracle babies," said the Roman Catholic nuns at the Edson hospital. I think many prayers were said over these tiny twins. The hospital kept the twins in a basket with a light bulb to keep them warm. The nurses used an eyedropper to feed Nioma and Nelson, as they were too weak to nurse.

The nurse on the night shift often held Nelson because he would quit breathing and needed immediate attention. I guess his lungs were underdeveloped.

Nioma cried a lot; Mom never found a reason why. Their constant care was one of the many challenges Mom would meet in her life. Mom walked to the hospital each day to hold and bond with Nioma and Nelson.

After three months in the hospital, the twins were discharged. This was late February. Mom said, "Premature babies are not cute. The twins were so small and skinny with big heads. Our one room house was not very warm. I kept the twins wrapped tight in a blanket for months. I bathed the babies in a small basin on the bed.

Nioma and Nelson needed much care. I learned to rest when the twins slept. Nights were long and at times very busy. Your dad was not a dad who helped with the babies."

Mom's life became diapers and bottles, as she cared for the twins. How was Mom to know that the bottles and diapers would last for almost twenty years? That seems to me like a long, hard commitment, and nobody would be willing to choose any part of that life. Today many new moms have help with their babies so the new mom can rest and grow stronger. Thanks Mom for all your efforts!

In a few months, Dad had some time off. Mom and Dad went to see Grandma Timmoth and show off Nioma and Nelson. The twins were Grandma's great-grandchildren.

Mom proudly removed the blankets from her twin babies. Grandma Timmoth had a harsh side and spoke what was on her mind; often not in the most enduring words at the time. Grandma gazed upon the twins and said, "My, they do look like little crows; so small and squawky."

Was it Mom's dropped jaw that made Grandma add, "But I know

every crow thinks that hers is the blackest." I take this to mean that for a mother, it is her own brood that is the best from all other birds. This holds true for all mothers today.

Chapter 11:
Great Grandma (Sarah Timmoth)

I remember Grandma Timmoth, as a sombre lady who rocked in her chair and hummed hymns. She must have liked babies, as she often held a baby on her lap. She also liked to play checkers; my bothers took turns playing checkers with her.

Grandma Timmoth said, "I moved West with my parents and my siblings. The Lord kept my family safe when we moved from Ontario; about 50 kilometres from the Niagara falls."

Mom recalled Grandpa Timmoth as a sickly man. I'm thinking that he was elderly when Mom was growing up because she remembers him being bedridden, and Grandma caring for him in their home.

Mom told me that Grandma said that Grandpa called her "Pet". It was a way of making her feel special. I don't know anything more about Great-grandpa Hellekson. I have not seen a picture of him. It is sad how family lines are lost and never recovered for the younger generation.

Grandma was a lady full of life and could see the best in all things. Grandma gave thanks for the awesome sunrise, as she washed her clothes on the rocks of the flowing river. Grandma said, "The glittering water of the river mixed with the lye soap removed all the dirt from the wash."

I wonder how hard that soap was on her hands, and what she used when her hands were dry; she didn't have hand lotion. Her fingers maybe bled at times.

Grandma spread her clothes over the trees branches to dry. I'm sure Grandma enjoyed her washday as she listened to the flowing water and the birds singing.

Grandma remembered lots of black crows and how determined they were. She remarked, "I needed to chase those pesky crows away from the trees first. Then I listened to those birds scold me from a distance. They didn't like me invading their space, where I sat nearby and clicked my knitting needles. I made socks and mitts for the long, cold winter season that always approached too soon.

"The birds were a bother, but God made the crows too, and we need to learn to live with them. All species play a role and have value in God's great creation. God intended everything to work together when He make the food chain complete. That included us doing our part."

Grandma had a good start on preserving the environment. Each one of us has a responsibility to pass on a clean earth. I have strong feelings about recycling and conserving our world for our future generations. I will try to do my part to teach others to enjoy but also conserve this precious land. Most areas have bins where you can place your articles—such as papers, bottles, cans, and plastic containers—to be picked up and recycled.

I thought that Grandma Timmoth's downfall was picking out her favourite grandchildren. Grandma called me the "good kid" because I liked to please her, and do as she asked. I didn't like to be singled out because I have always liked to help others. I don't feel that I need any recognition for doing what is expected of me. Everybody needs a helping hand sometimes, and it is our duty to help one another. My brothers and sisters called me "Grandma's pet"; I guess I was.

Grandma Timmoth was the grandmother that Mom recalled as a stern lady, but Grandma had another side that was full of gratitude. She taught Mom to see all of "life's little pleasures" too. Mom passed this special trait onto me. Thanks Mom! I look for the best side of things in every situation. I try to see the good in all people because

I know we all have an abundance of good to share with one another; God doesn't make junk.

I heard Mom say, "Today is a blessing because I woke up with all my senses intact to care for my family." I also give thanks, as my eyes open each morning, and I ask God to fill me with grace to meet every job in this day. Some days I felt that the day was too long and the many task were more than I thought I could handle; but I knew I wasn't alone at any time. God is my guide.

Grandma came to visit us, and before going to bed, she said, "I'll see you in the morning if the good Lord doesn't call me in the night." This statement frightened me. Grandma was so quiet in morning; I tippy-toed into her bedroom. I found her alive and well, reading her bible.

Grandma was a hard worker; she expected all people to work. Mom ingrained good working habits in us kids too. Mom repeated Grandma's words, "Work never killed anyone; it just keeps you out of trouble. Now get busy."

Grandma was living proof that work is healthy for you because she lived for over a century.

Now that I am a great-grandmother, I know why great-grandma was in a slow mode. Grandmas don't have the energy to play hide and seek or go on a nature hike, as often as kids do; our minds think we can, but our bodies aren't so ready as they once were.

Grandma Timmoth celebrated her one-hundredth birthday with family and friends in a nursing home in Mayerthorpe Alberta. When Grandma was asked what it feels like to be 100 years old, she said, "I think the Lord has forgotten all about me; my friends have passed on, and I'm still here. I know God has a plan for me."

Grandma's body was faltering, but her mind was intact. As a young girl, Grandma had memorized the psalms from the bible. She recited the twenty third Psalm on her 100th birthday before we had cake. Grandma voice was soft and weak, but she spoke with amazing accuracy. I guess we don't forget the things that are important to us.

The Lord called her name when she was one hundred and two years old. Grandma was confined to her bed for the last few months of her life. I know that she would not have chosen to have others care for her; she was the one who cared for others. Her work on earth was done and God called her name.

Chapter 12:
Moving To Grandpa's

Life was starting to come together as a family for Mom and Dad. Edson, Alberta was a good place to raise a family. Mom and Dad lived there with Nioma and Nelson until the spring of 1944, when Grandpa sent a letter to Dad asking him to return to Pierceland to help him with the spring seeding on the homestead in Pierceland, Saskatchewan. (Most areas didn't have phone service then.) Dad had worked in the logging camp while he was in Edson. The farmland there was not as fertile as where Dad and Grandpa had moved from in southern Saskatchewan. Dad may have been excited about returning to Pierceland and sharing the work with his father because he had worked on the farm fields before the drought of the dirty thirties hit. Maybe Dad thought he would someday own Grandpa's small homestead.

In April 1944, Mom and Dad and the twins moved into Grandpa's farmhouse in the Pierceland area. Mom didn't see any of her family for a few years and became homesick. What a struggle it must have been as she stared out the window and dreamed of Edson and familiar faces. Mom was known, as Joe Burge's wife; she didn't have any family or friends to turn to and share some woman talk with in this new district. I often think that she was like a cork pitched into the water and tossed this way and that, as her heart yearned for the time when she would once again become herself with loved ones near. Maybe she would be

Evelyn, a real person and not someone's wife who was from another location. I know Mom's heart ached, and her tears were many, as she cared for the twins.

The area around Edson has some farmland too; however it's the logging that is the primary means of income. The Edson area was better known for forestry because the terrain is swampy and the fields were small. Most farmers had animals to care for and not too many crops to plant — probably just enough oats or other grains to feed their livestock. Machinery was expensive to buy, and some farmers worked together; one man had a drill to put the seed into the ground, another had a disc to work the soil, and another man had the threshing machine that would separate the grain from the straw. Of course, they all had horses with which to pull the farm machinery.

Edson, Alberta is about 500 kilometres from Pierceland, Saskatchewan. Mom and Dad came by train to Cold Lake, Alberta. There was very little money, and Mom and Dad didn't have a reliable vehicle for travelling on a dusty gravel road. Did Mom have doubts about leaving her family and friends? Did she know that she wouldn't return to Edson for a visit after they were settled in at Grandpa's house? I'm thinking that Mom had many unanswered questions, as she packed the twins and their few belonging for the big move. It's a good thing Mom did not know that it would be years before she would see her Daddy or her sister again.

She kept in touch with them through letters; she wrote a letter every two weeks to her sister or her daddy. She waited for her sister's reply and opened Auntie Irene's letters as soon as Dad brought the mail home. I'm thinking that's how she got through all her forlorn feelings with the longing to return to her roots and the things that were familiar to her. Aunty Irene kept her informed about marriages and deaths in the Edson area too.

Mom recalled the move as tough; Mom's heart was with her family in Edson. Her daddy, sister, and cousins had always been close by to share in her life when she lived in Edson. Uncles and aunts lived around the Edson district, and she often rode a horse to visit them when she and her sister were growing up. How hard this must have been to leave her loved ones behind.

When my parents moved in with Grandpa Burge, he bought a rocking chair for Mom. He said, "Babies needed to be rocked." Mom doesn't remember having much time to rock her babies, however. That chair is still in the family and is displayed in a home of a grandson (Nioma's son).

This living situation was not ideal for my parents. The house was small and crowded. Mom and Dad had the unfinished upstairs level. Grandpa had raised his boys alone; he never had a woman around to fill his space or run his house. Did Mom do things different from what he was accustomed to? A woman can add frills and warmth to a plain and simple house, but she can also be viewed as domineering. Most women run a household differently from what a man does. Life also changed for Grandpa when Dad and his family moved into his home. Was it overwhelming to be invaded with a young family? Grandpa's silence was interrupted with the cries, squeals, and laughter of kids, and also a woman.

Remember: Grandpa raised his two boys alone; he didn't have a woman to cook, wash, or clean in his house. If Grandpa left the bread and butter on the table, it was there for the next meal. Mom would have had a place for the bread away from the table; everything had its own place in her kitchen.

I have never had to move from my house, but I'm sure that it must be devastating. Family and friends are left behind, and your life is focused on a different way to make a living in a new area with different demands — a new house, a change in the weather patterns, new neighbours, and different food supplies. This northern area has many trees, lakes, and cold winters. The deer, moose, and fish are plentiful for food, but a good gun was needed, and you had to learn to be accurate when shooting. The cold winters demanded more than a tent to keep out the snow, wind, and cold temperatures.

Then in 1945, for reasons unknown to me (maybe it was Dad's drive to become rich or a longing for the prairie roots that called him), Dad moved his family to a dairy farm in Saskatoon, Saskatchewan so he could work as a farm hand. The cows were milked twice a day, and the milk needed to be delivered each time. The cows were fed, and the barn needed to be kept clean too. He received a monthly salary of $200 and the family was given all the milk and eggs they needed.

Mom and Dad were provided with a one-room house. This arrangement worked well until another drought hit southern Saskatchewan. Many people experienced hard times, and didn't have any money to pay for a hired hand. Dad's employer was one of those people. Dad was let go. Mom and Dad were on the move again and went back to Grandpa's homestead in Pierceland, Saskatchewan.

I'm thinking there wasn't any other place for them to go with no job or money and two children. The farm had all the necessities needed to feed a family, and here in the north the hunting and fishing was good.

I see similar situations happening today for many young couples. Rent is a big expense for our kids who often spend beyond their means. Many adult children move to one of their parents' homes to make ends meet with one income. When the wife finds work outside the home, the young couple can continue with their high standard of living. Many couples buy expensive furniture and recreational toys. The kids are taken to childcare or if Grandma is healthy, she becomes the daycare. Many young parents are not able to share a lot of time with their children, but with two incomes, young couples are able to pay for a mortgage and live in their own house.

Grandpa and Grandma miss the kids when the family moves on, but I remember how life became more quite, and how special it was to have the grandkids come to stay the night and share their week events with me. As I became older, I didn't have as much energy for busy kids. They too grew older, and I saw the grandkids less.

My sister in-law, Marie Gonie remembers their milking days in Pierceland. She said, "My brothers and I rose early to milk the cows, and then delivered the milk around Pierceland before we went to school. We went from door to door and placed a fresh litre of milk on the doorstep each day. We picked up the empty bottle with a nickel placed inside for the litre (not quite a quart) of milk. The money was put into our pockets, as we left a full bottle of milk on the doorstep of the homes. A litre of milk cost 5 cents, but the bottle was worth 20 cents. It was important to get the bottle back each day."

Marie also remembers using a small enamel basin of water to wash in before going to school. That cow smell was a hard odour to remove; a strong soap was needed. (Often soap was made from beef tallow and lye that was boiled together outdoors.) I'm sure we all smelled the same, as the farm kids all did chores before going to school.

Chapter 13:
My Brother Lloyd

On February 5, 1946, my brother Lloyd was born in the hospital at Cold Lake Alberta. I asked Mom why Lloyd was the only one of her children who was born in Cold Lake.

Mom told me that Dad was going fishing on Cold Lake with Nick Toma, and that she was due to delivery her baby any day. (Dad also fished with Frank Collin's and Charlie Larson.) Dad took Mom to the Roundel Hotel in Cold Lake so she was close to the hospital. Mom said, "Your Dad had left about one hour, and my labour pains started. I couldn't find anyone to drive me to the hospital, and I started to walk. The hospital was then located about five blocks away (close to where the Cold Lake water plant is today). A man (John Pikowitz) stopped and picked me up and drove to the hospital."

I was amazed at this story. I experienced labour pains too, but I always had my husband around home to drive me to the hospital when the time came. I was filled with compassion; I know that this was only one of Mom's many struggles in her hard life. Mom did what she had to do.

Mom said, "Lloyd was a chubby and cute baby. He weighted over 6 pounds, and I'm sure he was as big as the twins were after three months of age. Lloyd was able to come home with me from the hospital. It wasn't too long before Lloyd slept all night too. This was so different from the twins."

Lloyd always seemed like the "pet" in our family. He often found a way to get out of his chores and went to town with Mom and Dad more times than any other child did.

Mom and Dad's challenges seemed to grow. Their lives didn't get any easier with time, and another baby added to the work. Dad worked at different trades without much success because he grew weary of the same work each day. Mom said, "Your Dad and Grandpa didn't work well together, but it seemed that it was your Dad who had a problem."

I can only imagine how hard it is to live with in-laws as you try to keep the peace and make everyone happy. I feel torn when my kids are "bickering" with one another, and I try to help each of them to see that we are not perfect people, but we do need to listen to each other and to work through our differences. It takes a lot of work to live together, and stay friends too.

Dad went to work on Cold Lake for a commercial fisherman, Nick Toma. Cold Lake is about thirty miles from Pierceland, Saskatchewan It is a large, deep and very cold lake, stretching about 48 kilometres from one end to the other. The lake is over 60 metres deep in some areas. The fish are plentiful, and Cold Lake remains a favourite fishing lake!

Horses were used on the lake to fish, and the men stayed at the lake for most of the winter season. The fish were sold at the lakeshore. Both men and horses were challenged as the weather was cold, and the old shacks didn't have insulation. Wood was easy to get as the lake is surrounded with poplar trees and a few spruce trees too.

The horses were medium-size workhorses that were used year round. Some horses were afraid of the ice if the ice was not snow-covered. This meant that the men needed to put horse shoes on the horses to keep them from slipping, as they pulled the sleigh with the nets and the boxes of fish. The day started at daylight and ended at dusk, but the men returned to the shore at noon to feed the horses and give them a rest. Wood was put in the stove to keep their food supply from freezing. At night, the horses were tied in a log shelter for the night. These barns were used each year, as the men returned to the lake to fish. The fishermen rose early in the morning to feed the horses before they ate a good breakfast of eggs, bacon, and biscuits or pancakes.

Winter parkas were worn to keep the men warm. In cold weather, the frost built up around the parka hoods, and the men's whiskers were white with frost too.

I remember going commercial fishing with my husband and being dressed in layers. I covered my face with a scarf that kept my face from being frostbitten by the bitter cold. Many times it was covered with the white frost too. The wind was always a factor on the lake. I struggled through the elements of winter, and I was thankful for the days I spent safely on the lake. Woollen mitts were used to take the fish out of the nets. Yes, the mitts froze with the water from the lake, and the mitts became hard to use. It was important to remember to take another pair of mitts along with you. At night, the mitts were washed and dried by the fire. A hot fire was a joy to all fishermen who warmed their bodies, which ached from the cold. Fishing was a hard way of making a living, but our forefathers did whatever it took to provide for their loved ones.

I am grateful to our pioneers for the pleasures I enjoy today; my insulated house is warm and cozy. I just turn up the thermostat on the propane furnace, cuddle into a warm bed with fuzzy sheets, and lock winter outdoors, as I listen to the wind howl at my door. If the noise is too loud, I turn up my stereo or the television set. I love my flush toilet too, no need to dress and go outdoors.

Great-grandma Hellekson, that gentle, warm, and compassionate lady, came to help Mom with the family. Mom said, "Grandma stayed with me about a month and helped me with the kids." Grandma was healthy and always willing to help wherever she could. I'm thinking that Lloyd's birth was the last time Grandma Hellekson came to run Mom's household. Grandma had taught Mom to meet all challenges, as she faced every situation head on and made the best of every day.

Five Plus Five Makes Fifteen · 39

How hard it must have been for Mom with a big family and not much money. How did my parents manage to give us all the necessities to keep us all comfortable?

As a mother, I know how I like my kids to have everything they need and a few extras too. Mom's heart must have longed for more, but she wasn't able to do a thing to change it. Mom continued to wash, clean, and cook for her large family. In a year or two, she would have another baby.

I often felt housebound when my children were young, as their care was constant. Each day is a repeat of the day before — cooking, washing, and cleaning house. I never had to worry about what I would serve for the next meal, as Mom did, but the yearning for some "women talk" was great. I found myself wondering if there was a life beyond my little family and home. Mom, did you talk to yourself just to have some woman talk? Mom had to be a woman of steel.

Chapter 14:
Welcome To My World (Barbara)

1947 PRICES		
AVERAGE INCOME	$	2,854.00
NEW CAR	$	1,290.00
NEW HOUSE	$	6,650.00
LOAF OF BREAD	$	.13
GALLON OF GAS	$	.15
GALLON OF MILK	$	.78
GOLD PER OUNCE	$	35.00
SILVER PER OUNCE	$	.71
DOW JONES AVERAGE		177

1947 prices

I, Barbara Ann, was born on December 12, 1947. I joined the Burge family as the fourth child. I am the second girl in my family. Mom recorded my baby years and told me that my hair was curly. This brings me to remember the nursery rhyme about the girl with the curl in the middle of her forehead: "When she was good, she was very good, but when she was bad, she was horrid." Was that me?

Mom said, "The winter you were born was a harsh winter. It was cold and snow drifts were huge, making the trip to the hospital challenging with a team of horses."

The local Red Cross Hospital was in Pierceland, Saskatchewan, and the doctor came once a week to administer to all the sick. (This Red Cross Hospital operated for about twenty years. It was later sold and is used as a home, but it still stands on its original spot today.)

The first doctor travelled from Cold Lake, Alberta to Pierceland, Saskatchewan. Cold Lake is about thirty kilometers to the west of Pierceland, Saskatchewan. The main highway was in poor shape. The road was maintained with a horse-pulled, steal grader, as a small amount of dirt was moved to fill in the ruts. A man rode on the grader and used his hands to turn a wheel so that the grader blade would turn and spread dirt into the deep ruts.

It was a cold day in December when Dad hitched up the team and took Mom to the hospital, about a 6-kilometre drive, because it was time for me to enter this world. I didn't wait for any doctor. Miss Robson, the registered nurse, delivered me. (Miss Robson delivered many babies, as the doctor wasn't always in the hospital.) Mom said, "It was almost two hours after I arrived at the hospital when you wailed your way into the world weighing about six pounds."

I still like to voice my opinion, and at times, nobody appears to be listening to me, and I'm just making noise.

Mrs. Hazel Little (the mother of the family that Dad and Grandpa helped moved to Pierceland) suggested my name. Mrs. Little said, "Barbara Ann Scott is making her name to fame in the figure-skating world." (She won in 1948.)

In the forties, there were no antibiotics to fight infection or other serious germs. The normal procedure for women who gave birth was to stay in bed for 14 days. Women must have gotten weak after lying in bed for so long. How hard it must have been for Mom.

My sister in-law referred to the stay in the hospital as "a holiday". I often wonder if this was like a holiday for Mom, or did she work harder to catch up when she got home? All women were expected to resume their duties instantly. Mom never had a real holiday for many years; her kids needed her each day, and she was always there as a pillar.

After my birth, Mom returned home to my three older siblings, who bounced with excitement, as they awaited Santa. Nioma and Nelson were four years old, and Lloyd was almost two years old. I'm sure that Santa was talked about and every good kid expected a present. Did Mom and Dad have any gifts for their children? I know that they didn't have any extra money to buy anything. Mom said, "I don't remember if Santa Clause came that year. I may have knitted some mitts or socks for all the kids."

Maybe Mom said that I was their gift. I like to think so; each of my siblings is a great gift to me.

Chapter 15:
My Sister Judy

My sister, Judy arrived on February 18, 1949. This was fourteen months after I was born. Mom said, "It's easier to have twins than two babies a year apart." Judy has blonde hair with brown eyes. She has always been very petite like Mom and isn't afraid of work either. She and I often share our clothing. Her feet are a size smaller, so we don't share our shoes. We are the "runts" of the family. Judy has always been a talker and expresses herself freely when in a crowd.

Judy was a tiny baby, but she grew into a girl with a big heart. She's often in disputes, as she defends the underdog. Today, people would say that she is an advocate against bullying.

Neither Judy nor I are easily swayed, and Mom was often challenged, as we held our ground. I often say that it's okay to be stubborn; you just have to learn to control it and know when it's best to back down.

Judy developed bronchial pneumonia when she was two and half years old and spent a month in the hospital. Mom said, "We all welcomed her home and watched her closely, as nobody wanted her to go back to the hospital."

I often think about Mom and wonder how she managed in those crammed quarters without anyone to reach out to. Dad didn't help much with the kids. He was not raised by a mother or with other kids.

Did he see what was needed to be done? Dad worked outdoors, came in, and rested. Mom worked nonstop, as a mother's work is never done. Mom didn't have a sister, a mother, or in-laws living close by to assist her. Mom recalls when, years later, she had yellow jaundice, and she lay in bed with a newborn baby (George); she couldn't even lift her head. Nioma was a big help, as she went to Mom's bed to feed and change the baby. Nioma was almost ten years old.

When my children were young, I had sisters and in-laws to help me and support me. Mom also lived close by if I needed a hand, any advice, or a shoulder to cry on. I thought I was busy with our four children, who arrived within five years (and no twins either). It was easier for me if I stayed home and kept a routine. (The world seemed to close in around me, and I often wondered if there was a life away from my home.)

Mom wasn't able to go anywhere even if she had wanted to because there was no vehicle and no babysitter either. Mom said, "One winter it was over three months before I spoke to another woman. On a warm spring day, I burst with joy when Mrs. Little rode her horse to visit me."

Today, many women keep in touch with phones or on Facebook on their computer from the comfort of their own home. Most women are social beings.

Mom said, "Going to town was a big deal." We went to Pierceland with the horses. I put the kids in the high wagon box after Dad had the team hitched to the wagon. We went to the co-op store where there was a hitching post. The Post Office was just across the street. It didn't take long to get what we needed. Often we stopped at our friends, the Little's farm, as it was on our way home from Pierceland. We always had a good visit and something to eat before going home."

The Little family remained close to our family. A few years ago, in the late 1990's the Burge family had pre-booked the community hall in Pierceland for our family's Christmas because today Mom's family is large; over one hundred people, with Mom's children, their spouses, grandchildren, and a few great-grand children.

The Little family approached us about sharing the hall on December 24th for Annie Little's funeral service. There was no problem about sharing the hall as Annie Little had remained a good friend to Mom and her family. Everybody visited with her son, George Little and his family before our family prepared supper. The Burge Christmas supper then continued, as it had each year. Christmas was enjoyed by all, and the Littles returned to their homes to celebrate Christmas with their families. Both of our families managed to use the community hall without any problems, as the funeral was at 1 p.m., and our supper was at 6 p.m.

Chapter 16:
Big Moves For All

Dad built a log frame building on the meadow quarter. My family moved to this shack for the summer months. There were poles on the roof, which was covered with straw and grass. This roof didn't keep out the rain. Mom said, "After a big rain, the roof got soaked and it dripped for a long time; there was not a dry place to be found." Nelson, my brother, remembered sleeping under the table, as that was the only dry place in the shack. I wonder, was the table large enough for the whole family to sleep under? This lodging wasn't warm enough for winter. The space between the logs needed to be plugged tightly with moss and mud. This was called "chinking". The mud and the moss needed to be mixed just so, and I don't think Dad ever did manage to master that skill.

I wonder why those hard times are often called the "Good old days?" It must have been the slower pace without modern vehicles, television, and cell phones. Maybe families enjoyed the simpler way of living. It's hard for me to envision those days as "good days".

Our house at the meadow was a cold and drafty shack. It didn't keep out the flies and mosquitoes. I recall Dad made a small fire in a pail with dry twigs and put grass on top to make a smudge (a big smoke). Dad carried this smudge throughout the house to chase the mosquitoes away before we went to bed. My brothers, sisters, and I would follow Dad and swing towels to move the smoke around. It was a blast!

Dad knew that he should have a warmer house for the upcoming winter. Mom was expecting a baby in October and a better house was needed to keep our family warm. It was time to pull a Hank Snow "I'm moving on." Charlie Larson, a neighbour, had moved to Pierceland, and his house on the farm was empty. He had lived about a half a kilometre from Grandpa's homestead. Charlie's dwelling was alongside the main highway to the Alberta border. The house was small with two rooms, but it had a good roof and would keep out the wet and cold season that was ahead. A good stove, a big woodpile, and warm hearts were sufficient to survive the cold winter of big snow banks and a howling north wind. This could last for about four or five months before spring would be welcomed.

Dad rented Charlie's house in the fall of 1950. The two-room house at Charlie's was a much better place than what we had lived in for the summer months. This was a house with a good roof, a barn, and a well with enough water for our family to drink and cook with. A large barrel was placed inside the house to melt snow. It was Nelson's job to bring the snow in to melt. Nelson was the oldest boy, and he learned to work at a young age. His small body was strong, and his determination was even stronger. Nelson would work at whatever job he needed to and not complain.

Mom said, "Nelson carried snow into the house with a gallon syrup pail. It takes a lot of melted snow to make enough water for two cows to have a good drink. Nelson made many trip with that little pail until the snow melted and the barrel was full of water."

Another bonus at Charlie's place was an outhouse just outside the door; the toilet was by the barn at the meadow quarter. I think that Mom may have had a chamber pail for the young kids to use, and she would empty it often to keep the smell down. Who would need anything more?

Mom remembered how the winter of 1950 had so much snow. The

main highway going past Charlie's house was closed because of the big snowdrifts. One night, the road to Alberta was closed; Mom and Dad had ten people stay overnight. I'm thinking that the night would have been memorable, as Mom cared for her twins while bodies slept on the floor. In the morning, Mom used her last flour to make pancakes for all. I think about using my last flour to feed strangers, and wonder if I would have been so giving. The overnight visitors were grateful and gave Dad 10 dollars for the warm sleep and hearty breakfast.

My parents were so obliged to the overnight visitors because the family allowance cheque was not due for another week. (The government introduced the family allowance cheques in 1945; each child received 5 dollars until they were in school, and then it went up to 7 dollars.) Dad was able to go to town for coffee, flour, and sugar. Mom said, "When we help others we will always have enough to eat. God always provided a way to care for our family." Today, my siblings are all willing to share with others, and I'm sure it is because my parents were willing to help everyone in need. They seemed to know that tomorrow would take care of itself. When we give to others we receive in return.

Chapter 17:
Twin Boys (Grant and Graham)

Mom gave birth to her second set of twins. Grant and Graham were born on October 1, 1950. The twin boys were welcomed into our growing family at the Pierceland hospital. Twin girls (Lorraine and Lucille Lepine) were also born that same day. This small northern town of Pierceland was famous. No other town had a set of twin girls and a set of twin boys born in their hospital on the same day! Grandma Timmoth came to help Mom this time.

Dad must have moved from the meadow quarter with five kids, two cows, and the bare necessities while Mom was in the hospital. Mom came home from the hospital to "Charlie's" place without the twins, Grant and Graham. Each baby weighed about five pounds. The nurse in Pierceland had said that Mom needed to go home to her other babies, as Judy was a year and a half old, and I was two and a half years old. Grant stayed in the hospital for one week longer than Mom, and Graham stayed for two weeks longer.

Mom said, "In seven years, it seemed like we stood still. The only things we accumulated more of were children. I never had time to get depressed. The diapers were washed each day on a scrub board and hung above the table on a string line to dry. That line was never empty. I washed about thirty diapers each day. The diapers were used from the line, as they were needed. One day rolled into another, and I did whatever I needed to do. I went to bed exhausted and got up tired to prepare for the next day full of the same routine." Times have changed in many ways, and I know that a woman's work is easier with today's modern appliances. I only need to put the clothes into the washing machine with some soap, return when the cycle is done, and place the clothes into the clothes dryer.

Mom told me that at night she poured the babies milk into a tin pie plate and placed it on the stove to warm, as there was always a fire to keep the house warm. The health nurse today would freak out and say that the babies might get sick, as that was not very sanitary, but we all survived. Mom had two babies to feed and change before returning to a warm bed.

Today I witness young parents discarding food items that have passed the expiry date that is marked on the container that it is in. Nobody checks to see if the food is still good, even though that date is only a suggested date for the food to be stored. I use my nose to smell, my mouth to taste, and my eyes to check the appearance of food before I discard any food that could still be eaten.

Mom told me that she recalled that she was always tired and promised herself that when she got old, she would sleep all day if she wanted to. Now I understand that Mom never had six hours of undisturbed sleep. I found it hard to wake up from a good sleep to feed and change one baby. I would have been tempted to give my baby cold milk to drink!

Chapter 18:
Time Away From Home

Mom and Dad's hard times were similar to all families. Dad kept enough wood to keep the fire blazing, and Mom kept the diapers washed and dried for the babies. Dad put a clothesline above the table for Mom to hang the diapers. The hot fires helped to dry the clothes; I guess there was no need to worry about the air in the house becoming too dry to breathe, as there was a lot of moisture from drying clothes.

Mom and Dad didn't feel any more deprived than any other family; everyone struggled with a meagre living. I recall that the chores were done, wood was cut and carried into the wood box, and food was prepared before any games were played indoors for the winter months. Mom said, "A large family consumes a lot of food. If the hens didn't lay eggs, I needed to cook what I had. I recall making porridge for dinner too. We always found a way to feed the kids. You learn to do whatever it takes to continue for one more day." What a positive statement!

Each politician seems to make a mark for us to remember; Tommy Douglas brought in a health care system to Saskatchewan, and it remains a great service. The John Diefenbaker government gave every child a case of Spork meat to help out with the food shortage. To me it seemed that our family got many cases of that canned meat. Mom served it cold, fried, and boiled, but that fatty taste remained. Some families were happy to give their portion of Spork to us too. When I see that blue-and-white, oblong can in the store today I remark, "There is that awful Diefenbaker meat."

There wasn't money to spend on entertainment; Mom and Dad didn't get out often. Mom said, "When there was a wedding dance, I put the babies to bed, and Grandpa Burge babysat so Dad and I could go."

Mom remembers how wedding dances were free, but you were expected to put some money into the groom's boot when it was passed around at the dance. This money was given to the bride and groom to help set up their future. The new couple didn't have much, and all items were cherished. Most gifts were small kitchen items, like a cream and sugar set, towels, or pots and pans. A special gift was a handmade quilt.

The orchestra consisted of a few neighbours who played an instrument and volunteered the music. Many times, the kids and babies were taken along to the dance. The coats were piled on the bench, and the kids lay there to sleep, as their parents enjoyed dancing into the wee hours of the morning. A friend told me that he would get home from the dance in time to do the morning chores.

Pierceland began to grow, as more families moved into the northern area. In the history book, *Our Pioneers*, I found some of Pierceland's firsts; they're listed below.

1931   Lillico family came north and started a saw mill.

1933   Hazel and Bob Little arrived with George Burge and his sons, Joe and Leonard.

1936   Gonie family arrived.

1937   Bill Davis came to the area. He married Edith Lillico.

1939   Red Cross took over the Pierceland Hospital.

1941 Fr. Schultz, a Catholic priest, came to Pierceland from Goodsoil with a horse and buggy to Wilhelm Gelowitz's house. Later Pierceland had a parish priest, Fr. Joe Boening. He held mass in the rectory. In the early forties, a church was built but was destroyed by fire in 1953.

1941 The first Credit Union opened in Pierceland. Walter and Loreen Pikowicz built their first store at Jiglem's Lake.

1943 Mr. Walter Pikowicz opens the Red and White store in Pierceland

1944 John Eistetter Sr. had a blacksmith shop.

1945 Mr. Baumgardner became the first agent for Saskatchewan government telephones.

1946 The first barber shop was run by Matt Gelowitz.

1947 I, Barbara Burge entered the world

1948 Pete Epp established a freight haul from St. Walburg.

1949 Mert Henetuik drove a truck for the co-op.

1950 The first high school was opened in Pierceland; the high school was in the old co-op store up on the hill by Swingley's meat shop (the former Eaton's meat shop).

1952 The first high school was built in Pierceland (in the

location where the community hall is now).

1952   The Esso bulk station was established by Arnold Hardy and operated by Ed Esau.

1953   Walter McClellan built a store. 100 pounds of flour sold for $2.85 and 5 pounds of sugar for .85 cents.

1953   The Roman Catholic Church burnt. Clarence and Sal Hickie had the last wedding held there.

1954   The second Catholic Church was built. The first wedding held there was Tony and Lorraine Gonie's. This church also burnt in 1970.

1956   John Britton operated the bulk station and 1964 A.O. Foss became the operator.

1959   A plebiscite voted in mixed drinking for woman and men.

1959   Frank Muelhbauer and Ray Seewalt bought the hotel from Mr. Baumgardner. I think it was 1959 before woman could walk into a pub on their own, as a man did.

1961   Catholic Women League was formed by Fr. Wagner with 18 members; how hard it is to believe that I've been a member for fifty years. I am available to bake, but I no longer bake 20 dozen buns for a wedding reception.

1964   Pierceland had a one-man police detachment.

1965   Betty Eistetter was the switchboard operator; my family was on a party line with nine other people.

1970   The new headquarters for the R.C.M.P. (with 3 members) opened.

1972   The Lakeland Library was formed.

1973   Natural gas was brought to Pierceland.

Pierceland's 1 st rodeo replaces the gymkhana.

1974   Pierceland had a flood; the Ducks Unlimited dam was blown up.

Melvin Coleman won the Canadian Saddle bronco

Dial phones were installed.

Pierceland has had some champions who made the area proud. I'm sorry if I missed other important events to the area. I have tried to write about the struggles of the earlier days, and I wish to thank the many pioneers for making life easier for me. I know my life is better because of the many people who made this world and my little corner a better and safer place to live. Thanks to one and all!

Chapter 19:
A Rough Ride

Mom and Dad lived on the meadow quarter with ten kids. Nioma was now eleven years old and was a big help in caring for her siblings. Mom depended on Nioma each day to help feed and change the babies.

Mom said, "Joe was going to town, and asked me to go with him. Nioma was eleven years old and could run the house for a few hours while I was gone."

Mom was happy as she dressed in a blue cotton skirt and a starched white blouse. Mom said, "I looked forward to a day away from the farm chores. Most days there was no need to look my best, as the cows and chickens never noticed; they only wanted to be fed. It was over one month, and I had not had a visit with another woman."

Mom's large family needed care, and with no family members to help out, Mom managed to wash, clean, cook, and supervise our household. A day away from the farm and all its responsibilities was overdue. Her trip to town would be with the Cockshutt 30 tractor and a two-wheeled cart. Mom would buy the groceries for the coming month, visit with other women, and arrive home feeling good.

Mom wrapped a blanket around herself to help keep her white blouse clean. Mom gave the eldest child, Nioma, some instructions for the baby's bottles, nap times for the toddlers, and said that we would be home to make supper.

Mom said, "I climbed into the two-wheeled cart with the high side; it was made big enough to hold a cord of wood. I heard the roar of the tractor, and Joe slowly eased out the clutch to allow the cart to move without a jerk, as I sat down on the little wooden seat. The tractor began to roll slowly along the bumpy dirt road. Joe shifted the tractor to a higher gear, and I watched the house become smaller in the distance. I was excited to have the chance to have some adult company. I would visit with the people in the store, as I waited for my list to be filled."

Mom and Dad rounded the big slough, and soon the rough road turned into a big mud puddle. "The slough was a short jaunt before we would be at the highway. I heard the tractor gear down for the mud puddle, and I sat up a little straighter. The cart hit the big ruts and swaged back and forth. The cart bounced high, and with a jolt, it came to a stop. I was tipped off my stool. My short legs flip over my head, and the blanket fell from my shoulders. I reached for something to grab, but there was nothing in the cart, and I hit the floor. To my surprise the cart tipped forward and came to a sudden stop.

"That rough mud hole had jiggled the draw pin out of the hitch of the tractor, and me and the cart skidded to a stop, and plunked to the ground. I crawled onto my feet and out of the cart; there was water all around me. I managed to take a step big enough so my feet wouldn't get wet, as I stepped from the cart.

"The sound of the tractor was getting fainter. I looked down the road, and Joe was looking straight ahead, as he continued on his way. He had never looked back. How would he know that the cart was not behind the tractor? I was shocked to hear the tractor shift into another gear. Soon Joe and the tractor were out of my sight."

Mom decided to dust herself off, and stomp toward home. She said, "I was disappointed that my vacation ended so soon, but what else could I do but have a quiet walk home. I wouldn't let my time alone be defeated or turned into a total failure. I took the wooded area home, and I listened to the birds sing, saw some pretty flowers, and enjoyed the quiet. My day away was not what I had anticipated. I never knew when my husband discovered that the cart or I was no longer behind the tractor."

Mom arrived home before Dad, but when Dad carried the groceries into the house Mom found a box of chocolates with the food items. Mom said, "I enjoyed one chocolate each day for a week."

Dad was not a man to talk about the events in his life. There was never a mention of when he discovered that the cart or Mom was not with him. He simply hooked onto the cart on the way home. He drove the cart to its usual place.

Main street Pierceland 1940

Chapter 20:
Another Work Day

Mom used slough water to wash clothes in the summer time. Mom said, "My kids didn't have all the clothes that the kids of today have. Each child had one change of clothes, and often my kids shared their clothes."

I remember changing my clothes, as soon as I got home from school. In the wintertime, snow was carried indoors and melted on the stove in the copper boiler, which had a permanent place on the back of the cook stove. This provided warm water for the families, as the cook stove had a fire at all times to help to keep the kitchen warm. Mom did get a new stove with a reservoir that held warm water. We also had an airtight heater in that larger room where the table was kept. That heater helped to keep the rest of the house warm. Our bedrooms didn't have any heat.

My Aunty Darlene told me that Dad didn't work well when he was alone. He needed someone to work with. Mom filled that gap too and often was outdoors helping Dad with chores, gathering wood, and supporting him.

Who said that women didn't work out of the home? Mom hung the clothes on the clothesline outdoors to dry and propped up the line with a stick that had a branch like a "Y". The line ran between the "Y twigs" and held the clothesline higher from the ground, as the blowing wind made the clothes flop to and fro. I enjoyed the smell of the fresh and soft towels, as I wiped my face after a bath. I recall how a puppy had great fun when he got hold of some clothes on the line and tore them to shreds as he swung back and forth. I think that was the end of our puppy.

Mom washed clothes twice a week to keep up with the laundry. I remember a peddler, Frank Collins who came with his goods — pots, pans, and some dried goods. Dad bought some orange concentrate to make juice. This was a specialty, and it was saved for birthdays.

The peddler saw the line full of pants, and said to Mom, "Your wash has ten pairs of pants all about the same size hanging on it. Your child must a lot of clothes."

When he entered the house and saw our many head peeking from behind the bedroom door, he was embarrassed, but he understood why there were so many pants on the line that were about the same size.

Mom said, "Your Dad helped me by bringing in the clothes from the line, and he folded the clothes too. He stacked them in piles for me to put away."

I recall learning to hang clothes on the line. Mom was fussy and told me, "Hang the tea towels together, the pillow cases next, and be sure the pants are hung by each leg so that the wind can blow up the legs to dry them faster." I couldn't see why any of that was important, and I was sent back outdoors to hang the clothes the proper way. Today I do hang my clothes in the way Mom told me.

Mom had apple boxes nailed in a corner by the bed. (Apples were shipped in a large wooden box, and those boxes were used for nightstands, cradles, and storage boxes too.) Mom was always organized, and all things had a place to be stored; there was no extra room anywhere. I know Mom never had a bedroom suite, but nothing was left lying around. Mom still likes her stuff organized and put away; everything has a place in her world.

Mom has given away many of her treasures to her children and grandchildren. She tells me that she no longer needs to have her place cluttered with knick-knacks; it's just stuff. I know that we enter this world with nothing, and I guess we will all leave this world with nothing; some of us will not have a good mind or a good body. Nobody can know when one of us will wither away in a bed. That's just how it is.

Chapter 21:
Mom's Love For Poetry

As I helped to clean Mom's room, I found this interesting saying that was marked "1946" among Mom's scrapbooks:

> A heart full of thankfulness,
> A thimble full of care,
> A soul of simple hopefulness'
> An early morning prayer,
> A smile to greet the morning with,
> A kind word as a key,
> To open the door and greet the day,
> Whatever it brings to thee,
> A patient trust in providence,
> To sweeten all the way,
> All these combined with thoughtfulness,
> Will make a happy day.

Today Mom is 93 years old. She repeats poetry from her school days along with many poems that she recalls learning throughout her life. There is an odd time when she may miss a few words. Mom said, "It was important for me to memorize these poems and repeat them to my kids. I wasn't a singer, so I said my poems."

Chapter 22:
Grandpa Burge's Homestead Is Sold

Grandpa Burge lived alone when Mom, Dad, and the family left his home and moved to their meadow quarter. Grandpa's arthritic joins were painful; he was getting tired, and he found it hard to manage the chores on his farm. The hip that had been broken when he was a young lad was now wracked with pain. As I get older, I have a few aches and pains, but Tylenol soon takes away that pain. The pioneers didn't have those drugs and most likely could not afford such luxuries; they suffered through the day.

Grandpa didn't have any pain relievers, and he made plans to sell his farm. Dad had no money and was not able to buy Grandpa's homestead, and it seemed that working together was out of the question. Mom said, "I witnessed many disagreements that the two of them had." Wow, Mom was there to listen to each of their sad stories too.

Dad liked to play cards for money. Mom said, "Joe walked to town and was gone for a day or two. When I asked where he was, Joe said, I couldn't find a ride home." I guess he forgot that he had walked to town. I don't know if Dad made or lost money, but I know that it took a lot of money to buy food, clothing, and shoes for the family!

In 1951, Grandpa sold his little farm. His assets were few, but he earned enough money for a trip back to Prince Edward Island to visit his cousins. He had not been back since the time he and his boys left on that train.

At Grandpa's sale, Dad bought a team of horses, a sleigh, and a wagon. This provided a way for Dad and Mom to go to town for supplies. Dad now had five horses with the filly.

Grandpa sold his homestead to Mr. Wilhelm Baumgardner who lived in Pierceland and owned the local parlour. This man never moved to Grandpa's homestead, and later he sold Grandpa's homestead to Rosa and Bill Gonie Sr. The Gonie children were adults and getting married to make a life with their spouses.

One of his sons, Tone, worked as a carpenter, and was a newlywed. My Grandpa Burge's place had a house and a few fences, and it was close to the highway that ran to Alberta. Grandpa Burge's homestead place became the home of Tone (the son of Bill Gonie Sr.) and Lorraine Gonie.

Tone and Lorraine were so special to us older kids. Tone had a tinge of red in his hair, and when his whiskers grew, they were red too. Tone's hands were big and strong when he pulled me up on his saddle horse to ride to his place.

The meadow quarter was about 1 kilometre from Tone's house. Tone rode a horse back and forth to our place, and I remember he sang old cowboy songs, as I rode with him to his home. I would stay with Lorraine because she didn't like to be alone when Tone went to work, and he would be away at night.

Lorraine was a slim lady with dark hair and dark eyes. She showed me how athletic she was, as she walked on her hands and stood on her head. I would try to copy her, but I never managed to walk on my hands. I liked sports and could run with her across the meadow when she walked me home. Lorraine was a good cook, and I loved to stay at her house. I felt special, and I loved the attention that Lorraine gave me. I recall the many times when I went with my siblings to Lorraine and Tone's house; they were our closest neighbours. I remember when I stayed with Lorraine, she let me use her blue lunch kit when I went to school. This was better than my lard pail. Lorraine was good to me, and I enjoyed my stay. Another time I spent the day with Lorraine when I fell on the ice and got soaked with water. I walked home with my family that night. Mom was not happy with me when I told her I had missed school, but I enjoyed my day.

Tone and Lorraine took Nioma, Nelson, and Lloyd to the Grand Centre Theater. Nioma told me that was the first time she had been at a theatre. They all had a treat too —a bottle of orange pop!

Years later, as fate would have it, I married Tone's younger brother, Lloyd Gonie — a local farmer. We raised our four children in Pierceland. Our kids all live nearby. It is a joy to have our children close today.

When I grew older, I thought it was great to walk with Nelson, Nioma, and Lloyd to visit the Gonie neighbours. Tone and Lorraine played ball, kick the can, and cards too. Tone could hit the ball farther than any of us could. Lorraine always made a lunch for us before we went home. She made goodies that we didn't have at home. Mom told us to mind our manners. She said, "Don't eat like pigs; one treat is enough."

Tone often slipped us a second cinnamon bun with icing or another piece of Lorraine's burnt sugar cake with caramel icing. I never refused the delicacy.

After a few years, Tone and Lorraine built a new house on Grandpa's homestead. They raised six kids on Grandpa's old homestead. I remember going to babysit, and I enjoyed playing ball with their children too.

Time has a way of moving fast, and all to soon our bodies get tired, and we can no longer do want we would like to. The mind thinks we can, but the body is stiff and slow. Tone said, "If you wake up in the morning and nothing hurts on your body, don't move." Tone and Lorraine built a new house in Pierceland. I watched this couple make the adjustments, and thought of the days when I too would need to leave my farm.

Tone said, "The lights and sidewalks make it easier to go for a walk, but the barking dogs were not a plus when night fell and rest is due. On the farm, I listened to the frogs croak and the birds sing, as I dozed off to sleep. Yes, I needed to start my Ford pickup truck and drive for the mail each day, but my sleep wasn't interrupted." Tone's son, Bill Jr., took over the farm when Tone retired and moved to Pierceland, Saskatchewan.

Today, Bill and Joann Gonie are raising their four children on my old playground. Their kids can explore and experience the joy of country living. I am an Aunty to Bill Gonie Jr. and his wife Joann, as I married Bill's Uncle Lloyd. I can visit my "roots," and I remember the old homestead as I see it is again filled with the joy of a thriving family.

Chapter 23:
Back To The Meadow Quarter

Money was tight in the forties, and my family moved back to the meadow quarter in the spring. At Charlie's place Mom and Dad had paid rent. It was the summer season now, and the brutal cold of the demanding winter months were over.

I was curious about the big adventure of Mom and Dad moving to their old log shack at the meadow quarter, and I asked Mom about it. I know Dad needed to do some work on that log frame structure before the family moved back in.

Mom said, "We didn't have a lot to move. I guess a few possessions were loaded in that high steel-wheeled wagon box behind the seven kids, as we went on an adventure to our new home. The milk cows walked in water up to their udders in the deepest part of the meadow. The old sow was ready to have piglets, and she followed the wagon. The laying hens were shoved into a gunny sack. I guess the hens roosted in the trees until a shelter was made for them. I can't recall, but it must have been quite a sight."

A barn was needed for the horses, pigs, and chickens. Mom questioned Dad about building a barn. She said, "Can't we build a lumber house for our family, and use the log shack for a barn? That log shack needs much work." Mom had lived in a log house with her Dad, and she knew how hard it was to keep mice out. Mom told me that she won the conversation about building a lumber house for the family to live in, and the shack was used for a barn to house the animals.

In 1951, Dave Riddell, a neighbour, helped Dad get logs to build a lumber house. Dad built a house that was about 8 metres wide by 6 metres long. Dad needed windows and a door for the new house. I remember going to Bonnyville with Dad and Dave. I sat in the middle. I felt like a little peanut between the two big men. All I saw was the sky!

Dave was a tall man, over six feet tall. He liked to tease. He told me the Easter Bunny wasn't coming because he saw him running away from our place and he never went back to a place after he left. He just had too many places to go to. I asked Nioma to tell me that wasn't true; she would not speak of the Easter Bunny.

Our new house had three bedrooms and a combined kitchen and dining room. I remember the two windows that were side by side near the kitchen table. When winter set in, these frosted windows became a drawing board for us. Not one of us kids was an artist, but we drew what we knew, the toilet and snowmen. Mom placed towels on the wet windowsills when the warm sunshine melted the frost because the water began to run down the windows.

Mom must have enjoyed having a bigger area than what Charlie's two-room house had to offer her family; I wonder if she had time to notice.

The move back to the meadow quarter had some challenges. Mom feared the dense bush around the house at the meadow. Would the kids wonder off and get lost in the willows and tall grass? Where would a frantic mother look for a small child? Then there was the fear of a fire starting and burning everything to the ground. How would they save the kids and animals and start to build over again?

Mom said, "To keep the kids safe, when I worked in the garden, or went to milk the cows, I put the kids in the high wagon box; Nioma was in charge. I listened for the different cries and knew when I needed to run to check." Wow, Mom invented the first playpen! Hers was outdoors.

I remember when my daughter, Angie, was two years old and she was out of my sight. I called her name and she didn't come. The tears streamed down my face, as I searched the yard. I ran to spots of danger like the dugout, the pigpen, and the old well by the barn. How could a small child wander away from her brothers in such a short time? I had just gone indoors to get a drink of water for my son. I was hysterical until I found her. She had sat down by the hedge and was picking flowers. I understand Mom's great fear with many small children in the tall grass and willow bushes.

Much work was needed to clear that bush quarter. Dad was able to clear the trees and break about five acres of land that first year and seed some oats. Dad harvested enough oats to feed the chickens, pigs, and horses for the winter. I'm sure Dad planted potatoes and other vegetables too. Our pioneers worked hard to provide for their families.

Dad worked for a neighbour and earned a cow. The cow was due to calve in a few weeks. Dad took the cow home, and she calved, but Dad found her and her calf a few days later; she had died of milk fever. The neighbours went together and gave Mom and Dad another cow. Mom and Dad milked cows and sold cream to help buy the groceries.

I remember Dad tied a rope to the cream can and lowered it down the well. This kept the cream cold. Sweet cream brought a bigger price. As the boys grew older, Mom and Dad milked 16 cows. The milking chores were done by hand at 8 a.m. and 5 p.m. There was no exception. We knew we had to plan our day or free time around these chores. Mom said, "The cows must be milked on time to get the most milk. I always liked to milk and helped the boys. There were days when that was the only time I sat down all day."

Nelson was a responsible kid and was in charge of taking the cans of cream to the highway where the cream truck would load it and transport it to Bonnyville Alberta. I remember an event when Nelson was about fourteen years old; it was Friday and the day to take the cans of cream to the highway for Mr. Swingley to take to Bonnyville. Mr. Swingley waited in Bonnyville until the cheques were made out, and then he brought the cheques home to Pierceland with him. The farmers picked up their cheques on Saturday night when they went to town for their weekly groceries. Saturday night made Pierceland come alive. The ladies could visit at McClellan's store or the Co-op store while their list was filled. Nobody walked around with a cart to pick up their goods; the stores didn't have any shopping carts. The stores were full of many items, and there wasn't room to push a cart between the isles. The store manager or the help was given the list, and they filled the grocery list.

Back then, Pierceland had a barber shop, a pool hall, and a shoe maker, who repaired all leather goods. There was a garage too and a community hall where I watched a movie for 10 cents. What a thrill that was when I could save the 10 cents for the admission fee. It was special to go to the movies with my friend Gerry Swingley. It didn't happen often.

The scary event that I remember took place on Friday when the cans of cream were to be delivered to the highway. Nelson hitched the team of horses to the wagon. I was one of six kids who waited to go along for that 1.5 kilometre ride to the highway where the cream truck picked up our cream.

Nelson loaded the cans of cream. One over-anxious kid picked up the reins that were used to drive the horses. The horses started to move ahead, as they were trained to do. Nelson made a fast dash for the lines, but another kid screamed, and the horses jolted ahead and began to run. I was the first kid to jump off the back of the wagon. I met Mom in the doorway of the house; she had heard the commotion outside and was coming out to investigate. Mom was anxious, as the team of horses turned the corner by the barn. Mom and I instantly ran in hot pursuit after the team. The planks on the wagon bounced high and made more noise for the horses to hear, and they galloped toward the lumber pile west of the barn. Two of my brothers tumbled off at the barn. Mom grabbed each of them, stood them on their feet, and told to go to the house. Around the corner of the barn another kid hit

Five Plus Five Makes Fifteen · 71

the dirt. She too was dusted off, told to stop crying, and run to her brothers. Mom and I ran after the horses and prayed, "Hail Mary Full of Grace."

I saw the fear in Mom's eyes, as she stumbled and caught herself before falling down. Another sister was retrieved from the briar patch, near the place where I had picked raspberries. I know that my sister Judy has not been picked up yet. Why had she not fallen off and been picked up?

Mom was out of breath, but pushed on in search of her missing daughter. I'm an adult now, and I know a mother's pain when your child is in danger. We jogged toward the old lumber pile, and Mom spotted the horses close to the poplar trees. The horse's neck yoke was jammed between two trees and that made the team stop. The rig was at a standstill, but it wasn't the wagon Mom was worried about.

There still was not any sign of Judy. Judy was the sister closest to me in age, and we were always together, much like the twins were. I longed to find Judy and dust her off. Could she have fallen into a bushy place where Mom or I could not see her? I followed Mom to the horses. I saw a small bundle on the wagon. Was it possible that Judy could have managed to ride the wagon to a standstill? I raced to the wagon, and I was stunned to see my sister, Judy laying flat on the wagon. Mom rushed ahead of me.

Judy laid face down and motionless on the wagon. Her hair was windblown and dust covered her clothes. My heart pounded, as Mom called her name and reached out to touch her. I took a deep breath, as Mom rolled Judy over. Was Judy able to reply or was she dead? My mind ran wild. In an instant, Judy flung her arms up to Mom's open arms. Judy was safe, but a little traumatized. Mom checked her over for broken bones or head injuries. Judy appeared okay. Mom put her on the ground and told her to hold my hand, as we started for home.

Mom reached for a bridle of one horse and led the team home. As we journeyed home, Judy told me how she was the only kid to ride the wagon to a stop. Judy had experienced a memorable ride. I guess she was the first one of us to have a chuck wagon ride.

Later in the evening, Mom removed the slivers from her feet because she hadn't taken the time to put shoes on her feet when she ran from the house. What great blessings this day had, as not one kid was hurt from this incident. Mom was so thankful; she stoked up the fire and popped some popcorn for us to celebrate.

The water well was a large hole that was dug into the ground to where the water level was. The hole was about 1.2 by 1.2 metres. It was dug deep enough for a pail to sink down and be filled. The pail tipped and was filled with water. Our well had enough water for cooking and drinking only. The drinking water was lifted from the well with a rope that was strung through a pulley on a frame that stood above the well—like a wishing well. Dad tied a galvanized pail to the rope, lowered it into the water to be filled, and then pulled on the rope when the pail was full of water. He lifted the water to the ground and filled the water pails to be taken into the house. I remember a mouse floating in one pail of water. Dad emptied that pail of water and lowered the pail for more water. Not one of my family thought that the water was unsafe to drink.

I told my grandkids about a white enamel dipper that hung on a nail near the water pail. Everybody used that same dipper to take a drink, as did any company that came to visit. My grandkids thought that it was a terrible thing to drink water from the same dipper as everybody else. Each person should have their own drinking glass.

Mom raised her own baby chicks from the clucking hens (a hen who has laid about a dozen eggs and wants to sit on her nest to keep the eggs warm so as to hatch little chicks). Mom told me when she set hens on the nest to hatch their eggs, she covered the hen with a box for a couple of days so the hen wouldn't leave her nest and allow the eggs to get chilled. It takes 21 days for the chicks to hatch. The eggshells become weak, and the chicks are then able to pick their way out of the shell that had held them as they matured. The hen's nest always needed to be cleaned, as she eats the eggshells that the chicks hatched from.

Mom tied one of the hen's legs to the chicken coop to keep the hen from dragging her babies into the wet grass and any danger that lurked nearby. I remember Mom cooking eggs so that they were hard and mashing them up to feed the young chicks. In a few days, the chicks could eat mashed-up grain. One summer, Mom raised one hundred chickens from ten hens. That must have been a record!

A rooster was needed to make the eggs fertile. I did not like that rooster. He chased me, and I hid in the closed shelter; the outhouse. That rooster pranced around outside. Every time I opened the door to come out, that rooster was there. I felt like I was in jail. I hollered and cried until Nelson rescued me. I was so thankful that I tagged along with Nelson when he went to get the cows for the evening milking.

I remember smelling the roses, feeling the cool grass on my bare feet, and listening to the robins chirp. I walked and talked with Nelson until he told me to stop talking because he wanted to listen for the cowbell. (Mom had a bell tied around the cow's neck so that we could hear where the cows were grazing.)

Nelson threw a stone into the water to make the frogs stop croaking too, as he listened for the cowbell. He heard the "tinkle" of the cowbell. I followed Nelson toward the bell sound and found the cows eating in the shade of the willow trees. The hunt was over; we arrived home in time for the evening milking.

I feel that many children today don't always have a farm to visit where they can watch farm animals with their babies. Animals with babies need to be watched, as they are always ready to protect their babies.

me by our first house

Chapter 24:
Fun Chores

Mom washed clothes twice a week with slough water. I went with Nelson to get water for washday. He hitched one horse to the stone boat that had a big barrel placed on it. A stone boat is a flat-bottom structure made out of two by six planks that are spiked together. It slid along on the ground on other planks that acted as runners. Because it was so low to the ground, large rocks could be rolled on to the stone boat so they could be removed from fields being prepared for crops.

We drove to the slough that was a few hundred metres from the house. Nelson used a syrup pail to dip the water from the slough and fill the barrel, which could hold about 170 litres. Nelson had to drive the horse back slowly so that the water wouldn't splash over the edge of the barrel.

The water was warmed on the stove, as Mom made breakfast. Mom said that the water needed to be hot to get the white clothes clean; today I wash my clothes in cold water.

The slough water was also used to bathe once a week. The bathtub hung outdoors on the side of the house until needed. Saturday night was bath night and the tub was brought into the house in the afternoon to warm up. The little ones bathed first, and were put to bed. That round tin tub served us all; the water did too. Some hot water was added after each bath.

The older kids had a very quick splash because there was no privacy. I felt like my body was on display for all to see. I like the privacy that a closed door brings today. The only warm spot was by the old airtight heater, as the bedrooms were not heated. The houses didn't have insulation like today; only tar paper or wood shavings were used for insulation. That's why we had sheep wool quilts on our bed. With three or four kids in one bed, we had body heat too. Today, one of my biggest pleasures is when I soak in my Jacuzzi tub.

In the daylight hours of winter, my family all took turns at fetching wood. If anyone got in trouble, they needed to fill the wood box that was placed near the cook stove. What a useful punishment because the wood stove was filled often as Mom's washday was also her day to bake bread and other good food to keep the family fed. The cook stove also was a part of our heat in the house.

When darkness set in, Mom used a wooden match about three centimetres long to light the coal oil lamp. The matches were bought in a small cardboard box. There were no propane strikers or lighters to use. Later we had a gas lantern for light. I remember Dad pumped air into the fuel tank of the lantern to make the light burn brighter. The lantern had two mantles that were very fragile if they were touched. The special material sometimes fell apart, and the light could not be used until new mantles were bought. I was afraid of the burst of fire when the lamp was lit and before the mantles produced light.

In the dead of winter, we sat around the table and near the airtight heater to keep warm. Dad got the mail once a week, and when the *Free Press Weekly* paper came, Mom read Woody Woodchuck, Reddy Fox, and Peter Rabbit to us from the paper. Dad finished his work outdoors and read books like *Hardy Boys* to keep us entertained. I liked the mystery stories.

Mom made a special dinner of stew with fluffy white dumplings. Mom browned the meat with some onion added, and put in carrots, potatoes, and turnips. When the stew was cooked, Mom made gravy. Then the dumplings were added. It cooked for about 10 minutes;

nobody was to open the lid before the dumplings were done because the dumplings would fall and be heavy instead of fluffy. Those fluffy dumplings melted in my mouth. Mom used her biggest pot to cook with, and the stew with dumplings was always cleaned up too.

After we ate, Mom would put the little ones down for a nap and the older kids were kept quiet with jigsaw puzzles. The puzzles were placed on cardboard so they could be moved to the bed at mealtimes. Mom used every bit of space she had. Mom taught us that, "Everything has a place; now put it away."

All was quiet, as Mom listened to her program on the radio. *Ma Perkins* was a radio drama that was continued each day. I'm sure that Mom did her ironing or folded clothes as she listened to the drama on the radio. Mom filled every minute of the day with something constructive.

Many of her kids are now at retirement age. I find it hard to get a cheque for no work, but I do enjoy the extra cash. I'm thankful for my good life; I have never experienced the struggles that my parents had. I do give them thanks for all their efforts that made my life easier.

Mom stated: "People are stained glass windows. You can sparkle and shine when the sun is out, but when the darkness sets in, your true beauty is revealed only if there is a light from within." What a statement!

Chapter 25:
The More The Merrier

After selling his farm, Grandpa Burge enjoyed spending the summer months and the fall harvest with family in Prince Edward Island. While Grandpa was down east, he stayed with his cousin Laura. Before leaving, he offered Laura some money for the summer stay. Laura refused and said, "You helped with the seeding and the harvest. I don't want the money. Use that money to buy Joe's wife a washing machine."

Mom and Dad went to Cold Lake, Alberta to the McLeod's store and bought a gas-powered washing machine, complete with a wringer. There was no electricity in Pierceland at that time. That gas-powered motor putt-putted for about 2 hours when Mom did her laundry. Mom said, "That gas-powered washing machine was like a gift from heaven. The tight wringer squeezed out the water. My hands didn't blister from wringing clothes anymore. I think I washed everyday for that first week." (Mom had used a scrub board in a tub to wash for nine people.)

I remember Mom putting the exhaust hose from the washing machine out the window. Mom stepped on a lever at the bottom of the machine to start the motor. I have memories of the piles of washing that Mom had lined up on the floor to wash; there were the whites, diapers, coloured, and dark clothes to wash. Mom used "liquid bluing" from a bottle with Mrs. Stewart's picture on it. Mom said, "My wash was whiter when I used that magic bottle of bluing. I used 1/4 cup of bluing to a tub of water and added it to the final rinse water for the white clothes. I liked my diapers to be sparkling white." She started her wash with the white clothes and went on to coloured clothes, and then onto the very dirty pants. I thought that the pants would never come out clean, as the water was dirty from the many loads of wash that had already been washed. The clothes were also rinsed in a large tub and put through the wringer on the machine again.

Graham and Grant were the babies when Grandpa bought Mom that wringer washing machine. The twins slept, as long as that motor on the washing machine hummed. When Mom was done washing, the twins woke up. Now the babies needed their diaper changed. Mom was never out of a job; she went from one necessity to another and cared for her large family.

Mom said, "My kids didn't have a lot of clothes like the kids do today. They each had a set of good clothes for church, and they often shared with one another. Grandma Hellekson helped with the clothing. She went to the second-hand stores in Edson and bought good second-hand clothing and mailed the big box to me."

Oh, I can remember all the excitement when that big box arrived; it was like Christmas! We all gathered around that box, as Mom lifted out each item of clothing. I recall a blue frilly dress with embroidery down the front. I loved that dress, but it didn't fit me and was passed on to Nioma. Mom often remodelled the clothes, and fixed an outfit for each child to wear. Sometimes she added a frill for length or cut off a piece to make it shorter. What a task that must have been. I remember that I liked all my clothes that Mom made over for me.

Grandpa Burge needed a place to stay when he returned from down east. He moved in with Mom and Dad. Mom said that this was a better time, as now Grandpa was living in "our" home. Mom and Dad had lived with Grandpa for six years prior to him selling the farm.

Grandpa and Dad worked together and got enough logs to saw into lumber to build a house in town for Grandpa. When Grandpa Burge's little house was finished, he moved to Pierceland. I wonder what Grandpa had to move.

Grandpa's small manor had a kitchen and a bedroom. Near Grandpa's little red house was a big garden without weeds. He hoed every day to keep down the weeds. Grandpa's raspberries were so good! I stayed with Grandpa; we had tea and store-bought cookies before going to bed.

Grandpa married Sophie Ollenberger in 1954. I went with Grandma's granddaughter and her dad to get some things from Cold Lake. He drove fast, and I was afraid. I was not fond of Grandma Sophie. She had a German accent and spoke funny. She was old and had grey hair. She cooked different than Mom did. I was not her grandchild by kin, and I felt that Grandma didn't have time for me; she just had more to do when I stayed with Grandpa.

Grandma needed more room, so Grandpa built a living room onto the end of his house. I remember I walked through the bedroom to get to the living room with a chesterfield and a big armchair. Grandma had some pretty ornament, a pair of birds, and some snowmen to display on the dresser.

Grandpa and Grandma relaxed and enjoyed company, as they played cards and served tea to their guests.

Grandpa and Grandma had twenty happy years together. As time passed, Sophie could no longer manage a home. Grandma spent time in the hospital with a chest infection. She soon was too weak to cook, clean, and do laundry. Grandpa and Grandma moved to Edmonton, Alberta to live with Sophie's daughter, Florence. This arrangement lasted for Grandpa until Sophie passed away. Grandma Sophie died in September 1975.

Grandpa returned to Pierceland when Grandma died. Soon Grandpa began to experience poor health. He struggled to walk downtown for his mail and his groceries. I wondered if Grandpa was still able to cook healthy food. Grandpa's memory was failing too. I remember the time Lloyd and I took Grandpa some firewood. He wanted to pay Lloyd three times. I know Grandpa needed help, and I wondered if anyone took advantage of his forgetfulness. I had a young family and did not make a move to help Grandpa. Today I feel bad about not taking time to help my Grandpa Burge.

Dad took Grandpa home for the summer months. My sisters, Laura and Josie, were home to look after Grandpa, as they were out of school. My sister Laura remembers how hard it was to keep Grandpa from running away. She said, "I had to watch him like a baby. He always wanted to go home."

School started in the fall, and Dad was able to find a seniors place for Grandpa in Bonnyville, Alberta. Grandpa spent about 18 months in long-term care in Bonnyville. I was young with a husband and kids, but not once do I remember going to visit my Grandpa in Bonnyville. With age comes wisdom, and regrets and I have many.

Grandpa Burge died January 26, 1978. Grandpa is buried in St. Antoninus Cemetery in Pierceland.

My mother is 93 years old, and at the present time, Mom is in the Cold Lake Lodge. I try to visit Mom every week. I try to put myself in her place, "What if I was in a lodge or a home for the elderly and no one came to visit or play cards. I would need more than a warm place to sleep and good food to eat. Loneliness is hard for the elderly; they lose mobility and some feel that there is no reason to live."

Many elderly people are like historians who give us insight into the days that are gone by as they reminisce about their former life of work and play. Some stories seem to be a little farfetched, but today's world is different for them and who am I to judge them?

How hard it is to think that one day our kids too will be the parent or grandparent who sits at the window and waits for a visitor to come and spend time with them. I pray that I have showed my children how to make the time to share in another's life and make new memories with the elderly. Lord, bless those who make time for others.

Today, I find myself not wanting to play games that have a lot of action. I would rather play board games. My energy level isn't what it once was.

Chapter 26:
My Family Faces Death

Mom always rose early each morning. Her work started as her feet hit the floor. She knew the day ahead had many jobs and challenges too.

In the summer of 1952, Mom was more tired than usual. Soon she discovered that she was pregnant again. I'm thinking that this was not good news. I'm told that Mom never showed any signs of regret about more babies, and I'm told that Dad supported her; but I know another baby meant a bigger workload. What women could handle anything more?

Mom said, "It's hard to look forward to a new baby when you still have a baby."

I too experienced this incident with my family when I had four babies within five years; I hear you, Mom!

Dad struggled to support his family. Another income was selling wood for the schools and homes in Pierceland. The cook stoves had small blocks that fit into the smaller firebox, but larger blocks were cut for pot belly heaters that were placed in the schools. This bigger wood took longer to burn, and the hot fire would last for many hours. Dad charged $10 for a cord of wood. A cord of wood approximately fits into a box that measures 1.2 metres long, by 1.2 metres wide, by 2.4 metres high. The wood was cut to measure about 15 centimetres in diameter. The wood had to be piled tightly into the cart without any spaces to make a cord.

On Saturday, when the boys were home from school, the long trees were cut and brought from the bush and piled up to be cut later. Dad started to cut wood with a handsaw, but when he was able to purchase a power saw, the work was much easier and a lot faster.

Mom and Dad sawed the wood into blocks with a buzz saw. (A buzz saw is a large blade that turns with the power of a tractor as a belt ran from the saw pulley to the pulley on the tractor.) Dad pushed the long wood into the saw blade on one side, and Mom stood on the other side and threw the blocks away from the end of the whirling saw blade. Mom said, "It is too dangerous for anyone else to stand close to that spinning blade. I knew I needed to stay focused at every minute." Mom tossed the blocks from that saw when she was nine months pregnant; one week before George and his twin were born. Mom had asked the doctor if it was safe and he said, "It won't hurt you if you have always done it." Safe boundaries were unknown to many of our pioneers; they did what they needed to do, but care was taken to be safe.

How tired Mom must have felt, as she stretched her arms past her growing womb. Mom must have had strong arms from milking cows and throwing blocks of wood.

Pierceland didn't have a doctor; the doctor came from Goodsoil twice a week for the doctor's clinic days in Pierceland. It was time for Mom's doctor's appointment, and Mom went along with Dad when he went to town to sell firewood. Mom's baby was due the end of January.

Mom said to me, "I rode on the load of wood to Pierceland. I remember that the ride was so rough." When I was pregnant I rode in the big truck as far as Mom's—about 5 kilometres. Lloyd was hauling some milk cows for Dad. I found the ride rough, and it was hard to step so high into the three-ton truck. Wow Mom, a cord of wood? How did you get up there? I guess I shouldn't complain.

The doctor examined Mom in his clinic in Pierceland and said to her, "Your baby is due soon, and I hear two heart beats; are you prepared for another set of twins?"

What could Mom do, but accept the news; she would manage like she had before with two babies. Mom willingly went with the doctor that day to the hospital. I'm thinking Mom was ready for a rest and to have some time away from the many duties she had at home. Did she have a bag packed? I don't believe she had a thing for her or the new babies.

Chapter 27:
The Third Set Of Twins
(George And Leonard)

Mom said, "I arrived at the hospital in the late afternoon. I'm not sure how long it was before I went into labour; I was put to bed, and I soon fell asleep. I lost track of time and woke up with pains. On January 28, 1953, Mom went into labour. Twin boys were born. George and Leonard became the third set of twins. All was not well with this delivery.

The first baby, George was born strong and healthy. Mom remembers being so tired. About one hour later, Leonard, the second baby, was born. He had a strong heart beat that continued to beat for about an hour. The doctor and the hospital staff worked hard to get Leonard to breathe, but without any success. Leonard suffered from collapsed lungs and the hospital did not have any machine that would inflate his lungs. Hospitals today are prepared for that.

On January 28, 1953, my baby brother was named, only a first name, and baptized in that hospital room. Mom was alone as the doctor said to her, "I'm sorry, but I could not save your baby." Each baby is a blessing, and Mom was shocked at the news. Leonard died a few minutes later. Mom suffered her loss alone; Dad was home with rest of the family to help Great-Grandma with their care. I wonder who and how

Dad was told about the death of his infant son. Dad too would suffer his loss alone, as he choked back tears.

Mrs. Slager, a registered nurse in Goodsoil, dressed baby Leonard and put a ribbon around his head. She took Leonard to Mom's bed and placed him in Mom's aching arms.

Mom said, "He was a picture perfect baby. How could he die? I knew that my baby son would not go home with me." Mom often held two babies; but now one arm was empty. Mom's newborn was taken away, and that was all that Mom saw of him.

Mom's tears fell, as she grieved Leonard. She clung to George, pressing him close to her broken heart. Every child is unique and special; Mom would never have the joy of sharing in Leonard's life. How would she get past this loss? Sure, Mom had a baby to take home, but it didn't make it any easier when she knew that she should have had two babies to show her sons and daughters at home.

Leonard's death was the first death to be experienced by our family. We had chickens and animals die, but I didn't know of any person who died. Now death became a part of our family. I don't remember talking about Leonard's death, but I knew it was a dreadful event that was filled with pain. A dark "cloud of gloom" hung above our home. Leonard's name seemed to vanish, as Mom and Dad suffered in silence. Mom told her family that Leonard was taken to heaven to be with God. Leonard would be happy. I was 7 years old, and I struggled to understand why a loving God would take Leonard home when he was only a baby.

Dad had a local carpenter, Adam Hickie, make a small coffin for Leonard. Dad told Mom that Adam fixed it up nice. (Mom stayed in the hospital for about ten days, as was the custom in those days.)

Dad took his newborn son, Leonard, from the hospital to Pierceland. A nurse had placed his tiny body in a small cardboard box. Dad was an emotional person, and I know he sobbed and wiped his tears, as he drove home alone. (Mom was still in the hospital and did not go to the cemetery.) Dad dug the small grave in frozen ground with a pick and a shovel. What a lonely task for a father without any other family to give him support; only Dad and the priest laid Leonard to rest in St. Antoninus Catholic Cemetery in Pierceland, Saskatchewan. Leonard, rest in peace.

Great-grandma Timmoth had come from Edson to help Dad with the kids while Mom was in the hospital. The eldest twins were just ten years old, but they were a big help in a full house of active kids. The weather was -40 degrees most of this time. Can anyone imagine a household of seven kids all cooped up indoors for one week in a small house? The cooking and washing was hard enough; now add a stern great-grandmother to the mix. Is it any wonder that Grandma went home soon after Mom was released from the hospital? I know she was in need of a rest and some quiet time.

Chapter 28:
The Fourth Set Of Twins (Lillian and Lewis)

The Burge family of twins was not complete as yet. On February 24, 1954, Lillian and Lewis were born. It had been just over one year since Mom had her last set of twins. What women today could manage that kind of a household? (Four babies in thirteen months!) Each of us girls agreed that not one of us would even like to try.

Mom's daily menu consisted of three wholesome meals — breakfast, dinner and supper, as there was no time or extra food to have a lunch. Most days were repeated; make breakfast, clean house, and wash diapers before it is time to make dinner. Mom's life was filled with much work and not much play. She got through one day and dropped into bed to prepare for the next day. The washing of cloth diapers would have been a big job; there were no Pampers to use and throw away. (George was just over 1 year old and Grant and Graham were about three years old; I'm thinking they probably still had a few accidents and needed to be changed too.) Mom's life would have been diaper, diapers, and more diapers. Mom, your hands should have turned colour!

Mom knew that she couldn't change anything that was presented before her, and she tapped into that positive attitude and said, "I am thankful that not one member of my family ever had a serious injury or a sickness where I was told it would be fatal. Many mothers are told that their child will always have a handicap to work through."

Mom had three sets of twins in about 4 years. How was Mom able to give thanks for her health and the health of her family when all she did was work?

Chapter 29:
Another Baby (Debra)

In just twenty months there would be another baby.

Debra was born on October 25, 1956. I remember Mom babysitting for the Hewlett baby in the summer months. Mom was always ready to care for another baby. The Hewletts had a hay meadow near our meadow and Bert and Alfred Hewlett both worked at cutting and stacking the hay. Mom cared for their baby, Robert, during the day. Robert was a sweet little boy, and he fit into our family. The older kids played with us too, and often we were back and forth to the meadow, less than a kilometre away. The Hewlett oldest kid, Charlotte, was 6 months younger than I am. The oldest boy, Alfred Henry, was about Grant and Graham's age. Bertha was the girl who was closest to Lillian and Lewis' age. Harold was about two years old when baby Robert was born. Our family waited for haying time so that our friends would return again. Our families were connected through the summer months, and I recall many happy days, as we all walked to the meadow, and back to Mom and Dad's. I have good memories of our summer fun with the Hewlett kids.

Mom told us that she was having a baby in the fall. I wanted a little boy like Robert Hewlett. Rob had big blue eyes, dark hair, and liked to be held by each of us kids.

Mom went to the hospital and gave birth to single girl. Mom, was it maybe a pleasant surprise to give birth to one baby? The only one that was disappointed was the doctor. If Debbie had been a twin, the doctor would have delivered four consecutive sets of twins for Mom.

Mom came home from the Goodsoil Hospital to Pierceland with the doctor. Dad picked Mom and the baby up in Pierceland. I remember that I wanted Mom to bring home a baby boy just like Robert, but Mom carried a baby girl into the house. Mom removed the blankets for us to see our new sister, Debbie. This baby was not like Robert; she was a tiny girl, she didn't smile or make any noises, but just lay in her bed and slept.

Debbie, my baby sister had big blue eyes and dark hair like Rob. She grew fast, and soon I was happy with Debbie, our special baby who fit into our family. Debbie was our unique baby to keep; she didn't go home in the evening like Rob. I soon felt that I would not trade my sister Debbie for any other baby; not even Robert Hewlett. Debbie remains special in our family, as she often organizes family events without any failure. Debbie has a strong will, a great personality, and she is a person who gets things done on time and in that perfect way.

Today I'm the Hewlett kids' Auntie, as I married their Uncle Lloyd. Bert Hewlett was Lloyd's sister. Bert and Alfred lived about 2 kilometres from Lloyd and I, and we often visited each other. When the Hewlett kids come to visit Uncle Lloyd and Aunt Barb we share good childhood memories. The hot summer days we spent together are a treasure. Charlotte and I remember the walks to the meadow and back to Mom and Dad's too. Not one of us was afraid of any animals or of getting lost in the willows or the tall grass. I am connected to my childhood friends in a deeper way, as their Auntie. The Hewlett kids come about once a year to spend some time to visit and have coffee.

Chapter 30:
A Tough Year

Life was hard, and money was hard to come by. Dad needed a way to make some cash. Dad was of Irish descent and he recited this poem:

> "Did you ever go into an Irish man's shanty,
> Where money was scarce and whiskey was plenty?
> A two-legged stool and a table to match,
> A string in the door instead of a latch."

Dad knew how to make home brew. Dad resorted to brewing a batch to sell (Maybe he drank a little too.) I know that it was illegal to make and sell moonshine. Dad was desperate, and I'm sure he thought he was too wise to get caught. One day, Dad shared a drink with a customer. This man wasn't very considerate of Dad's financial state. The man reported the sale to the authorities. Maybe that sale cut into *his* sales too; surely he didn't think of Mom and how hard it would be for her to manage a family alone?

Was Mom able to cut wood to put in the stove for cooking, hitch the horses to the wagon to go to town, and keep all her children safe? Yes, Mom was a strong lady, and she always found a way to survive.

The policeman came to our farm and searched the place. They found what they were looking for, and Dad went to court. He was charged $200. Dad could not pay this fine. He was sentenced was for three months in jail, and Dad was taken to jail immediately by the RCMP. No one bothered to tell Mom where Dad was.

Mom received a letter from Dad about a week later in the mail. Dad was in the Prince Albert, Saskatchewan jail to serve a three-month sentence. I don't recall Mom falling to pieces; she just did what she needed to do. Mom did not drive or own a vehicle, but she hitched the horses to the wagon and went to town. Mom went to the Local Improvement Office for assistance. When Mom arrived in Pierceland at the office. the secretary asked Mom, "How much money do you have in your purse?" Mom replied, "Not even one penny, that's why I'm here."

Mom received $250. She bought some groceries and sent an order to Eaton's for some sheets and new material to sew clothes.

Mom was a determined lady, and she managed to keep wood for the fire, water to drink, and food for everyone to eat. Mom and her kids managed the outside chores too. Nelson and Nioma were about ten years old and were responsible people. Dad was released from prison in six weeks due to good behaviour. I recall Dad showing me a leather belt that he made while he was in Prince Albert and serving his time. The time Dad spent in jail left a scar on him, and he felt that he was viewed as a criminal.

My life continued, as it always had, and I don't recall those dramatic months. I was about six years old.

Dad came home and went to work with the harvest crew and any other place he could find work. He worked for farmers, helped fishermen, and worked at the Cold Lake Air Base. I'm not sure what kind of job he did there. Dad was a proud man and never again received assistance. Dad changed jobs many times, but we lived as well as any other family in the early fifties. My family milked cows, fed pigs, raised chickens, and had a big garden. There was always enough food for us to eat and any other people that came to visit.

The outdoor toilet brings back a few memories too. My flush toilet today is great, and that soft paper is a big treat. Back in the earlier days, there was no such things as Kleenex, napkins, or toilet paper. Yes, we used the old Eaton's catalogue. When we had Christmas oranges that were wrapped in little square pieces of paper, we saved that paper for the toilet. It was wonderful, but it never lasted very long with so many bums to wipe, and soon we were back to the catalogue paper. Mom probably didn't buy many boxes of oranges.

I recall playing games after the work was done. We often played "hide-and-seek" or "Auntie I Over." "Prisoner's Base" was also a favourite. We had enough players for ball too. No one had a ball glove or a bat; we used a round stick. Lloyd hit the ball into the bush and the search was on as it was the only ball we had to play with. Lloyd sat back and laughed, as Judy and I rambled through the underbrush and came out with the ball. Now it was Lloyd who had to pitch, as Judy and I hit the ball.

My sister and I made a fort out of willows. Judy bent the tops over to the ground, as I rolled a big rock on top. There were many willows close together, and we made a three-room castle. The patch of willows was a cool place to play in the hot summer. Each kid had great imaginations. It was Grant who made himself the king. He gave everyone a parcel of land to live on. Grant said, "My kingdom is a safe place for both men and horses, but you must obey my rules." I rode a stick horse and chased my siblings around in the bushes. I found a burnt stick and made it my special pinto horse with many patches. Judy pealed a green stick, and it became her palomino horse with a flowing white tail.

Judy and I went along to the meadow with the older boys, Nelson and Lloyd, when they went to haul hay home to feed the cattle. We stayed on the hayrack to tramp the hay into the corners. We walked up and down on each forkful of hay that the boys threw onto the rack. That was hard work, stomping the corner tight so the boys could load more hay. Our little legs soon tired, but we continued to walk on the hay. When we saw a mouse, we were done tramping hay. My brother Lloyd stabbed a mouse with the pitchfork and dangled it in front of our faces. I saw that mouse wiggling, and I heard it utter a squeal that I have never forgotten. Judy and I both screamed in unison and jumped off the rack. We held hands and ran home. Nelson and Lloyd called us a pair of "sissies". We arrived home about the same time as my brothers. Mom never knew that we had abandoned the boys because of a little mouse that she said couldn't hurt us.

I recall another mouse story from when I was an adult and had small children. My sons, Dan and Joe, were about 8 and 9 years old. A mouse managed to find its way into my house. I set a mousetrap to catch that pesky guest, but the mouse didn't go where the trap was set. I guess I wasn't much of a trapper. In the evening when all was quiet, a mouse ran across the floor. I don't like mice. I jumped onto the table and said to the boys, "Don't be scared, a mouse can't hurt you; just hit it hard on the nose and kill it."

Both the boys could swing a broom and hit a ball. Joe grabbed his dad's big boot, and Dan got the broom. The chase was on, as I gave instructions from my high perch on the table. "Catch it before it runs under the stove. Don't let it go under the fridge either." The boys found that mouse chase a very interesting game. Dan swung at the mouse, but it scurried the other way. Joe threw Lloyd's big boot at the mouse and hit its long tail. Those beady black eyes seemed to eye me up too. The mouse was too fast for Dan and Joe, and it squeezed under the door, and out of range of my little warriors. I don't remember if the mouse was killed that night, but the walls had a few battle scars.

Chapter 31:
We Welcomed Each Season (Fall)

fall harvest scene

upgraded today-swather

Five Plus Five Makes Fifteen · 97

Fall was a time to harvest and prepare food for the long winter months for both the animals and for our family. I have some harvest memories of the earlier years. In late September and early October, the harvest was on the way. The binder was used to cut the crop and tie the oat sheaves into bundles. The bundles were dropped in single file, but close together for stooking. The binder was pulled with horses. A man rode on the binder, drove the horses, and tripped the bundle carrier. It was tripped when there were six or eight sheaves to drop into a single row to stook later. Eight sheaves or bundles were stacked with the grain heads facing upward so that the grain and the straw would dry. The sheaves were piled close together to hold each other up; this was called "stooking".

I recall walking along the rows of sheaves in the field and lifting up the bundles for Nelson and Lloyd to stook as they plunked them on the ground. In a week or two, the threshing crew came with their teams and hayracks. The men drove their teams close to the piles of stocks and pitched the bundle with a fork into a hayrack. In the field there were two men who were field pitchers to help load the racks quickly. When the hayrack was full of sheaves, the men hauled the load to the threshing machine. The threshing machine needed to be full at all times for the best performance. One load of bundles went to each side of the threshing machine, and the men pitched the bundles into the threshing machine that separated the straw from the grain. The straw was blown into a stack, and the grain went into a bin. Dad had a small wooden granary by the barn with a hole near the top of the granary for the grain spout of the threshing machine to be put in. The grain ran into the granary, and the straw was blown into a stack by the barn. The straw and the grain were near the barn to make it easier to feed in the winter months.

One of our neighbours had a threshing machine and a tractor. Many men worked together (a threshing crew was about ten men), and the men travelled to each neighbour for the harvest season. Dad was happy when he could thresh enough grain to fill the granary to feed the chickens and pigs. On a poor year, when Dad didn't have enough grain for the winter months, he made a deal with a neighbour and traded a pig, chickens, or potatoes for some oats. The neighbours were all willing to help one another.

I remember the men from the threshing crew. They all wore those grey, striped, bib overalls. Each man wore gloves to protect his hands from getting blistered from the forks twisting, as they pitched the sheaves into the hayracks.

I liked threshing time. That was the only time all the neighbours came to our house, and Mom had good food like warm buns, lemon pie, cabbage salad, and canned corn. That food looked sooo good, as I waited in the bedroom with my siblings. It was my job to keep the younger kids out of sight until the men were gone. I tried to keep everyone quiet, but I'm sure little giggles were heard, as we took turns, and peeked through the cracks of that old wooden door on the bedroom. My siblings and I ate that scrupulous food after the crew left the house; we cleaned it all up!

Mom must have crawled out of bed extra early on the harvest morning to do her farm chores before she prepared all the food. Mom said, "I made the pies and the bread the day before the threshing crew came." Mom made dinner and lunch in the afternoon, as supper was late. She also needed to do the evening chores because Dad was out in the field.

I helped Mom in the morning, as I mixed that orange package of colouring into a brick of white margarine. That made the white margarine look like butter. (Mom didn't make butter because she needed all the cream to sell and buy groceries.) Margarine was cheaper than butter.

I have a memory that isn't so good to recall: the straw from the threshing machine was piled high on one side of the barn. We were instructed not to play on it. Of course we enjoyed a slide down the straw stack. Dad saw us and we all lined up for a "whooping" from Dad. I was crying before my turn came. I can remember this happening only once because nobody wanted to take the chance of going through that again. I guess we must have learned fast.

Mom's memory of her uncle who was buried in a straw stack helped us to see how dangerous a straw stack could be. Kids think that nothing will happen to them.

Mom said, "My uncle dug straw from the same side of his stack all winter. Toward spring he had a hole in one side. He went to do his morning chores in the spring and continued to dig into the same side of the straw stack.

"He didn't come in for dinner. His wife went to look for him. She saw the fallen straw stack and went to get help. The neighbours found Mom's uncle buried in the unstable straw stack. The straw fell onto him, and he was not able to move away from the large pile; he suffocated. That story stayed with me longer than the little strap that Dad used to teach me a "good lesson".

After the fall harvest was complete, Dad had time to build a kitchen on to the west side of the house. I recall coming home from school and seeing the progress each day. First the floor was done, then the walls went up, and at last the roof was on. Now the addition was closed in, and Dad could work indoors where it wasn't so cold. My birthday was in December, and I was so proud to invite Sylvia Bear, a classmate, to come for a sleepover for my 10th birthday. Dad and Mom had just moved the stove and kitchen supplies into this new area before we came from school. Now Mom had another room to cook and prepare the food.

I told my teacher that we had a new house. A teacher must hear many stories from her students, as they share and stretch some of their home life events.

I recall the measles germ came home from school. My brother Lloyd and I were sick at the same time. It seemed that we spent many days in that dark bedroom, like an eternity. Mom said we needed to protect our eyes. When one kid got a sick, we all took our turn at being sick, as the germs travelled through our whole family. Mom, how did you manage with the added work of sick kids?

In the fall, we dug the potatoes, let them dry, and carried them into piles in the garden. Then we covered the potatoes with the potato tops to allow them to be cured. (Grandpa said the potatoes needed to be cured.) The following day, we carried the potatoes to the cellar. (To me, it seemed like a make-work project.) Today I dig my potatoes and let them dry in the garden, but I carry them into the cold room that same day. My potatoes keep until I grow new potatoes.

When it was time to pick up the potatoes, we had many little wars as we threw the small potatoes like snowballs. The potatoes hurt when I got hit. When I screamed, Dad threatened me and said, "If you kids don't quite throwing potatoes, I'll take away all your privileges." I didn't think I had any privileges to lose, but I learned not to yelp, as the war continued when Dad wasn't looking.

I don't remember our family having a "cold house" outside with ice in to store summer food. Our family had a cellar under the kitchen floor. The houses in the earlier days didn't have basements like we do today, but they did have a root cellar (a hole was dug in the dirt under the floor of the house). A square was cut into the kitchen floor, and a hinged door was put over the cellar opening. There was a ring put on top of the door for easy opening. The cellar was a cool place for keeping milk and cream for the coffee, the canned fruit, and the root vegetables for the winter season. Mom put the milk on the top step of the cellar so that she could easily get it when she baked. Mom saved fresh milk each time she milked. Today the store milk is dated about two weeks ahead of the present date. My, it must be full of preservatives to last that long because I know that unpasteurized milk will sour in a couple of days.

When it was my turn to get the potatoes for supper I was stressed because I didn't like to go down into the cellar. I said to Mom, "I saw a big black tail crawling behind the jars of fruit when I went to get potatoes."

Mom said, "It just a little mouse and that mouse won't hurt you."

A few days later, I was in school and Mom needed to go into the cellar for supplies for dinner. That night at suppertime, Mom said, "I saw an uninvited guest with a big, flat, rubber-like tail in the cellar today. I know that it was not a mouse." A trap was set and in the morning the trap was set off. Dad said, "It must be something larger than a mouse." A larger trap was set, and in the morning, Mom had a big surprise as she lifted the cellar door. As a monster varmint was in the trap; it was a muskrat. No one knew how a muskrat found its way into our cellar. I told Mom that I was traumatized as a child because she sent me into the cellar for potatoes and that muskrat made me afraid of mice. All mice appear big to me.

I remembered trapping muskrats with Dad on the slough. The one in the cellar looked much larger than the ones that Dad caught in the traps out on the trap line.

Chapter 32:
Winter

Soon the cold winter days came, and I was cooped up indoors. There were no ski-doo suits to wear outdoors; and my family couldn't have afforded them if there were. Nelson said, "I wore a woollen sweater, and the wind blew right threw it. I was always cold." I left my pyjama bottoms on, and pulled those ugly, long, brown stockings overtop. I tried so hard to get the wrinkles out so that no one knew that I had my pyjamas underneath. I often think of walking over a kilometre to meet the bus. What if the bus was late or if it didn't come? I don't remember going back home.

I'm a mother, and I can't imagine sending my kids to walk a kilometre to meet the bus. I guess Mom was concerned too, but she didn't have time to walk with us. Her babies needed attention and household chores kept her busy.

The cold weather had me and my siblings indoors after our chores were done. The younger kids had waxed crayons to color on old newspapers, as they sat by the table. The older kids enjoyed puzzles, Chinese checkers, and card games like "Go Fish" with all their siblings.

Judy and I had the same passion of cutting out pretty clothes from the old catalogues and spreading them on my bed to look at. I don't recall any paper dolls cut-outs. Judy loved nice clothes, and she enjoys shopping today. I don't have much need for nice clothes, as I am a farmer's wife; jeans are more practical. If I buy a new outfit, I don't get much wear out of it, and it is soon out of style.

Mom and Dad played "Hearts," with the older kids. I recall many disputes, as to why a certain card was played or not played. Dad remembered each card that was played and said, "Why did you play that card?" Nobody else remembered or even cared much about the outcome. I have played many card games through the years. The Gonie's love their cards, and I've played along with the rest; however it isn't my favourite pastime.

On the meadow quarter, there was no hill to slide down in the wintertime, as it was flat ground. Summer had rolled into fall and the autumn into winter. Winter meant snow and sliding down the big hill. Our new fortress had a big hill to slide down — what a treat. I liked to jump on pieces of cardboard and whizz down the hill. I looked for lights, and if none were seen, I could make a fast run and cross the highway. Lloyd and I jumped on the cardboard and went across the highway before any vehicle; waxed cardboard went faster. Nobody ever told Mom where we were sliding. I now recognize the dangers.

Chapter 33: *Spring*

The daylight hours grew longer and spring arrived to start a new season. I thought spring was the best time of year. The days were warmer, the animals began to shed their winter coats, and the fresh smell of spring was in the air. Soon the snowbanks melted, the frogs croaked, and the birds sang; new life was everywhere. On our small farm, we had soft, fuzzy chicks, cute little pigs, and black calves that raced about in the meadow. The whole world was transformed.

The old airtight heater was taken out of the living room for the summer. Our house seemed so big now. The wood cook stove was cleaned of that black soot. The black soot was a big mess to clean, but Mom said the bread baked better.

Spring also meant mud; it was all over, as many boots were placed by the door. Our house didn't have a porch, and so the outerwear was stacked by the door in a whopping pile. Not all of our boots matched, but that didn't matter, as we all didn't go outdoors at one time. We wore whatever boots we could slip our feet into. Dad pounded nails in the wall by the door to hang up our coats; they weren't used often.

Good Friday and Easter came; Dad brought in some black dirt and placed it under the cook stove to warm. Dad said, "Good Friday is the best day to plant any seeds for the summer crop. The moon is right, and the garden will thrive because the moon is growing." I plant my tomatoes whenever I'm ready to do so.

Dad filled some small containers with dirt, made a hole in the centre, and pushed those tiny tomato seeds into the hole and scattered dirt over top. The plants grew bigger and Dad transplanted them into larger pots with well-rotted manure. This acted as a fertilizer and allowed the little plants to grow faster. The plants were placed on the windowsills so that they could get a lot of sunshine. Dad's bedding plants often got upset and replanted. Dad always knew when this happened. Not one of us owned up to spilling the plants; it was always that "Mr. Nobody" who caused the disaster.

In late May, Dad cut the potato eyes for planting. We always planted a gigantic amount of potatoes. When it was time to plant potatoes, everybody helped. Dad made a furrow with the plough, and we walked along, and dropped the eyes of the spuds into the furrow. Then Dad covered the potato eyes with dirt. I thought that our potato patch was about an acre big. Dad was from Prince Edward Island where the potatoes are the best. He said, "No one should ever run out of potatoes."

Chapter 34:
Summer

Summer was a free time with no school to attend. I ran around in my bare feet all summer. The mud would ooze between my toes. Mom had a basin of cold water on the step for me to wash before I could go into the house. I liked to wade or raft in the slough. If I came home wet, I needed to scrub the outdoor toilet, a job I didn't like.

Dad laid some large trees across the wet part of a slough so that he could cross to the field on the other side. The horses would find their way on the new bridge, but when he had a truck; he then had to go around the slough.

A job that I remember doing is riding our horse, King, as Mom walked behind the garden plough to hill the potatoes. Mom would get angry when King stepped on the potato plants. I could not make King walk straight down the row; maybe the row was not straight.

Mom recently told me that there were so many flies in the summer that she sewed earmuffs for the horses to keep the bugs out of their ears. I recall Dad rubbing grease around the horses' ears too. Dad also put "baskets" on the horse's noses. These were made of a screen, which fit over the horse's nose, and a strap was slipped over the horse's ears and under the bridle to hold it on. This helped to keep the flies from getting into the horses' noses when they were used for work.

Dad bought a car that he had to leave parked at the highway because the road was impassable for a car. Mom was upset because he should have known that a car was meant for the highway. After a few years, Dad was able to buy an old Ford truck, but he got stuck a few times as he tried to cross the wet meadow.

Berry picking was a big job. We picked strawberries, raspberries, Saskatoons, and blue berries. I didn't like to pick berries when we went to the bush for many hours. It seemed that the pail never got full very fast. Today I like to pick berries; I go for about an hour, and if my pail isn't full, that's okay.

Nelson was allowed to drive the team of horses, and he would take us to the highway where we went to the Alberta border and picked beer bottles to sell later. It was about three kilometres away. When we got home, we washed the muddy bottles before Dad took them to be sold. Bottle picking was a job, and we made some money too.

Chapter 35:
More Twins (Lance and Laura)

family picture

The fifth set of twins was Lance and Laura. They were born on April 9, 1958. The same doctor was in Goodsoil, and he delivered four sets of twins for Mom. Mom came home from the hospital with the doctor as far as Pierceland. Dad and I met Mom and the twins in the Pierceland café. I was ten years old when these twins were born. Mom said that I was small for my age, but I was capable to help.

I remember going to town with Dad to bring Mom and the twins home. It was my job to hold one of the new babies. Dad drove the tractor with a cart behind, as that was our means of transportation. I held Lance on the way home. I remember being upset when the man at the café said to Mom, "And who is going to hold her?"

I was angry at that man for thinking that I was a little child and unable to hold my baby brother. I know that it was Nioma, who loved babies, and she helped Mom the most at home, but I made out just fine, as we travelled those 11 kilometres home to our farm. Mom told me that the man was not being mean; I was a small child, and he spoke what was on his mind.

Lance and Laura were about two years old when we moved to our new fortress. They didn't like the move with the unfamiliar places. My brother Lance said, "Home now," when it was time to go to bed at night. Mom often put the twins in her big wagon box to keep them together and safe as she worked in the garden. Laura was content to play with Lance in that big "playpen".

Laura was an easy child to care for; whatever came her way was okay with her.

Lance was the twin who liked to be the leader. He took Laura's hand and led her to the garden. At Mom's 90th birthday celebration, Lance and Laura walked into the hall holding hands.

Chapter 36:
Hair Day

Mom always provided both the girls and the boys with their hair care. The boys were lined up for a haircut about every two months. Mom used hand clippers to trim the boy's hair short. Dad took his turn too.

The girls' hair day was more outstanding. Mom bought a home perm or a Toni to try and make our hair pretty for picture day. I hated that day! Judy and I shared that wonder solution, as we sat in that stinking solution until our hair was set. That strong smell lasted for a few washings too. Mom rolled those tight curlers and poured on the smelly solution. After a few minutes, the curlers were taken out. I had frizzy hair that stuck out all over. I wanted to wear a hat to cover my head. Mom tried to tell me how beautiful my hair was, but when I looked into the mirror I knew that I hated every bit of my head. I could feel how "fried" my hair was. Judy spent more time with her hair, but I know that she too hated those home perms. Maybe that's why Judy became a hairdresser. Her golden locks are always well done, and she is happy to have a mirror to reveal the beauty of her hair.

Chapter 37:
Moving From the Meadow

farmyard house

The meadow quarter was Home Sweet Home for nine years. Now Mom and Dad made the decision to move away. The road across the meadow was impassable for a truck when it was wet; that was most of the summer. When Dad got a truck he had to drive around the meadow and come in from another direction. Dad asked the L.I.D. (Local Improvement District) to build a road. The municipality told Dad, "No road can be built this year because there is no money for roads in the L.I.D. budget."

Dad and Mom looked for a place near the highway. The neighbours, the Buchans, were moving from their farm to Cold Lake in the spring. Mr. Buchan worked at the air base and his wife, Sadie, was a cook at the Cold Lake hospital. So in June of 1959, Dad and Mom bought the Buchan Place, which was closer to the highway and about three kilometres from the meadow. The house wasn't any bigger, but this new lodging had an old barn with stalls and straw on the roof. There were two granaries with a good roof. The log house was located on top of a big hill. The meadow was flat land, and we never had anywhere to slide in the wintertime. We often made snow forts or igloos from the crusty snow, but now we could use the toboggan to slide down the hill when the snow came. The toboggan was used for us to bring wood from the woodpile to the house when we filled the wood box indoors.

It was a thrill to sit on the hill and count the cars that went by on highway 55; none of us had ever seen many vehicles. This didn't last long, as we were expected to work and help with family matters like babysitting, gardening, hanging out the wash, and picking berries. The work never seemed to be done. Nioma worked indoors and was great with the babies. Judy was Nioma's helper in the house. I was four years younger than Nioma, and I was never fond of babies. I was a tomboy and loved the outdoors. I managed Grant, Graham, George, and Lewis to try to keep them safe. I helped the boys with chores, and then the games began. Hide and go seek, wheelbarrow races, and tag were favourites. The two sets of twins—Grant and Graham and George and Leonard (who had passed away)—were about twenty-seven months apart and close to the same size. Grant and Graham took George to a school party. A teacher from the next class asked George, "Are you Grant or Graham?" George replied, "I'm George."

These boys could think of many unsafe adventures. I became their shadow, caregiver, and a supervisor. I refereed too. I must have been like an army general. I used my shoe on their backside when they needed to be disciplined. George talked about that shoe at our reunion, as we sat around the campfire. He claimed that it must have been a high heel shoe, but I know that it was not, as Mom said I had to be sixteen years old before I could buy or wear heels. I'm not sure how I could discipline boys who were as big as, or bigger than, I was. I guess my growl must have scared them. I like to think that they had respect for me. Today I get along fine with all my brothers.

Lewis was younger and smaller than his brothers but he kept up to them. He tried whatever was suggested, and he was often in trouble, as he made a drama out of every situation. I rescued Lewis from on top of the barn when he was afraid to climb down the way he crawled up. I learned later that the boys had taken the ladder away so he couldn't get down. That ladder appeared quickly when Lewis screamed that he was stuck on top of the barn.

I recall the time he crawled onto a raft, and the older boys pushed the raft in the slough. The boys walked to the shore and dared Lewis to jump off the raft into the water. Lewis wanted someone to catch him when he plunged into the slough. Lewis was stranded and yelled to me. I retrieved the raft, and the boy's water fun came to an end. The boys were not pleased with Lewis for spoiling their cool fun. The raft was "off limits" for the rest of the week. I had planned to make teaching my career, as I had learned much about handling mischievous boys. And a classroom would have some girls in it too! However, as I matured, I thought that more schooling was just too much to endure.

The log house at the Buchan place had a larger room with the stove at one end and a table and couch at the other end. There were two bedrooms, one for Mom and Dad and the other was for Nioma and the younger kids who slept in the house close to Mom and Dad. The granaries didn't leak, and they became our outdoor bedrooms — our own summer cabin. I liked the girl's granary where we slept. My brothers slept in the other granary.

There was a power plant at the Buchan place, but the batteries were dead. Dad didn't want to put any work or money into the plant because electricity was soon coming to the Pierceland area.

The water well didn't have enough water for the cows to drink, the house was small, but there was a gigantic garden space. Dad could drive out the lane and to town with the old Ford truck with no fear of getting stuck. Wow! Was this a step up in the world?

The barn in our new place had poles on the roof. Straw was placed on top of the rails, like that first shack in the meadow. That roof dripped after a rain. Mom said, "I would rather milk the cows outdoors in the pouring rain than have my head soaked with that yucky brown water that dripped for a week after it rained."

Later in the summer, Dad moved our lumber house from the meadow. The house was put on the west side of the old log house at the Buchan place. Dad made a walkway to join the two houses. We had six rooms now and enough bedrooms indoors for both the girls and the boys. Dad bought a chesterfield for our front room. We had a bigger kitchen too, and Dad made a large table from an 2.4 by 1.2-metre sheet of plywood. He glued some Arborite over the plywood top; it was beautiful and easy to wipe. I was happy because it was like my friends', Chris and Jerry's, table — only much larger. Dad also made a bench, as long as the table; we all sat together to eat. Judy and I no longer held our plates and sat away from the table.

Chapter 38:
Homemade Entertainment

My large family learned how to make their own fun. My brothers found some old nails and made a cart. They didn't have any wheels, so it was pulled along on the grass. This land buggy pulled heavy, and the boys teamed up and became the horses, as we each had a turn at riding. I was tipped out when my turn came, but my bruises healed.

When the family grew older, we were introduced to hockey at school, so we played a game like hockey at home, but it was on the grass in the summer months. We used our own rules. In the wintertime we used frozen horse dung as a puck. Our hockey sticks were any stick we could find with a club on the end.

Gus Wagenhauls, our bachelor neighbour, lived about a kilometre away from our farm and often came to our home for Sunday night supper. Mom fried four chickens, made coleslaw, and mashed potatoes too. Gus wanted to join in the fun, and he would go in goal. What a good sport he was. I know on some occasions he went home with bruises, as he was knocked from his feet. I still have this image of Gus rolling around on the ground and trying to get up. George was a big boy, and he often helped Gus to his feet. Our household was full of action; if there was free time, there was always someone who wanted to play catch or ride a horse or go rafting. Dad made a rope swing from a tree. He also made a teeter totter for the smaller kids. A game of tag in the dark was mountains of fun; not one of us kids was afraid of the dark. Dad said, "There's nothing in the dark that will hurt you."

Judy and I made mud pies in the summer months. Our hand would get sore, and Mom made us rub pork lard into the dry and dirty cracks. Judy and I also danced and sang about the yard. Judy used a skipping rope for her microphone when she sang. I introduced her as a Hollywood star. The stone boat was our stage, and we could bow to any curious animals that wondered by. There always was something to do.

Another game we played was a castle game. We would live in a mansion as royalty do. My brother, Graham draped a towel over his head, and said he was a lord. Grant was the king with a crown; a bowl placed on his head. My sisters and I would pick rhubarb leaves for our heads because we were rich ladies in the kingdom where all fancy ladies wore hats. In this castle, every child had his own bed. (We slept 3 and 4 kids in one bed.)

Today my grandkids have their own bedroom and bathroom too. It's hard for them to believe that we were three or four kids in one bed. I know this helped to keep each other warm because there was no heat in the bedrooms. Sometimes the water froze in the water pail in the kitchen. In the morning I dressed by the airtight heater in the main room. I remember jumping from one foot to the other because the floor was so cold. Mom always had a roaring fire in the airtight heater for us to get dressed by.

One morning, my sister Lillian backed into the hot airtight heater. Lillian's tender skin was burnt instantly. She screamed in pain because the one cheek of her bum was burnt, and the skin was rolled up to expose that meaty flesh. Mom and Dad took her to the Goodsoil hospital. Lillian's backside was burned badly, and the doctor placed some ointment on the burn and wrapped it up. He told Mom, "You can take her home, but keep the bandage dry, and do not take it off. Bring her back in two weeks to see me."

Mom worried about infection, and she thought that she could smell an odour around the burn area. Lillian appeared okay, as she played with her siblings and joined in their fun. The last couple of days were long for Mom, as she waited for the two-week period to be passed. My parents took Lillian back to the doctor and the bandage was removed from the burn. Mom anxiously peered toward the injured flesh. The doctor said, "It has healed well and no scar will be left." Mom's worries of infection were over, and she was pleasantly surprised that the burn had completely healed.

Chapter 39:
Prayer of Gratitude

old 45kg bag of flour

I marvel at the many loaves of bread that Mom baked and once wrote a short story about Mom's large bread pan, where she mixed her bread until it was not sticky any more. She emptied the bread on to the table to knead. A big batch of bread needed to be mixed well. Mom rolled and pressed the ends of the bread dough from one corner of the pile to the other until it was thick enough to make into loaves, rise, and go into the pans.

I have added a short story about bread called "Prayer of Gratitude" that was printed in our local seniors paper.

"Do I hear one, now two, and then three," the auctioneer shouted. This auction was a hard day for our family, as each piece of our past was held up for the world to view and give their price of what it was worth with a raised hands or a shout. A twinge of loss crept over me, as the many items crossed the bidding block. I thought it would be easy to get rid of all the pieces of clutter that filled the old farm house; others would carry it away with joy.

The old wooden stool sold for one dollar. Mamma said with a sigh, "Nobody wants this junk in their modern-day kitchens. Today's house is full of sparkling glass and brass that speaks of riches in the twenty-first century; everything is fixed to meet today's code."

My family gathered around Mamma to support her big move. We visited and enjoyed coffee with many old friends who ventured to the sale. The auctioneer shouted, "Look, here is something we don't see very often."

Like a jolt from the past, my heartstrings were tugged. I saw a blue enamel bread pan held high. It was on display like a useless article that no one used or wanted any longer. This was a pan that was used every three or four days. A grandchild, with her arm around Grandma asked, "Did you use that big pan to mix your bread?"

"Yes dear, I baked every three days, and I used 100 pounds (45 kg.) of flour very two weeks for over fifteen years. Money was short; we ate whatever we could grow in the garden or make in the kitchen."

From my perch on the old porch, I could see the child's mouth fall open in disbelief, as she said, "That's a lot of bread. I like homemade bread. Do you think you could teach me how to make bread?"

Grandma hugged her granddaughter and said, "I sure could." The flour came in 100-pound cloth bags back then. I recall remember how frustrated Mom was when she would pick and pull at the little white string; sometimes the string was pulled out easily, and her flour bag was opened.

There were times when Mom used a knife and cut that string. Today I see that same kind of string on dog food bags. I too am frustrated when I can't pull the right end of the string and have it unwind easily.

The flour bags were later bleached and used for dishtowels. Women were creative and found a use for many things you know. Nothing was thrown away. Mamma served bread for breakfast with scrambled eggs or oatmeal porridge. Lunch was a slice of bread with our favourite potato soup or another vegetable soup. At supper, we had bread with roast pork, fried pork, or chicken. We also had potatoes with gravy. The older children sat by the little tykes at the table. They dished their plates up and buttered bread for their younger siblings. Mamma's bread brought unity to our family.

Grandma smiled and patted her grandchild's hand. She was proud to share the story of her prized bread and a big part of *days gone by*. I closed my eyes and recalled Mamma's soft voice, as she said grace. She pointed out, "There's always something to be thankful for."

We can make a bad day better, if we are willing to help others. It was at the family table that we learned to help others, share our adventures, and cry over failed relationships. "Family is our support system, often it is taken for granted. Always remember following the letters of bread."

"B" was for all the blessings a big family received as we learned to share.

"R" was for the responsibility we learned, as we did our daily chores.

"E" was for the everlasting values we learned, as we reached out to the needy.

"A" was for the art of forgiveness, as we learned to replace broken toys with a hug.

"D" was for the divine power that watched over us and kept us healthy and safe.

Once one meal was over, Mom planned for the next. My brothers became teenagers and couldn't seem to get enough food to eat. The kettles were filled to the top, and when supper was over, there wasn't any leftovers. One of my brothers invited a friend to stay for supper. This friend saw a large cookie sheet full of fresh buns. The buns were passed around the table. He said, "I wanted to mind my manners, and I didn't grab a bun like the other boys, but soon the bun pan was empty." It seemed that it was impossible to fill up the growing teenage boys. They ate whatever was placed before them.

Mom made desserts that used milk and eggs because that is what she had to cook with. Dad only liked rice if it had raisins in it. Mom made rice pudding with milk, raisins, sugar, and cinnamon. I still like rice pudding with raisins.

Mom made a chocolate cake for supper when it was someone's birthday. I can remember her sending me to the corn broom to get a straw. Mom poked that straw into the middle of the cake to test and see if the cake was completely baked. I wonder what our health fanatics would think of that unsanitary procedure!

My family was raised on eating pork or chicken, as that was what we could raise on the farm. We butchered one hundred chickens throughout the summer. We needed four chickens for one supper. Lewis, who is younger than his four brothers, said, "I was the last one to the table, and I always got the ends of the chicken. I didn't know that a chicken had anything but the ribs and back for many years."

Mom said, "Dad butchered a hog every two weeks. It was the kids and I who cut that pig into meal size pieces." When Mom made supper, she placed three frying pans on the stove and fried the meat for supper. Gravy was made by adding flour to the grease in the frying pan. Mom added potato water to make the gravy the right thickness.

Dad used cure called "habit-cure" to preserve the pork as bacon and hams. I remember that slimy juice dripping back into the crock, as Dad lifted out the ham leg. The cured meat was good. Dad sometimes took a bite before it was cooked. I didn't try to eat raw meat.

Some folks thought that we never had any fun, just work, but there were many hands to help. The small kids set the table and carried small blocks of wood. We worked together, and then we played together.

I remember going to the cow pasture and taking a lick of that salt block that was placed there for the cows. Dad put it in the pasture for the cows to lick, but none of us ever thought that it was not clean enough to lick from the same block as the cows did. My tongue was sore from the salt, but I knew not to complain to Mom because Mom told us not to lick the cow's salt block.

Saturday was a day of work. Mom and Dad had jobs for everybody on Saturday; it was not just a day off from school. Clothes were washed, the floors were scrubbed, and so was the toilet. Nobody wanted that job, so if we were in trouble, that was our punishment.

I believe that work is what you make it to be; a picnic was great, as we went to the hay meadow or to the field to pick rocks. A cool drink and some egg sandwiches were appreciated when we had a rest. The family all enjoyed the down time, as we sat in the shade. The local machinery dealer went by on the highway, as our family picked rocks with the team of horses. We were about ten bodies who walked along the wagon and threw rocks on. He said, "I know why I cannot sell that man a rock picker." On Saturdays, the boys helped Dad haul the wood in long lengths, butchered a pig, or picked rocks and roots from the fields. In the evening, we all had a bath and prepared for Saturday night and a trip to town if it was our turn. Our shoes were lined up and polished for church on Sunday.

Mom and Dad went to town to get the cream cheque and to buy the week's groceries. McClellan's store had groceries, hardware, cattle supplies, and anything else that a person might need. The store manager, Mrs. McClellan said, "If we don't have it, you probably don't need it." This store was a meeting place for friends to visit and share in the week's events.

Mrs. McClellan was a kind lady, and sometimes she put candy in with the groceries. Mom said, "There were times when we could not pay for all the weeks' groceries. The items were listed in a bill book, and we paid what we could. The store bill got large over the years, but the McClellan's never refused us any groceries. Dad paid as much as we could after the fishing season, and when we sold our calves in the fall. Mom said, "The outstanding bill was paid off when I went to work at the air base as a cleaner about 10 years later."

Chapter 40:
Grandpa Hellekson

As the pages of time were flipped over, our Grandpa Hellekson became a bigger part of our family. Grandpa retired from farming in the Edson area. He sold his small farm and had a little money and time for travel. Grandpa came to Saskatchewan to visit Mom and her family. He rode the bus to Edmonton and enjoyed "Klondike Days" for a day or two before he continued to Cold Lake where Dad and Mom met the bus. Grandpa's visits were heartwarming, especially when it was my turn to go along and meet the bus in Cold Lake Alberta. It was a long wait if the bus arrived late.

Grandpa was a cheerful character. He found joy in his grandchildren and took time for us kids who craved his attention. I remember Grandpa had some cool stuff — like that brown leather bag with a straight razor. I recall him rubbing his straight razor back and forth across a long leather strap. He said, "That's how I sharpen my razor." I never could figure out how that could sharpen his razor.

Grandpa played the harmonica, and Mom taught us to dance. My younger siblings remember Grandpa showing them card tricks. Not one of my brothers found that special way to make cards appear in places that they should not be. Grandpa would chuckle and tell them to practice for a year until he would be back again. I don't remember Grandpa saying he was tired, but I think he returned to his home with good memories and very tired.

The years rolled along, and many of Mom's kids were gone from home and living their own life. Grandpa gave Mom a scribbler with his poems that he had written. Mom knew that Grandpa wrote some poetry, but she had not read them. His penname was, "Queer Fellow". Mom was happy to read Grandpa's poems although she was sad when she read about her daddy's many trials and how he had suffered alone. He had not told anyone of his pain. He was taught to suffer in silence. Mom said, "Your Grandpa didn't talk about his long or lonely days, but he could write poetry about them." I guess that's how he managed to get past his hurts.

I read some of his poems. He expressed some of his inner views in ways that were painful, but at other times he was comical. I enjoyed his gift of words as I tried to place myself in a few of his life situations too.

Grandpa married a second time to Annie Mae in 1945. Mae worked in Edmonton at the cancer hospital for a few years. Mae returned home to Edson area on her days off. One day, Mae heard about someone who worked at the centre being diagnosed with cancer. She assumed it was her and said she wouldn't go through that kind of pain. In 1957, on one of Mae's days at home, Grandpa was outdoors working when he heard a shot. He knew that Mae was a good shot and thought that he would have a coyote to skin when he came indoors. He opened the door and saw his wife stooped over in her chair. He ran to her and picked up the gun. Mae tragically died from a gunshot by her own hand. There was an investigation because Grandpa had picked up the gun when he saw Mae in the chair. His fingerprints were on the gun. Grandpa spent a few devastating months thinking that he could be accused of murder. He was never charged, but that someone could think that he could do such a thing, took a toll on him.

In 1972, Grandpa married a third time to a lady named Amy. They shared many years together. I remembering stopping at Grandpa's house when they lived in Edson, Alberta. Lloyd and I had four kids; we didn't stay long, but I have a picture of us all with Grandpa Hellekson.

Amy was the Grandma that was there, as we visited Grandpa. Amy passed away before Grandpa, but I couldn't find any papers with a date of Amy's death and Mom can't remember either.

All too soon, my Grandpa Hellekson grew weary. He sold his house in Edson and needed help to care for his basic needs. His last few years were spent in a care home in Edson. Now it was Mom's turn to travel to visit Grandpa, as he found it too hard to travel by bus to Pierceland. Mom went once a month to visit her daddy. Grandpa always enjoyed her visits and appreciated her efforts to make the trip. Mom went to Edson to visit Grandpa to share in his ninetieth birthday celebrations. Mom's sister Irene was there too. Mom spent the night with Auntie Irene, who lived in Hinton, Alberta. (It's about a one-hour drive away.) In the morning, as the girls were having breakfast, the phone rang; Grandpa had passed away in the night. Auntie Irene and Mom got the news together.

My Grandpa, Harry Hellekson, passed away on May 4, 1991. Grandpa is buried in the local cemetery in Peers. That is the area where he lived most of his life. Many of his family members surround him in that county cemetery.

Nioma and I visited that cemetery in 2014 with one of Mom's cousins, Shirley. Neither Nioma nor I had the opportunity to meet many of Grandpa's siblings. Grandpa rarely talked of them, and I thought that the family wasn't very close. It was like a family history lesson for us, as Shirley was a local girl, and she told us many sad stories of family members who were laid to rest in that country cemetery. The afternoon with Shirley was a great family time, as she filled us in with Grandpa's family history. Thanks Shirley — that's a day that I shall always remember!

Chapter 41:
Grandma Ruth Visits

Mom had moved to Pierceland in 1943 when Grandpa Burge needed help. Aunty Irene had come to visit Mom before she was married and had her family, but it was not possible to travel back and forth due to lack of funds and a reliable vehicle. Mom and Auntie Irene had not seen each other for fifteen years. Then a letter came informing Mom that Auntie Irene and her family would arrive in one week.

I remember that Dad went to town and bought some oilcloth to cover the bottom of the dark mudded walls by the table. He white washed the top of the wall, and made our house beautiful for our company. I was so happy with our "new house" when my cousins came. There were five kids in their family. I guess we must have made room for a few more bodies in the bed. Auntie Irene and Uncle Ben and their family stayed for about a week. I'm sure the sisters, Mom and Auntie Irene, had many topics to cover.

In the summer of 1959, Grandma Ruth Stahl (Mom's mother) came from B.C. to visit us. I was amazed when Grandma Ruth could saddle up and ride a horse to get the milk cows. I remembered the other grandmas who had come earlier and only read to us or played checkers.

Grandma had her two sons with her, Jack and Dean. Jack was a little older than Nioma and Nelson. He may have been in his late teens. This was cause for a little excitement. Jack had been worked in a logging camp and had lost his arm above the elbow. He now wore a "hook" for a hand. He could open that hook and reach out to pinch me. I was afraid of that hook, but Jack only laughed at my fear. I never liked Jack, but later I understood why he was not a warm and loving person. Years later, Mom told me about his early childhood and how he had accidentally killed his sister. Jack never received any counselling to help him move on. I think he may have had horror dreams of his sister lying motionless on the floor. How did he get help or who came to his aid? There are many unanswered questions, and maybe Jack felt that Grandma never forgave him for Alva's death.

I recall Jack laughing at strange things, like when Nelson and Lloyd fell off the roof of the old barn. He didn't ask if they were hurt; he only laughed. That may have been the way Jack found to cope with his pain. Jack came to our house with his yellow Ford truck. He sped around the yard freely. He said, "Nobody is my boss. I'm an adult and go where I want when I want."

Jack liked to play tricks on the boys. One time he tied a rope to a bucket of water and put it on top of the door of the granary where he and the boys slept. Then he tied the rope to the door latch. The first boy to open the door and go into the granary was drenched. Jack stood back and laughed. Mom was not happy.

Jack went to high school in the fall to meet some girls. That didn't work well for him, and he quit school; and soon he was gone from my life.

Jack's younger brother, Dean, was about two years older than I was. He spent much time with Lloyd, Judy, and I. Dean was always willing to try any suggestion. He was that town boy that never dreamed of being a "redneck".

Lloyd, my brother, told Dean to hit a bee's nest with a stick and run. The bees could fly faster than Dean could run, and Dean had many stings. Judy and I made mud pies to put on his stings.

Another time Dean rolled the raft when I suggested that he should stand on one side. He pushed the pole into the swampy bottom, and as

Five Plus Five Makes Fifteen · 129

he tried to pull it out, he lost his balance and fell into the water. Mom was upset again.

Judy told Dean to slide down the horse's tail, and he would land on his feet. Dean hit the ground with a "ker-pluck". The old horse ran to the barn, and Judy had to retrieve him. I don't think that Mom was told. Why did Dean continue to trust us in whatever we suggested? Did Dean want to be a part of our hillbilly fun?

I liked Dean, and we bonded. I missed him when he and Grandma returned to B.C. after three weeks. I'm sure Mom must have breathed a sigh of relief.

A year later, Grandma and Dean returned. Grandma moved her trailer to Cold Lake and worked in the hospital. This lasted for about a year, then Grandma and Dean went back to British Columbia. Grandma had waltzed in and out of Mom's life.

Mom was never close to her mother, and she was too busy with her own family to wonder about Grandma's life. Mom didn't have time to dwell on "why" her mother returned to B.C., and maybe she had her own problems to work through.

Chapter 42:
Life Improves

The years rolled along, and in about 1957, Saskatchewan Power came to Pierceland. Electricity allowed us to have electric lights, a toaster, and an iron. Life was good. With six rooms between the two houses, there was room for a deep freezer for our meat and vegetables.

Dad went to Pierce Lake, the local lake about 20 kilometres from our home, and set a fish net. Each fisherman was allowed one net to catch fish for their own use. The net caught a lot of fish; about 100 white fish. I remember cleaning those slimy fish all day long. We gutted, washed, and scaled the whole bunch before they were put into the freezer. It's a good thing there were a lot of hands to help. We worked outside and used lots of water to clean and wash the fish.

Another big chore was butchering about 150 chickens. The boys chopped the heads off, and the birds jumped around, which ensured they were well bled out. We never had that dark colour around the bone like the chickens I buy in the stores today. Are birds not bled properly?

Mom had a tub of hot water that she dipped the chickens into, this loosen their feathers. The water had to be just the right temperature so that the feathers were easy to pull out, but not too hot so as to take the skin along with the feathers. After the chicken was dunked in the hot water for the right amount of time, Mom would pass that hot chicken on to one of us to "pluck". We each needed to pluck three chickens. I remember pulling out the wing feathers first before I started on the rest of the bird. I shall never forget the smell of those wet feathers. I tried to hold my breath. Judy suggested that we put clothespins on our noses. After the feathers were off the chicken, Mom would "singe" the hair off the chicken. Mom held each bird over brown paper that was twisted and set on fire. Then she would cut off the legs at the drumsticks and place them in cold water. We needed to wash the chickens and rub away the pin feathers before it was time to remove the craw and the guts. It was Mom who did the gutting, but I recall putting my hand into that cavity to remove the lungs and the kidneys, as those organs didn't come out with the rest of the guts.

It was important to have all the chickens clean, and ready to eat before they were put into a bag and placed in the freezer for the long winter. Butchering day was a big day; Mom did about 25 or 30 chickens each time until they were all done.

Dad went commercial fishing on Primrose Lake in the winter. Dad had a good fishing season in the early sixties and he bought a television set. He made a shelf across the corner by our large table. The TV was in a chest casing and was placed high enough for everybody to see. I recall waiting for the black and white picture to come on. There was a click and a static noise before the snowy picture was seen, but it was worth the wait. We only had one station, but that was okay, as we all watched whatever came on.

Can you picture that long bench full of bodies, as my large family stared at that "box" waiting for it to blink on? The first show I remember watching was *Don Messer's Jubilee*. It was great!

Our nightly ritual was to watch the 6 p.m. news, wash the dishes, and do homework before we could perch ourselves in front of the television.

I don't remember Mom or Dad reading to us or doing any more puzzles; that black and white box took away our former ways of entertainment. The drive-in movie was no longer a big outing; we could watch many shows on TV.

On Sunday nights, our neighbours, the Haywards, came with 6 small kids to watch *Bonanza*. They lived about eight kilometres away and had a young family. Mom often made a large coffee cake or a puff wheat cake to share.

Our home always had room for one more body, and a baby was always a joy. Mom kept baby Randy Hayward for a week, as the Hayward parents, Roland and Melva, were in Edmonton with their two-year-old son Brian. Brian wasn't real steady on his feet, and he fell into a grass fire. He burnt ninety percent of his small body. Brian lived about a week.

I remember Roland Hayward bringing that little white crib for Randy to sleep in. Randy fit right into our family, and I enjoyed his little smiles when I spoke to him. I think Randy was about 5 months old. Mom was always ready to help and make room for another baby.

Roland Hayward returned the generosity by taking us older kids on a sleigh ride. Roland pulled us behind the truck. When we were cold, there was a big fire and a wiener roast. Roland also took Dad moose hunting. I recall a moose that was skinned, cut into four quarters, and placed on the floor to be deboned. It was a big job to help cut and debone that moose into meal size pieces, wrap it in waxed brown paper, and place it in the freezer. I liked moose meat when it was rolled in flour and fried brown in a big pan.

It was about this time when the old Ford truck was getting tired from the many kilometres of hauling pigs to market and going to the berry patch and to town on Saturday nights for groceries. To start this truck, the older kids went outdoors, and Dad pushed in the clutch, as we got the truck rolling. After the truck was moving, Dad "popped" the clutch, and the motor started. Dad was on his way. I didn't like to push the old Ford to start it at the drive-in theatre.

"Yes," Nelson said, "I also felt embarrassed because Dad didn't wait until all the cars were gone at the drive-in show before he insisted that I get out and start pushing the old Ford so that Dad could pop the clutch to start the motor." That truck had a standard transmission; I don't recall any automatic trucks back in my little area of the world in the early sixties. There were so many cars at the drive-in, about 20 cars in a line, as we left the show. Today, I go to the Cold Lake Mall to shop and there are 20 or more cars just travelling on the road on either side of me!

Chapter 43:
Boogie Bus

school bus drawing

Mom and Dad talked about getting a new vehicle, as the old Ford truck was not working well. Nioma and Nelson were about fourteen years old and able to run the household and do the chores for one day, so Mom and Dad left early in the morning to go to Edmonton in search of a better truck. Nioma suggested that Dad should buy a red station wagon.

Mom and Dad went to Edmonton and were gone all day. Edmonton was about 320 kilometres from our farm, and the road was not paved like it is today. It took about five hours to travel one way to Edmonton. Mom and Dad would be gone all day in search of "new wheels".

In the evening before the sun set my brother Lloyd saw a small bus coming to our house. He said, "There's a yellow bus coming, but there is no school today." We all rushed outdoors to see who it could be. Soon Mom and Dad stepped out of the bus. Dad lifted his straw hat and with a chuckle he said, "Now we have room for all the family; it's a 20-passenger bus."

Mom was a little more reserved, as she told us how a tire had rolled past the bus when they were coming home. Mom said, "I could see a tire passing us; it was going up into the bush. I wondered who could have lost it."

Soon the bus plunked down on the right-hand side. Dad brought the bus to a screeching stop and got out to investigate. Sure enough, that tire was from the bus. Dad retrieved the tire from the ditch where it had flopped down. He used a few choice words and bolted that wheel back onto the bus. I wonder if he had to take one bolt from each of the other wheels. I'm sure the bolts for that tire were not to be found. The bus worked fine the rest of the way home.

I remember that I thought our "Boogie Bus" was a great way to travel. The oldest twins were teenagers, and I know that teenagers are embarrassed easily.

Nioma was not happy to see a bus, and she said "It's a school bus, and I'll not be caught dead getting out with a bunch of kids in town; everybody will see us." She threw her arms in the air and stomped into the house with Laura, the baby, in her arms.

Nelson's reaction was a little different. He closed his eyes, blinked, and said, "I'll stay home and do the chores."

The insurance company had a rule that said a bus that is used for private use must not have a school bus sign.

Dad bought a can of black paint and with a swish of his brush, he covered the school bus words on the top and on each side of the bus; now we had a yellow bus with a large black pin stripe on the sides. He said, "That was an easy fix."

We didn't need to take turns; there was room for all. We faced each other, as there was a long seat on either side of the bus to sit on, and there were lots of windows to view the landscape. We all picked our places across from each other. Mom rode in the front seat by Dad and opened the door for us, as we joyfully stepped on; all except Nioma and Nelson. After a lot of talking and Dad making a promise not to stop in town, Nioma and Nelson climbed aboard. We dressed in our good clothes for our day away from the farm. I remember sitting in our boogie bus, across from each other, as I went to the lake for a summer swim. I know Mom didn't think that the lake was a big outing; she didn't like the water. Mom had all those wet towels and swimming cloths to contend with. Sometimes Mom packed a lunch too.

The bus proved to be a good vehicle for our big family; we all went to the lake, the drive-in show, and to town. I think we were the first to own a "minivan".

When we went to the show, the younger kids enjoyed the playground and the "funnies". Soon after we had popcorn, the younger kids fell asleep, missing the show. Dad liked Western shows and often they were shown on Wednesday nights. I do not like all the rooting, tooting, and shooting parts of a Western show, but I wasn't going to miss out. Wednesday night was dollar night; it cost a dollar for each vehicle, and we had money left for a treat too.

The bathroom at the drive-in was a big event. I had never seen a white porcelain toilet with water inside. I remember when my sister Judy pulled the handle, and the water swirled round and round. I was frightened, when the water kept on running. Judy and I ran out to our comfort zone, the old bus.

Dad used the school bus to go commercial fishing too. He was happy to put the boxed fish inside so that the fish would not freeze before he went to the lakeshore at night. The fish plant wanted fresh fish. There was room for about 30 boxes of fish. It was a good all-around vehicle.

Chapter 44:
I Take The Wheel

I matured and became a teenager like my brother Lloyd. I had my first driving lessons on the big open lake at Primrose. I drove almost 100 metres from one hole with the fishing nets to the next. I learned to step on the gas, as I let the clutch out slowly.

One day Mom and Dad were gone from home and my brother Lloyd took me to the field by the barn. Lloyd said, "It's time to drive around the yard and not on the wide open lake. You need to learn how to dodge rocks and posts."

I was excited, as I went with Lloyd to drive Dad's old truck. I thought that Lloyd had a good idea; but I knew that my parents would not approve of me driving their truck. This was a good experience, and when we returned to the house Lloyd told me to use the corn broom and sweep over all the tire tracks before Mom and Dad came home. Another time when Lloyd and I went to practice, it didn't end so well. Lloyd told me to turn as I went through the gate. I turned too soon, and I hit a fence post by the gate. The post scratched the truck. Lloyd told me to rub some mud over the scratch. I thought it was a good idea. I reached for some mud from the puddle, and I rubbed it along the mark. I thought it looked pretty good and the scratch was covered.

At the supper table, Dad asked, "Who tried to cover the mark on the truck with mud?" Lloyd's idea of putting mud over the mark was a mistake because it caught Dad's attention. Dad looked straight at me; I began to cry. I couldn't blame "Mr. Nobody" this time. Dad knew who did it.

Saturday night was a big deal for all farm families, as it was an outing with our parents to get the weekly groceries. We all took turns going.

A large family consumes a lot of food, and Mom often made pancakes for supper with fried eggs. Rogers Golden Syrup was thinned down with water before it was placed on the table. Eggs and milk were stable foods. I recall a custard pudding made with eggs and milk too; it wasn't my favourite, but we were taught to eat what was on the table. I also taught my kids that they should eat what was on the table. I can only imagine how many meals Mom cooked.

Mom said, "I liked to milk cows. That little milk stool was a great place to rest, and I could do a job that needed to be done; life was full of demands."

The milk was separated and the cream was sold. The money from the cream cheques and money from selling extra eggs helped to buy the groceries. Mom bought things like coffee, flour, sugar, and tea. If there was a few extra dollars, Dad bought bologna for supper or puffed wheat for breakfast; what a treat that was from the mushy oatmeal porridge that was on the menu most mornings!

My family had ten kids attending school at one time; Mom made ten lunches each day for two years. Lance and Laura started in 1964, and I was in grade ten and attended school for grade eleven too. The bus driver said, "That family filled my bus."

I never liked to make lunches, and I thought of Mom, as I made school lunches for my own kids. I know that I never had to worry about what to put in my kids lunches unless I neglected to go to town and buy what was needed for the week. I also had the benefit of the bus picking up my kids at the end of our lane. They never needed to walk.

I discovered Lloyd Gonie when I was sixteen years old, and soon he filled my dreams. Lloyd was my only boyfriend. Marriage became my career and I had three sons and a daughter to teach. In five years,

I was blessed with four children. My career was more than a teacher, as I became a cook, counsellor, nurse, taxi driver, and the list goes on. To be a wife and a mother is a rewarding job, but it does have many challenges too. Ask a mother which of her children she would want to be without and she will instantly reply, "Not any one of them; they are all precious to me." I know that is exactly how I feel. Each one of my children has different talents to make me proud. The things that I enjoy with one child are different from what I enjoy with another; they are all unique. I grew in strength and determination through the hard times and in the joyful times too. I tried to absorb knowledge from each child. When one door closes another door opens, and I always looked for the best part of every situation.

It was fifty years ago that I became a wife and then a mother; a career that I would never have wanted passed me by! I am happily married and have a good family. In my life, I had years with very little material stuff, but I learned to share with others, and I worked to become a person who is happy with a simple life. I have found my place in this little corner of the world as I discovered that I am happy just to be ME.

Life is full of the unexpected, and I've learned to take each day when it comes and give thanks for that day's opportunity and blessing with my family and friends. Life is a gift, and I don't want to waste it on living in the hard times from the past.

Chapter 45:
Leaving The Nest

Nelson and Nioma worked hard; they both said, "All I ever remember about living at home was that the work never ended." Nelson went to Fort Kent, Alberta to work. Nelson was the first one of my siblings to go away from our large table. George Malhalchen had a relative that needed help on his pig farm. Nelson worked away from home for the summer and came home for the winter months. I was happy that he was home again and a place was set for him at the table.

My family was born close together, and now we were leaving about the same time. Nioma went to work in Cold Lake about a year later. I started to work at Haase's as I attended school. There was more room in the beds, and I felt that once I left, I no longer had a spot at the table or in bed; it was filled with a sibling.

My youngest sister, Josie, was born about 18 years after the oldest set of twins. Mom said, "The oldest twins are going to be eighteen years old. I was embarrassed to tell Nioma and Nelson that I was pregnant."

In October 1960, we were getting ready to go to the church's annual fall supper. Mom put on a new pink smock top. Nelson saw Mom dressed in her new top, and he said to her, "You can't wear that outfit because people will think that you are expecting a baby."

I don't remember Nelson's reaction as he learned the truth. Nioma was excited and said, "I love babies; it'll be like my own baby."

I was fourteen, and I remember washing Mom's feet for her. When I married and became pregnant, I learned how hard it was to bend over my large belly to put on my shoes or to cut my toe nails.

Chapter 46:
The Last Sibling (Josephine)

Mom told me that she was not happy at being pregnant so many times, but birth control was not available then like it is today. Families today are smaller with a child or two because there are many means of preventing another birth. Today, I do not think that most women would choose a big family and such a hard life; although there are many machines to make a woman's work a lot easier than it was back in the forties.

Josie was born February 23, 1961. Josie is Mom's last child. Mom bore children for almost twenty years; Josie is eighteen years younger than Nioma and Nelson. What a great joy Josie was to each of her siblings.

Josie grew fast and always cooperated as Nioma dressed her and combed her hair into ringlets. Josie said, "Every picture I saw when I was little was a picture where I had curlers in my hair."

Lillian was in high school when Josie boarded the bus with the rest of her siblings. Lillian sat with Josie on the bus, as we rode to Pierceland School. Josie followed Lance and Laura to their classroom. It took a few days before Josie was comfortable to go by herself to her classroom. Nioma was close to Josie and remains so today. Nioma was out of school, but Nioma said, "Josie was my little sister who always ran to meet me. At my wedding dance, Josie ran to the door and walked in with me and Bill."

Josie was always cared for by someone in the household. Josie felt like she was mauled to death like a small pet. She said, "I must have been like that little kitten that each kid wanted a part of; one kid pulls at the tail and another reaches for a leg as that kitten is passed to another child. Each child has a turn at enjoying the soft fur as they cuddle the kitten."

Josie travelled with Mom and Dad when the rest of the family was in school. I considered her spoiled; nobody else got to go to Bonnyville auction mart or to McLeod's store to shop.

Nioma went to work in Grand Centre when Josie was about a year old. She worked for a hairdresser and watched a small boy named Danny. Danny became close to Nioma. When it was time for Danny to go to school, Nioma's job was done. When Nioma left home to go to work, I needed to step up and do some of the work that Nioma had always done. I never liked babies, but I could help Mom with gardening and cooking. I recall fighting with Mom because she thought that I should be responsible like Nioma was. Those were hard days for me. I was fourteen years old and a rude and selfish teenager. I had a lot to learn to fill Nioma's shoes, and I hated being in the house. I knew I wasn't as capable as Nioma was when it came to working in the house or caring for a baby.

Mom seemed to be upset with me all the time. I didn't care if I did anything right; I just wanted it done so that I could run outside and enjoy the outdoors.

Still life was easier in many ways. Here are a few changes that I have experienced:
- An enamel dishpan to a dish washer
- A rope clothes line to a dryer
- Cold, hard wood floors to warm and soft carpet
- The little outhouse to a flush toilet
- The lard pail I carried to money for the cafeteria
- A warming oven to a microwave
- Catalogue paper to extra soft toilet paper

- Itchy woollen socks to thick, pile socks
- A fountain pen and bottle of ink to the ball point pen
- Note books and pencils to computers and cell phones
- Hair curlers to set my hair to gel and hair dryer's
- Ankle-high shoes to sandals and flip flops

I was happy for Nioma when she went to work; now she could have her own money to buy pretty clothes and girl stuff. Nioma had a boyfriend too. I enjoyed taking turns going with Bill and Nioma to check his cows in the pasture. Bill's cowherd was so big in comparison to Dad's.

I went with Nioma and Bill to the outdoor drive-in show too, but I felt that Judy went more than I did. Did I clash with Nioma? Nioma and I often had disagreements.

It was about three short years later when I married Lloyd Gonie, Bill Gonie's brother. Nioma and I became sisters-in-laws. I turned to Nioma for many things through the years. Lloyd and Bill worked together on the farm, and Nioma helped me with my young family. Nioma and I had some memorable trips to the hay field; we took lunch to the men with eight kids. I went with Nioma and the kids to Pierceland to sell eggs and get the weekly groceries too.

When Lloyd and I were able to get a car, I went to town with my kids. I remember a time when I had left the kids in the car close to the door of the Red and White Store. I ran inside to get a few things. When I came out, I couldn't find my car. The kids had pulled it out of gear, and it had rolled down the hill about 40 metres away. When I got to the car, all four kids were in the back seat, and of course, nobody had touched a thing in the car. I was so pleased that no one or anything was hurt. In the winter it was easier if I took the kids to Nioma's and went to town by myself and did my shopping. It was always a fast trip.

Judy left home when she was seventeen years old. She worked with me at the bakery, and then went to Calgary, Alberta. Judy took a hairdressing course. This was the same year that I was married.

Graham left the following year, but Grant stayed in school and went on to college.

George found a job on the pipeline, and worked around Pierceland for a while but soon he too was gone from home.

Lewis quit school and went to work about a year later. Lewis was not yet seventeen but he wanted his own life and school could hold him. He claims that all the teachers were happy to see him close the door behind him.

Lillian continued in school and graduated three years later. Mom had a house full of teenagers for the next while and nobody moved away from home for a couple of years.

Debbie also graduated from high school before she went to Edmonton to work. The Burge family was getting smaller.

Lance dropped out of school at a young ag, as did Laura. Lance went to work, and Laura babysat for a while. Soon she met Warren Somers and she too moved from home. Mom said it was like a double "whammy" when both twins left at the same time.

It was about this time when tension was high in the house, as Mom and Dad were constantly arguing. Mom went to work in Cold Lake, and soon she moved there. Josie was alone with Dad after Laura and Lance left. Josie moved to Lillian's and went to school from there. Josie graduated from high school too.

Chapter 47:
Fishing Day

commercial net fishing

My dad worked at many jobs to keep us all fed. Commercial Fishing brought a good income. Dad was a fisherman, and worked for other men until he could afford to buy some nets and run his own outfit. Each year at Christmas, Dad loaded his vehicle with nets, shovels, and other tools to go to Primrose Lake to catch fish. Primrose Lake is located in the Cold Lake, Alberta Air Weapons range and approximately 85 percent of this lake is located in Saskatchewan. This was why permission was given to Saskatchewan residents to fish on the lake during the Christmas break when the air weapons range was shut down.

Dad and the older boys travelled about 40 miles to Primrose Lake Alberta to commercial fish. The boys, Nelson and Lloyd, were Dad's first helpers, but each boy took their turn as they grew older.

Nelson said, "I drove that Cockshutt 30 tractor with a cart behind to the lake for the fishing season. I had two flat tires before I got to Pierceland. I had money from working out in the summer. I went to Northland, the local garage, and bought two tires before I continued.

"Dad told me to stop at Cold River, about the halfway mark to Primrose Lake. "I ate a frozen sandwich, and I don't remember having anything hot to drink. There was no cab on the tractor and no place to get warm. I crossed the bridge and continued on my way."

I, Barbara, was twelve years old when I first went to the lake. Dad needed another license so that he could set more nets. The rule was that each person with a license needed to be at the lake. I remember that little 2 by 2.5-metre shack. The airtight heater was used for heat and for cooking. There was a bunk bed across the end. The table touched the bed. That little shack was home for about ten days. After a cold day on the lake, it was a welcomed fortress; we ate and rested in a warm place. The next day would be much the same.

My husband Lloyd told me that the shacks were left behind by the logging crew. The saw dust pile was made by Oscar Eiekle, who managed the logging operations in the early fifties. Lloyds brother, John and Tone were young men; they drove the trucks, loaded with lumber, to Meadowlake Sask. Lloyd remembers his dad bought a new international truck for the haul. The same road to Primrose was used to go fishing when the lake opened for the fishing season. Their was a fish plant on the lake shore managed by Eloise Gross. He booked in the number of boxes of fish that each fisherman brought in. The Gonie's had the fish hauling contract. Lloyd recalls the Martineau hill was a challenge for the powerless trucks.

After the fishing season, the nets had to be dried, straightened, and stored for summer. We all helped Dad, as he stretched his nets out on the floor in our house. The nets needed to have the knots taken out before they were set again. The nets were straightened and placed back into the box for next year. This was an evening job.

Dad was not a very patient man. I only imagine the immature help he had, as we were young, and not experienced. I remember working on a net well into the night, and the twisted knots were not coming out. Dad got mad, swore a lot, and threw the net into the blazing fire of our large heater. Mom stayed up until that fire burned down.

I recall another, not so pleasant spring fishing season on Primrose. We were allowed to enter the lake for one weekend before Easter, four days at Easter, and one weekend after Easter. The weather was warm, the sun was bright, and the lake was wet. My family camped in a tent on the Alberta side of the lake. The airtight heater dried our clothes at night. The trucks could not be used because the snow was so deep. Dad, Nelson, Lloyd, and I walked out from shore and set our nets. The next day we walked to our string of nets and carried some boxes for the fish to be packed in. We pulled the nets and placed the fish into the boxes to be picked up later. That was a long and hard day on the lake. I remember being so tired.

The Gonie family had set their net a little ways past us. They were using a team of horses and a sleigh to fish. In the evening, Lloyd transported our fish to the shore where the fish truck could haul them to the plant for sale. What a joy it was to have our fish on shore for the truck.

The sun was warm and bright on the lake. I got snow blinded because I didn't have sunglasses to wear. Tears ran from my eyes, and down my cheeks, as my eyes watered. I recall how my eyes burned. It was better if I kept my eyes closed and didn't allow any light to get in. When I got home from the lake, Mom put warm tea bags on each eye. I stayed in a dark room for three days until my eyes were able to stand any light again. My eyes are scarred now with spots like a welder often has; but I'm not bothered today.

Chapter 48:
Instilling Faith

my first communion

I always thought my baptism was special. I got to share my special day with Mom and six of my siblings, who were all baptized on the same day. Our local priest was Father Seewaldt. He came to our house a few times to give Mom some instructions about the church. Mom said, "I was shocked when Grandpa Burge and Joe came home with the priest. Mr. and Mrs. Adam Hickie were present to be sponsors for the baptisms. I had nothing to say in this matter, I just went along with it; they all moved in and the ceremony began." Mom was twenty-nine years old, had six kids, and didn't protest, as she had better places to spend her energy; she barely had time for her thoughts.

Mom met the challenge of a different faith, and lived up to her faith commitment. She sent us to catechism classes to learn more about the Catholic religion, and we attended mass often. I'm thinking Mom didn't want to make any ripples in her home or with her father-in-law.

I remember that I walked with Mom across the meadow to meet the Puech's, our neighbours who lived about 2 kilometres across the meadow. They had a car, and they picked us up for Sunday mass at the highway. Their daughter Carol always had a pretty hat, and their son, Robert, wore a suit. Mom never had a hat to wear, but she wore a scarf on her head because at that time women were expected to have something on their head when they attended mass. I rode in the back seat of the car with the well-mannered kids who never talked. I don't recall much more. Another custom that I recall about the church is that the men and the boys sat on one side of the church, and the girls and the women sat on the opposite side of the church. I wonder what that did for unity and family life. I'm happy that changed.

I liked to attend religious studies, but it seemed like I went to school longer than some of my friends. Catechism was held the first two weeks of July. The nuns came from Goodsoil after school was out for the summer. Each weekday morning, we trekked across the meadow where Marguerite Melalcheon picked us up with her car. Marguerite was a short lady with dark hair. I felt all grown-up when I stood beside her. She was from a French family, and she always wore nice clothes too. She was kind to us and never complained about taking us to town. Her husband George drove our school bus.

Mom taught us our prayers around the kitchen table. My first communion was memorable too; Mom had forgotten my veil and the flowers for my hair. I recall being upset at seeing my mother cry, and I couldn't do anything to help her. We went to the church in a wagon pulled by the tractor. How hard it must have been to keep a white dress clean, check eight kids, and prepare a diaper bag for the youngest twins—no wonder she forgot the flowers and veil for my hair.

I was in a class with good friends. Their parents, Betty Eistetter and Mrs. Kretz, took some flowers and part of a veil from their girls' hair and gave some to me. I was dressed up as well as the other girls when I lined up with my class and we walked up the aisle to the altar. I was so proud, and I felt like a little bride as I approached the altar to receive Jesus for the first time.

Christina Kretz has been my best friend for many years. We have been blessed with a lifelong friendship without any demands of the other person. We don't visit a lot, but we understand each other in a special way. We work together in the church with the youth, teach religion, and help the elderly. We have planned wedding banquets and other catering for three hundred guests too. I chose Mrs. Kretz as my confirmation mother. Today, I have the pink rosary that she gave me almost sixty years ago. This rosary is a treasure that is kept in my jewellery box, as it has been broken and tied back together with string. Mrs. Kretz also gave me a white rosary before she died. This is the rosary that I pray with today; it is so special.

I joined the Catholic Women's League the year I was married. Lloyd said, "The C.W.L. meetings were important to my mom. I drove Mom to Pierceland on the first Tuesday of each month so that she could attend the meetings." Lloyd called these meetings the "Hens' Meetings." This club is a big part of the community.

It's hard to believe that I have been a member of the Catholic Women League for fifty years. I enjoy attending C.W.L. conventions. The C.W.L. is active in Pierceland, and many members are counted on to help cater, serve funeral lunches, or lead a prayer service for the sick of the parish.

In January 2000, I was interviewed and accepted to take a theology class in Meadow Lake. It was a three-year program that started on Friday night and ended on Sunday afternoon (20 hours a weekend).

The classes were held once a month for eight months. This involved much hard work and reading. There was so much information to work through, and at times I was overwhelmed, but I did enjoy it.

One of the class activities was to study and pray with a special object in my home; something that I wouldn't want to be without. I needed to record my feelings each day as I prayed and looked deeply at my object. I chose an old lamp that had been in my husband's family for many years. This lamp is extraordinary, and today I display it on a shelf in my living room. The first day I saw some imperfections in the handle; I saw thicker glass on one side of the lamp. The lamp was fragile and could break if I dropped it. The last day I discovered that the very centre of the lamp with the wick to soak up the lamp oil was made of metal. This centre part would withstand a fall and remain after the glass parts were shattered. Wow! I can see my body is only a shell and my central core is unbreakable! I was dedicated to doing my homework, and I learned so much from this project. I received good marks for my efforts.

When our C.W.L. parish took our turn at hosting the annual convention, I took my lamp and presented this article to the ladies. The Catholic Woman's League sang, "Lamp unto my feet." It was a great devotion exercise. I entered a writing contest with this story. My story was chosen and printed in the *Insight* magazine. I was paid for my lamp story and can say, "I am a published writer."

My husband Lloyd and I attended mass each week in Pierceland, Saskatchewan. It was a challenge with four young children, but I believe I received graces for my family, as we went through our daily living. Everyone has a purpose for being on this earth; it's up to each person to find their talents and excel in that area, as they achieve their goals.

I had my turn serving on the parish council where decisions are made for the good of our parish. This too was a learning experience and opened my eyes as I listened to and served others in my parish. Retreats helped me share with other people, and I grew inwardly, as I tried to live my faith. I realized that we are all on a journey.

I took a course in palliative care from my home. This was a great help when I sat with family members, as they prepared for death. Death is always hard and leaves us with pain and a loss. Grieving people need healing time before they can move on. Be patient and pray. Today I am a member of St. Antoninus Parish Cemetery committee and am available for choosing grave plots. This cemetery is well kept by our parishioners.

Chapter 49:
School Days

old classroom scene

I was almost seven years old when I started school. My birthday was in December, and I was a small child. I needed to walk 1.5 kilometres across the meadow along with three siblings — Nioma, Nelson, and Lloyd. We met the bus and rode for one hour to Pierceland, Saskatchewan. The hay meadow was wet, and we needed to wear our boots most of the summer. We stored our shoes under the willows by the highway. I don't recall having wet shoes when it rained.

I was terrified when I started to go to school because I didn't know anyone; not one of the neighbours' kids was my age. My siblings went to another class, and I was expected to go to an unfamiliar desk and sit down. I remember being so afraid and all alone. I recall that I couldn't reach the large water fountain to push the button and have a drink. Someone needed to help me. Was I a "bushed" kid?

My first year of school was in the old band school, upstairs beside the combined grade eleven and twelve classrooms. I remember my teacher Miss Schellenburg wore a sparkly black dress. I thought she was so pretty, and she never shouted at us. I was one of twenty-seven kids who learned to sit down, hold a big fat pencil to write our names, and memorize the alphabet. Much of this year I stayed with Gerry Swingley. Her mother said, "That child is too small to walk a mile."

The Swingley family owned the local meat shop. Gerry's dad, George, took the cream to Bonnyville each Friday and brought the cream cheques home. Gerry sat next to me in school, and we became good friends. Her sisters were older and gone from home. Gerry was like an only child, and we soon bonded. I often stayed with her as the winter was cold with lots of snow, and I had no ski pants or ski-doo suits to wear. Mrs. Swingley was a tall, thin lady who managed the butcher shop, cut meat, and sold processed meat in Pierceland. I remember her being so annoyed when the power was off. Pierceland had a power plant that was run by Mr. Van Howard. He and his wife Cecil didn't always see eye to eye. When the power was shut off in Pierceland, Mrs. Swingley said, "That man must have been in the bar and his wife was angry with him because the power went off." I liked Mrs. Swingley; she cooked good food too. It was at her place that I ate my first "steak". We ate chicken, fish, or pork at home. She also gave us ice cream that came in a brick like our butter does today.

The Henetiuk kids were Gerry's neighbours in town. Beverly and Barry came to play cards with us at the Swingley house. Beverly was a year younger than Gerry, and Barry and I were two years younger. We all got along well.

Our class—the class of 1954-1955—planted trees at the end of the school yard. These trees are big today and are located near the Josie Britton Centre. I look at those trees today, and I think that they too look a little bit old and shabby, as do many of my classmates. I remember wintertime with my friend Gerry Swingley. I liked to skate at the Pierceland outdoor rink. Gerry had some skates that I could use. The rink had a string of light bulbs strung down the middle. When I got cold, there was a small shack with a long bench along two sides of that small room. I warmed up around the airtight heater. I don't remember a caretaker; some adult put wood in the heater to keep it blazing. I don't remember anyone ever sharpening my skates.

Grade two classes were at the old library with Mrs. Madge Foss as our teacher. (Up Town Treasures sits on that lot today.) Mrs. Foss was my favourite teacher. I remember that Mrs. Foss brought her son Harold to school. He crawled onto her desk and sat there while Mrs. Foss continued to teach us how to do addition on the blackboard. After Christmas, the new school was ready, and we were moved there (now the Josie Briton Centre).

Grade three was taught by Mrs. Berg. We attended the new school again but in another classroom. I didn't like Mrs. Berg. I was not a good reader, and I was embarrassed to read in front of the class. She had me and other students repeat things until it was right. I still have a fear of reading in front of others; I feel like I'm back at school. I recited a poem, "Has anyone seen my mouse?" I was chosen to go to Goodsoil to recite. Didn't I have a passion or deep fear of those fuzzy little creators? I hated mice!

In the late fifties, Pierceland had a school population growth. Many of the baby boomers were starting school. The school board made a decision to bring in the rural school children to Pierceland by bus, so there was a need for more classrooms. These classrooms were different, and the boys in my class named the country schools "the barns." I attended these schools for grades 5, 6, 7, and 8. This was a change for us country kids because before we had known all the students who were our neighbours. Now there were kids from town who had never milked a cow, fed pigs, or gathered the eggs each day.

In our classroom, there was a big wood stove to heat the room. The boys carried in the wood, and the teacher stoked the fire.

Yes, there was an outhouse out back, and it was similar to mine at home, but it had two holes. I remember being locked inside that little house and calling out to be rescued.

We were taught by Mrs. Forsyth in grade four and five. I recall acting in school plays; I was Gretel in the story of "Hansel and Gretel". I acted in many school plays, and I loved it. I had dreams of becoming an actress and thrilling the world with my talent.

In grade five, my class attended the school across the road. Janice Seland became my best friend. We rode the bus together, and we both loved to play ball. We took turns going to one another's houses for sleepover's. We walked or rode a horse to spend time together. Janice's brother Jerry was younger, but he often stayed with us on the weekends and joined in the family fun.

I recall a scary incident when Janice, Judy, and I walked home from her place. Along the way, we needed to walk past a house with a big dog that barked. Janice said, "There's a witch living in the house." There was a cemetery close to the witch's house, and Janice was afraid to walk past the area too. We needed to come up with a way to by-pass that troubled spot.

I was terrified of the dog, and Janice was afraid of the cemetery. She suggested that we find a new way to get to my house. Janice, Judy, and I walked through the bush. It was hard to find our way. We didn't try that again.

Soon the year passed, and I was in grade six. Mrs. Brady taught us for grade six. She was an older teacher, and the boys challenged her many times. I recall how the girls giggled because we thought her breasts rested on her waistline. It seemed that her belt held up her breasts. Now, fifty years later, I never wear a belt, but I think all my classmates appear similar, and I too am a bit saggy. I wonder if the young girls giggle at me.

At recess we played soft ball every chance we had. The class in the school next to us played too; it was great! Dad took me to Meadow Lake and bought me a ball glove. I felt as special as a queen. I knew how short the money was in our family, and I picked out a glove for $5. Dad said to me, "That glove is no good."

Dad picked out a glove that was $12. This was the best gift I remember receiving, and I valued my glove very much. Thanks Dad!

Janice and I played catch all the time when I stayed with her. I also remember walking with Janice to Pat and John Rewega's. They were her neighbours who lived about a kilometre away. They were newlyweds taking over the family farm. Pat had worked in Edmonton, and before she was married, she had purchased a television set. It was a small TV, and the picture was black and white. There was only one channel to watch. Neither Janice nor I had such luxuries in our homes. We walked to Rewega's to watch *Wagon Train* or *Dr. Ben Casey* and then walked home to Janice's. We were never afraid of the dark, as we walked about a kilometre home on the quiet road. I don't remember Pat and John ever telling us that we should go home. Teenagers don't think, and today I wonder if we invaded their special time together.

I recall that Pat had a wild rose flower growing behind her chesterfield in that old log house. John's parents were Ukrainian, and had built the log house, and filled the cracks in the logs with mud and straw. Pat said, "That wild rose thrived in the warm house with the straw and the mud." That pretty pink rose was a joy to Pat. She said roses were her favourite flower, and John didn't need to buy her any.

In grade seven, I had Mr. Barnes as my teacher. He was a young man without much experience. The boys often challenged him too. I don't remember him making an impact on anything that he taught me or in any sport that I participated in. We also had Mr. Clements, as a teacher. (I don't remember why, but he wasn't my favourite teacher.)

My friend Janice and I were in grade eight when we are asked to go along to Maidstone with the high-school team to play ball, as a spare pitcher and catcher. Janice was the pitcher, and I was the back catcher. We were so proud to play one inning with the high-school team! Now my new career was to be a professional ball player.

Two years later, I left my ball glove on the fender of the bus. Dad started the bus and drove off to town without seeing my glove. I walked the highway in search of this precious mitt. I didn't find it. I was devastated and my dream of becoming a ball player ended, as did playing ball. I didn't want to tell anyone why I no longer played ball. I couldn't ask for my ball glove to be replaced. It was hard to leave behind a sport that I loved so much.

I bought myself a ball glove when I was older, and I tried to play when I had four kids. That was too hard; my kids were always on my mind. I soon quit, as I felt that I was a handicap to the team; I could no longer play the way I once had. This was my first lesson in learning to move past a big disappointment. I thought that I would play after my kids were grown, but I played a few times at family functions, and I hurt my fingers, and I got stiff. It wasn't worth the few hours of fun.

I started to play volleyball in grade eight. Mr. McNaughton was my grade-eight teacher. He was a polio survivor and much older than our former teacher. I passed grade seven on condition; meaning that if I couldn't keep up to the class in grade eight, I would need to go back to grade seven. I learned to study. The fun was gone from school. The only fun left was when I joined the volleyball team. It was great fun, but we played outdoors, and it was often cold. It was hard when we went to Meadow Lake to play volleyball in the gym. The ball often hit the ceiling, and the play was called. That was different for us.

In the summer of 1960, I started to work for Lorraine Gonie. I babysat, helped in the garden, and milked the cow. I made enough money to buy my first pair of jeans, G.W.G.'s, at the Co-op Store in Pierceland. I loved those jeans, and I pressed them each weekend with a damp cloth. I didn't want Mom to wash them and make them faded.

I longed to be thirteen and treated like a grown up. I had issues like many teenagers do. Mom seemed too strict and treated me like a child. I recall some hard rules that I was not willing to follow. Mom continued to rule my life, but I was determined and struggled through the hard times. Each day seemed to have a different challenge.

I had my birthday, but nothing changed. What a letdown it was to be thirteen; I was still one of the kids. I did mature and eventually learned that my mother was doing her part to keep me safe, as I matured. My teenage years passed quickly with lots of fun, sports, and disappointments; I had many tears. Nelson was gone to work, but his car was in the yard. One day when Mom was gone, Judy and I took Nelson's green Ford car to visit Janice, about five kilometres away. I had to drive a short distance on the main highway before I turned down the back road to Seland's place. I never met another car. I was a year older than Judy, but it must have been Judy's idea.

Teenagers often do not stop to think of any dangers. They think that accidents only happened to other people. I was fortunate enough not to have an accident.

Chapter 50:
Mom Said Goodbye To Grandma

mom and aunt Irene

Niomas wedding

In the summer of 1961, while I was at swimming lesson, Grandma Hellekson passed away. This was the gentle Grandma that had raised Mom until she was 13 years old. Nioma had a summer job; she was babysitting at Rolheiser's. Josie was five months old, and the Rolheiser's told Nioma to bring Josie with her to their house so that Mom could attend the funeral. I was staying at Swingley's, and going to the lake each day for swimming lessons. Dad came to give me the news. I cancelled my swimming lessons and went home to help Dad with the family.

Mom took the bus to Peers, Alberta, and Auntie Irene picked her up. Mom and Auntie Irene said good bye to Grandma together. The girl's grieved together for their mother figure. Mom never talked much about Grandma's funeral, but this must have been another heartbreaking event in Mom's life. Mom had a few days away from her busy summer, but was that a holiday? Mom returned to her busy household in Pierceland, and her old routine filled her life once more.

In 1962, I helped Mrs. Marge Little with the kids and the housework. Marge was a former registered nurse, but didn't work as a nurse once she was married. She was tall and slim. She and George lived on the Little farm, which was once his dad's homestead. Now Marge was sick and found it hard to keep up with the cooking, washing, and cleaning. I found Marge hard to talk to, and I don't recall a lot of time spent with her. George and Marge had four kids at that time; later another boy was born. This was a few years after I was gone. I rode the bus to school along with her kids.

George was a quiet, gentle, and patient man. I liked George, and I learned to drive the tractor for him, as he loaded small round bales onto a wagon. George never hollered or swore like Dad did. He never lost his temper when I released the clutch of the tractor with a jerk. Driving was much better than housework. Hauling bales didn't last long enough, but I made a few dollars, and I opened my bank account at the Pierceland Credit Union. I was fifteen years old and wanted to save my money because I wanted to go to college and become a schoolteacher. I started my bank account that year. This is the same account that I have today; now my husband Lloyd is my financial partner.

Lloyd my husband, has never had a bank account of his own. His dad ran all the business, and it was he who spent all the money. Lloyd is comfortable with me doing the banking. My kids find that so hard to believe, as they each started their bank accounts when they were teenagers.

I had made it to grade nine, junior high, and I felt proud that I had achieved another milestone in my life. Our class returned to the school where we had attended grade one, but now we were in the basement level at the old band school. This was referred to as the "bomb shelter".

Mr. Ilnesky was our homeroom teacher. He was a young male teacher. His girl friend worked in Loon Lake at the bank. He would blush when the boys teased him about her. In time, they were married, and his wife Hilda became Pierceland's bank manager for over thirty years.

In the summer of 1963, I went to Saskatoon with a schoolteacher, Mrs. Rosdalh, to care for her two preschool children while she attended summer school for six weeks. I remember being packed into her little Vauxhall car with a high chair, toys, and some food, as we drove to Saskatoon. I had never been so far from home; it seemed that we drove for such a long time. When we finally reached Saskatoon, Mrs. Rosdalh unpacked her car before she drove around the city to find a Catholic church close to the area where we were staying on Temperance Drive.

On Sundays, I walked alone to church about three blocks away. I felt so grown up to venture on my own in the big city. The next week, the thrill was gone, and by the third week, I felt lonely, as I watched families attend mass together. Each family had young kids like my family at home, small children and babies too. I got homesick and cried at night. I waited for Mom's letters from home.

Mrs. Rosdalh saw my loneliness, and when her friend come to visit her with a daughter Margaret, a girl about my age, she suggested that Margaret and I go to the movies and enjoy the big city lights.

That night, Margaret and I went to the movies. I felt like a country mouse in a big city. I had never rode a city bus or transferred to another bus. The city was so big, and I had never been to a theatre. I had watched movies in our town hall. There were so many people at the show. Not one face looked familiar. At home I saw people that were part of our community. In the city we stood in line for popcorn too. When the show was over, we rode the city bus home. Margaret and I didn't have much in common; I had never been to a city, and I didn't know of the fun places that she spoke of like roller skating rinks, swimming pools, and the gym.

Margaret had never lived on a farm and had never seen baby chicks, newborn calves, or baby piglets. We were two young girls, living unique lives, who were trying to share different worlds. I couldn't relate to her night of fun in the city, and she couldn't see how going to the slough with my brothers and sisters to catch frogs was so exciting.

After the show, we rode the bus home until we were about three blocks from the apartment that I stayed at. When we got off the bus, Margaret didn't want to walk me to the apartment. She told me to walk straight for three blocks, and I would see the hedge and the fence around the back yard. She abandoned me, and she walked her own way home while I ran toward mine. My heart raced for three blocks until I saw the hedge by the apartment. I sure hoped there was not another hedge that looked like the one by my apartment building. My hands jerked open the gate, and I rushed indoors. I was relieved that I had made it home all alone. The city was a scary experience. I didn't enjoy my night out. I longed for my small farm home and my family where I was comfortable and part of their fun on the farm.

Upstairs from our basement suite was a lady named Phyllis. She had a baby boy about a year old. She was pregnant with her second child; she didn't wear a wedding band. Did she see me, as I glanced at her left hand? Phyllis told me that she was to be married next summer. I was taught not to ask questions or to judge others. She and I played cards and become friends as we watched the kids play in the backyard with trucks and balls and in the sand box. I was comfortable with Phyllis, and we enjoyed each other's company each day.

Mom's letters encouraged me every week. Sometimes there was good news, and other times it was sad news. One letter told me of my friend Lorraine Balaberde whose mother had died. I felt so bad for Lorraine because she would need to help her dad raise her four younger siblings; Lorraine was the oldest child. I remembered Lorraine and her family came to visit my family. Lorraine's youngest sister was a baby. It was her dad who dressed the baby when it was time to go home. My dad never dressed any of my siblings. I read those sad words, my mind rushed to home, and I worried that Mom might die. I was so far away and couldn't go home, as I had a job to finish. What would my family do if we were to meet that kind of a challenge? Mom just couldn't die; the struggle would be too big.

The next letter Mom wrote had good news. Mom told me Nioma, my eldest sister, was getting married to Bill Gonie in November. Bill was Lloyd's oldest brother. I secretly hoped that I would get to be her bridesmaid, but I know that brides often pick their friend to be with them on their wedding day. I would soon be sixteen years old, but I felt that I was an adult, and I could help my sister with her dress, flowers, or any other need that she had. The time passed slowly, and I waited for Nioma to ask me to be part of her wedding party.

I went shopping with Mrs. Rosdalh, my boss. She bought me a lime green dress as a bonus for a job well done in caring for her children. How happy I was that I had pleased Mrs. Rosdalh. After six weeks of summer school, we were on our way home. I could hardly wait to see my family. We spent the night in Loon Lake, where Mrs. Rosdalh's Mom lived. I went to a wiener roast and felt out of place; I did not know anybody. I wished we could have gone home instead. The next day I was so happy to get home and join in the work, play, and conversation with my brothers and sisters. I never wanted to leave my family again.

Nioma did ask me to be her bridesmaid! Nioma and Bill were married on November 23, in 1963. This day was Nioma's 20th birthday. (A memorable day in history; one day after J.F. Kennedy was assassinated on November 22, 1963.) I was so excited about being a bridesmaid. I was almost sixteen years old and could hardly wait for Nioma's wedding day. I wore that beautiful lime green dress that Mrs. Rosdalh had bought for me. I was thrilled to help a bride! It was a cold day, and I was partnered up with Lloyd Gonie, the best man. In three years, Lloyd became my husband; he was the best man in my life.

The new Pierceland Central School opened in 1964. Our grade ten class attended the second new school. Mr. Heber, an elderly French teacher, was a small man with a gentle voice. He became our homeroom teacher. He travelled from Cold Lake each day. He always greeted us with "Bonjour". I liked his slow and gentle way.

I had my sixteenth birthday in December. I thought that I could do whatever I wanted to do because I was an adult. Not much changed, and I continued to do the same work and have the same rules. I didn't think that sixteen was as sweet as I once was told. I was disappointed. Life improved as Lloyd and I started to date at Christmas.

On June 20, 1964, I went to the Haase's to help with housework and cooking. Mrs. Haase was going through menopause and was very sick with rheumatoid arthritis. Most of her days were spent on the chesterfield. She took many aspirins to control the pain. Annie Haase was a short lady, had a full body, and she never spoke bad about anyone. She was well respected in our community. I soon became fond of her and her loving ways. I remember her husband, Art, telling me that he would give me a radio to have in my room. I said to him, "I don't need a radio because I need to study." He said to me, "There's only two weeks of school left." It seemed like a long time to me; I studied every night.

At the Haase's house I had the whole upstairs to myself — my own bedroom! That was the only time I had a room all of my own. I felt like a princess in a bed by myself. The bed had a frilly pink bedspread. The

Five Plus Five Makes Fifteen

window had pink curtains too. The clothes closet was big and beautiful. Later Art Haase told me that when his wife bought that closet he had a hard time to get it into their small house. I took in all the beauty, threw myself on the bed, and embraced all the space. Life was great. I promised myself that I would one day have a room that special.

Lloyd picked me up from the Haases on Saturday nights, and we drove around Pierceland and had a bottle of soda. Lloyd bought peanuts and poured them into his pop. I liked to eat the peanuts and drink my pop separately. Lloyd drove me home before midnight. Sometimes we went to a show. Lloyd didn't dance, but we did go to a few dances, and he would dance the square dance. I had a good time dancing, and I learned to follow him. Lloyd drove me back to the Haases on Sunday nights after I spent the weekend with my family.

I went to school from the Haases with their youngest son, Greg Haase. Greg was like an only child, as his brothers were older and gone from home. Greg liked to play games; he taught me how to throw a football, and we also played crocket on the lawn.

I was part of the high-school volleyball team, but I didn't stay for practice because I had a job. I went to Meadow Lake to play, but I soon decided that work was more important than a game, and I quit that sport and concentrated on my work.

My first big outing was with Lloyd. On July 4th, we went to the Meadow Lake stampede. I feared for the cowboys, but I liked all the action. I had never been to a rodeo. The stage show was so good. It was like a circus act followed by some great country singers. This was an outing! My sixteenth year was turning into fun.

There were a few trials at the Haases. I had never painted a building, used the garden cultivator, or made piecrust. I liked to work in the tree line with the cultivator, and the painting was good, but I recall making that first pie. I rolled out the crust, but it fell apart when I went to pick it up to put it into the pie plate. The tears rolled down my cheeks. I wanted so badly to please the lady who was so affectionate. I didn't bake at home, as Nioma was there to help Mom. Mrs. Haase was patient with me. She said, "The crust is just too rich." I don't remember if the pie ever turned into a tasty treat. I recall another incident while I worked at the Haases. Greg was a fussy kid and didn't like anything that was dirty or had a smell. Mrs. Haase had an old kettle that she kept under the sink to put her kitchen scraps in. The scraps were fed to the chickens. She asked Greg to take the kettle and empty it into the chicken fence.

I recall that kettle had a few dirty potato peelings, an onion that was spoiled, and a few red stains from some beet peelings when the beet pickles were made.

Greg went to the cupboard, opened the door, and peered at the messy kettle. He stepped back, and said to his mother, "I cannot carry that yucky pail. I will be sick." Greg stepped back and began to gag. Greg's mother, in her calm and gentle way, walked to the cupboard where she kept a few toys for the grandchildren. She opened the bottom drawer, and took out a child's gas mask. She handed it to Greg and said, "Put this gas mask on and be on your way." Greg was reluctant to put the mask on, but he knew that he needed to carry that pail. He placed the mask over his nose and mouth and fastened the little strap behind his head. He carried the pail outdoors, as Mrs. Haase and I watched Greg mosey to the chicken pen. The chickens rushed around him and enjoyed the treat that Greg gave them.

I worked for the Haases until January. I recall her old spatula with a broken handle. Mrs. Haase used to scrape out a bowl. I knew what I was going to buy her for Christmas; a new spatula. I gave it to her, and she thanked me. I never saw her use the new one, as the old one still did what she wanted it to do.

Today I understand because I too have a problem giving up my old utensils that are still working and my daughter, Angie, suggests that I replace them. I tell her, "Why, this one still works fine?"

Art Haase went to Primrose Lake in December for the fishing season; I did the chores. I threw a few square bales over the fence to feed his 40 cows each day. I tossed the frozen cow manure from the straw bed, as he had. Lloyd Haase, Art's son, and his wife Mable were home for Christmas. Lloyd was a tall man like his dad Art, but Lloyd went to university and had lived in the city for many years. His farm interests were not like Arts. Lloyd did the chores for two days, and Mable took charge of the house. Mable was a registered nurse, and she was able to handle any medical event. I went home for the festive season.

On January 30, 1965, I finished working at the Haases; she felt that she was able to get along on her own. I missed her warm and caring smile and the hymns that she sang.

At this time, my brother Lloyd had gone to work on an oilrig in Edson, Alberta. Mom and Dad drove him to Uncle Ben's. I went along too. I knew I would miss his sense of humour and the trips to the barn where I once rolled his cigarettes. I had helped him to hide the evidence from Mom and Dad too. Lloyd became a working man away from home. I went to school, helped at home, and longed for my brother, Lloyd. Lloyd didn't come home for months.

But after Lloyd Gonie and I started to date, my brother Lloyd Burge was no longer the number one Lloyd. My brother was not in our home any longer, and when he came home he had his own friends to spend time with. One day my brother told me that I was getting too "churchy". I told him, "You are partying too much." We didn't see much of each other, and we drifted apart. We both had our own dreams for life.

In grade eleven, our class moved across the hall from our grade ten room of the Pierceland Central School. This year our homeroom teacher was Mr. Ilnesky for the second time. I studied every night and was determined to graduate. When I picked up my term report card in June, I was missing two subjects. I wouldn't be allowed to graduate with my class, the twenty kids that I had started with in grade one. I would need to go to school for another year. This was a devastating thought, but I didn't think I could study anymore. I didn't want to go to school or graduate with another class; I had the summer to think about it.

In the summer, I went to Cold Lake to babysit for the Seager family. They had three small children — Cathy, Sheldon, and Eric. Frank and Charlotte were good people to work for. Frank was in the air force and was a good father. Frank was a big man, and he had a big heart too. Charlotte was an immigrant, and I found her hard to understand for the first while. She was a small lady, a hard worker, and I soon enjoyed her company. Charlotte helped me with any problem I had. I recall how she cancelled a cheque when I paid too quickly for an item. I learned to never allow a fast-talking salesman into my house.

My room and board was included in my job at the Seagers. I had a taste of making my own money. I was paid every two weeks. I had never made that much money, and I thought that I was on my way to making a living. Why did I need to have my grade twelve, anyway?

When school resumed in the fall I didn't go back. My parents never spoke to me about getting my grade twelve. Nobody helped me to see that I could pick up those two credits another time. I longed to graduate with my class. I liked making money, and I had made a big decision. I didn't think I needed school. I thought my head was full enough of Shakespeare and calculus. I was torn apart by having to make such an adult decision; not one person seemed to be there to talk to me. I felt like Mom was happy to have one more kid out from under her roof. Now I am a mother, and I know that was not true. I also feel, in hindsight, that every child should finish high school and graduate; it was one of my big goals. I promised myself that I would find a way to complete my dream and graduate from something.

Later in my life, I found that one more year isn't a lifetime, and I wished I had finished high school. Soon I wanted to make more money, and I searched for another job. On January 19, 1966, I started working at the bakery. It was here that I learned to make a good pie crust. Gus Timmerman, the baker, was hard to work for, but I enjoyed working in a hot environment. Gus said that the bread raised the best if the temperature was over 26 degrees Celsius. My shift was from

2 a.m. until ten a.m. I helped Gus make two batches of bread; each batch had 210 loaves. We used a milk pail of water, and .45 kilograms (a pound) of yeast that was in a brick form. The yeast was dissolved in the water. The bread needed to be mixed, rise, baked, and cooled before it was sliced; all before the bakery opened for business at 9 a.m. We also made doughnuts and cinnamon buns. I learned to roll buns too. I cried many mornings, as my left hand couldn't make that perfect bun, and I needed to reroll. I still roll buns with two hands. I don't want to forget the art of rolling buns; it was so hard to accomplish under the watchful eyes of the baker.

homemade buns

After my eight-hour shift, I walked to my former babysitting job. Charlotte understood, and she found a baby sitter for three hours in the morning. I cared for the kids until 5 o'clock, often sleeping in the afternoon with the kids. I had supper with the Seagers and then I went to the bakery to sleep. I got up at 1:45 and went downstairs to work. Gus was hard to work for, and he said, "No one can hold two jobs and do them well."

I was determined to show him that I could. I was busy and developed headaches, but I wanted to make more money because I wanted to buy furniture when we were married. I continued to work at the bakery and then go to babysit. I enjoyed the Seagers' kids; they seemed like my family.

Judy started to work at the bakery at the beginning of April. Judy worked the day shift. She also worked the till and learned to meet the public, as she sold the bread and operated the till. This was a good start to one day having to run her hairdressing business. I didn't like to work with money, and today I try to find a way not to.

On Easter weekend, we made 500 dozen buns. Gus, the baker, believed the people would buy locally if he could fill their order, however McGavins with their cheaper bakery products overruled. McGavins came from Edmonton with their load of Easter goods and filled the store shelves. I know that those fresh buns and bread sold well. I recall that some hot dog buns that Judy and I had made at the local bakery were not very well shaped. I wonder how those imperfect buns sold. That Saturday, Judy and I worked a twelve-hour shift. It was a long day, and the first time I had worked such long hours. After we were tired, Judy and I got giddy, and we laughed at all things that were said or done in the afternoon. Gus, the baker didn't get upset with us, he seemed to laugh with us.

Chapter 51:
Our School House Home

Lloyd-my future husband

Dad moved the lumber house from the meadow in 1959. It was placed alongside the log house, and Dad made a walkway to join the two houses. My friend, Chris remembers that we had many rooms now, and Judy and I had a bed all alone.

The Meadow Lake School Division offered for sale several of their rural schoolhouses as bigger and more modern schools was being built in the towns, and the kids were bussed to town. In 1963, Mom and Dad managed to buy the Glenville School which had been in Northern

Pine; about sixteen kilometres away. I don't remember how the school was moved to Dad's property.

The school closest to our farm was called "Black Raven School". This is the school that Nelson, Nioma, and Lloyd walked to for the first few years. I never attended that school. (This school is still standing, as it is part of Dave Scott's recycling business.)

When Dad purchased the country school, 9 by 6 metres, the log house was torn down and he sawed the logs for wood. We slept in granaries for the summer months. Later Dad poured a cement basement in that spot. Mom said, "Me and the kids washed all the rocks before they were put into the concrete to make the basement."

Dad made a cistern in one corner of the basement, which collected rainwater from the roof. The rainwater ran from the roof into a pipe leading to the cistern. The water was used to wash clothes, and for bathing and cleaning dishes and floors. Dad installed a hand pump upstairs. What a thrill to have water in the house. Dad added a drain hose to the sink for the summer. When it became too cold for the water to run outside, a pail was placed underneath the sink to catch the water. That sink held a lot of water and I remember wiping up water many times because the pail overflowed. Mom told us to put a dishpan inside the sink and carry the water outdoors so the pail wouldn't overflow.

Mom said, "We had a busy summer. Many renovations were done to our school house home before Nioma's wedding. Dad lowered the ceiling and made a bedroom on the main level." I remember the two cloakrooms that the school had when I went to school. Dad made one into a porch, and the other became our bathroom.

A wood stove was put downstairs and Dad cut a hole in the floor above the stove to allow the heat to go upstairs. I liked to stand on that grate; it was a warm place to dress because the warm air coming from the stove went upward.

Mom had a "clothes horse" to hang the smaller articles that she washed. Mom carried the clothes horse outdoors to freeze the washed clothes. In the evening, she brought it in and placed it over that heat grate. The clothes dried quickly over the heat, and there was no need for a humidifier. I liked the fresh smell of the outdoors in my clothes. Today I hang my sheets outdoors to dry.

In the basement, Dad made a cold room and two bedrooms, one for the girls and one for the boys. We also had a little room for a chemical toilet with a curtain across the front. That little space was referred to as the "throne". I thought this was great, but it was the boys who had to empty the pail each day. Mom put Pine Sol in that chemical toilet to keep the smell down. I didn't like the smell of Pine Sol, but it sure was better than the smell of body waste. Nioma, Nelson, and Lloyd were gone from our home. Now we were 11 bodies at the table each day.

I had my eighteenth birthday in December 1965. I worked in Cold Lake. Lloyd Gonie filled my thoughts all day long, as I worked, and at night too when I went to bed.

On March 12, 1966, Lloyd and I were engaged to be married. Lloyd and I shared many weekends with Nioma and Bill, as the brothers worked together on the farm with cattle and fieldwork. Mr. Gonie was in control, and he arrived early each day to plan the boys' day. Bill and Lloyd always respected their dad and followed his wishes.

Lloyd still does not want to plan things ahead. Lloyd did most of the farming and haying and tended the cows. Bill was a mechanic and fixed whatever was broken. Bill also was the chore boy who pumped the water with a pump jack (a motor mounted on a jack that went up and down to draw the water out of the well and into a large trough).

Chapter 52:
Nioma Becomes A Mother

Nioma told my family that she was pregnant. I was sooo excited to have a baby around our family once more. I was in school and so proud to be an auntie. Mom was thirty-nine years old, and said to Nioma, "Don't make me a grandma before I'm forty years old." Bill and Nioma's son Victor was born on October 4, 1964. Mom turned forty on October 29. Mom was always ready for another baby in her household and congratulated Nioma.

Victor is the first grandchild to my parents. He was so special, and he learned to walk and talk very quickly. Victor learned to say nursery rhymes. He was telling me the rhyme, "Hi Diddle Diddle, the Cat and the fiddle, the cow jumped over the moon." Victor was with Nioma when she milked her cow Niger, and he remembered the cow lifting her foot and spilling the milk. Victor's next line was: "Niger put her foot in the pail."

Bill and Nioma lived in Lloyd's house with Lloyd for two years prior to our marriage. Victor became special to my family and to his uncle Lloyd too. Victor sat on Lloyd's knee often. When Victor started to walk, he followed his Uncle Lloyd, as a little puppy follows his master.

Victor grew each year, and soon he became an adult. He took over the family farm when he was nineteen years old after Bill had a heart attack. Victor and his wife Celana live in the house that Victor was raised in, less than a kilometre from our home. Celana has redesigned and updated their home, making it a beautiful old house.

Mr. Gonie handled all the finances on the Gonie farm. I was embarrassed when Lloyd went to his dad on Saturday night and asked for $20. I was uncomfortable that Lloyd had to ask for money when he was an adult. Lloyd didn't seem to mind, as he said he had earned that money. I guess Lloyd had money for the rest of the week. Lloyd's mom spoke German to him. I don't remember talking to his mother, as I didn't speak German. I know she could speak English, but she didn't. I never got to know Lloyd's mother.

Lloyd had quit school in grade six because he was making trouble at school. The teacher told Mr. Gonie that Lloyd would be better off at home where he could do work that he was interested in. How blessed Lloyd was to have a strong mind, body, and good health. Work is still Lloyd's priority, and I had to learn not to make plans for occasions when I might be let down because Lloyd was at work. I try to be half ready in case Lloyd ever wants to take in some event. Now, I too am happy to work at home and wash my hair ahead of time in case Lloyd decides to take in some function.

My brother Nelson had a girl friend, Doreen Dilcox. Judy and I had a few sleepovers at Doreen's house. Doreen's mother allowed us to talk into the wee hours of the night and then we slept in the next morning. This was a treat as nobody slept in at home. Mom needed to have breakfast over all at one time because there were many jobs to be done. Doreen wore nice glasses, and her clothes were new. Doreen had nice curly hair too. She worn black patent leather shoes. I thought Doreen was a real princess.

Nelson and Doreen dated for about 2 years. I was thrilled when Nelson and Doreen asked me to be their bridesmaid. What a joy to be a bridesmaid again. On January 29, 1966, Nelson and Doreen were married, and the reception and dance was at Cherry Grove Hall. It was a cold day in January, and we needed to go to Goodsoil because a blood test was required for marriage. Nelson and Doreen forgot to get theirs.

Doreen's cousin, Raymond Ayers, stood up for Doreen and Nelson. This was six months before my wedding, and I didn't like to be with another man.

Nelson and Doreen had their children about the same time, as Lloyd and I did. Doreen is six months my senior, and Nelson worked with Lloyd when Mr. Gonie needed extra help. Their family and our family spent many enjoyable times in the outdoors, as we camped, fished, or boated together.

Lloyd and I had been dating for two years and together most weekends. Lloyd drove me to the Seagers in Cold Lake on Sunday nights so I could babysit their three children. I recall how shocked I was when Cathy, the oldest girl, told her parents that one of the girls in her class wore Kotex. Frank calmly said, "You will too one day."

Chapter 53:
I'm A Bride!

our wedding day

In June, I went to Bonnyville, Alberta with Lloyd and his parents. They bought my beautiful lacy dress. It cost $50. I never had any outfit that cost so much. I felt like a queen. I don't remember if Lloyd saw my dress. I thought life was full of joy and success; nothing would change. I soon faced some difficulties; marriage wasn't the fairy tale that I had envisioned. I was alone when Lloyd went to work. The housework, cooking, and chores were done in a couple of hours. I felt that I should have a job. Lloyd was against me working and said, "If you want to work, you can go to the field with me." I didn't want that. I learned to ask God for guidance each and every day, as I matured and faced the challenges of life. I know that I was not fully in control. God guided me and kept me happy and safe. Now, as I look back over the years, I know I was only a child, but I thought I was in control to fill my dreams.

Nioma was pregnant with her second child at our wedding. When we took our family picture, Nioma wanted to be in the back as her baby was due in less than a month. Norman was born about three weeks after our wedding.

July 6, 1966 was our wedding day. Lloyd and I were married in the Catholic Church in Pierceland. The day was very hot. Our reception was in the church basement where it was cool. I remember the photographer took so long. Supper was ready and our caterers, the ladies of C.W.L., called us twice. I recalled saying, "Let the people start without us." Today I would say that was a child's answer.

A photographer was important to me. Our wedding album cost $100, but it was worth it to me. Both of our families had family pictures taken. This would be the last family picture the Gonie family had taken. Mrs. Gonie passed away later in July.

Our wedding was in the middle of the week — Wednesday. I was told that the weekend was better, but I didn't listen. The priest had changed the date twice already because of special days for saints to be honoured with mass on weekends.

Lloyd is 13 years my senior, and I was told that our marriage would be rocky. This made me more determined, and I vowed to do whatever it took: I believe that love held in harmony would mould us as one. It has!

I modelled my dress twenty-five years later. I wondered how I stood that itchy lace all day long in the heat of July. Our vows were taken seriously; until death do us part. We worked at everything together, and today, love is so much more than I ever thought it was when I was that eighteen-year-old girl. A married couple does become one body. I feel that young people today are afraid to make a commitment and many couples shack up and don't marry.

The day following our wedding we went to Edson to see Great-Grandma Timmoth. She was in her nineties and had come for Nelson and Doreen's wedding in January. She said, "It's too hard for me to ride the bus for your wedding." I promised to go to Peers, Alberta to see her. I feared that Grandma Timmoth might fall as she ran outside to meet us when she saw the pink, windblown flowers that were still on the car.

Lloyd and I stayed the night with Great-grandma Timmoth before we went to Nelson and Doreen's in Edson, Alberta the next morning. Nelson had the Friday off. The four of us went to B.C. Neither Lloyd nor I had ever seen the mountains. Lloyd didn't like the huge walls of rocks above the road. I feared the steep slopes and the rushing water below. The highway was narrow; the mountains are not special for me.

We returned home on Sunday. Mom suffered a miscarriage and was in the hospital. I am told there were two fetuses. Mom had lost a lot of blood, and her life hung by a thread. The Red Cross donated blood for three blood transfusions to save Mom's life. Mom was so tired; she stayed in the hospital for a week.

Lloyd's mother, Rosa Gonie, went to the hospital that week too. She was a diabetic and suffered a heart attack. Lloyd's family gathered round and said good bye to their mother. Rosa Gonie died July 17, 1966.

I recalled her words to us at our wedding. She said, "Now I can die because each one of my kids has somebody." What a rough start to my married life; all within a few days after our wedding.

I felt all the weight of the world. How would I be able to care for Lloyd the way she had? I fell apart the night of the prayer service. I was over twenty years younger than most of my in-laws; Lloyd's four older sisters were married before I was born.

I had never attended a funeral. I did not wish to go past the coffin and view Lloyd's mother. Yes, I guess I was terrified at seeing a dead body. One of Lloyd's sisters said, "You are Lloyd's wife; you have to go past the coffin to pay your respects like all the rest." I wanted to fit into his family, and I obeyed. I walked past the coffin, and the handle of my big brown purse was caught. I screamed. I'm told that Lloyd carried me out of the church. I vowed to never have that happen again. I promised myself to learn more about this terrible thing called death.

I remember as a child that the neighbours' girl, Lena, died. She was sixteen years old and went into a diabetic coma. I went to a granary with Mom to see her body. Lena looked so pretty in her coffin. It was hard to believe that she was dead. I recalled the reaction of her mother Violet; she was devastated, threw her hands in the air, and was angry at God. I cried for Violet's loss and her great pain.

I am from a large family, and I realized that I would need to face death many times in my life. Parents often died before their children, and brothers and sisters didn't always die in the order in which they were born. I needed to face the future and prepare myself for whatever it held.

I read articles, and books about death. I listened to other people tell me of their experiences and how they coped. I visited people who were grieving.

I took a bereavement course; read anything that I thought could help me, but death remained a mystery to us. It's so hard to accept, but now I understand that whatever lives must one day die. None of us can know the time, place, or how we will leave this world. I matured and learned to accept death as a part of life. I did learn that life is a gift to be lived out each day, and we are to live each day as if it were our last. We are not in control of the hour when we leave this world. God is the giver of life, and God calls us in his time. I pray that I will be ready, but I feel I'm not ready yet. One bible quote is: *"Man is like a breath; his days like a passing shadow."* (Psalms 144:4)

I know that I must die to be born into eternity. I know, in my

Father's house, there are many rooms prepared for all who love him. Help me Lord to love you more with each passing day and thus be more prepared for my end. Send me the grace to not be afraid as I face the unknown.

Chapter 54:
Moulding Together

My dreams were big, and I planned to buy our furniture with the money that I had saved from my many jobs that I had worked at since I was thirteen years old. I bought an electric stove and a bedroom suite; most of the money I had saved was spent. Lloyd's godmother gave us money for a wedding gift, and we bought a table and four chairs. Our furniture was minimal, but slowly we were able to get what we needed, thanks to Lloyd's dad who went to auction sales. He bought us a couch that we used for six years. I had a dowry; I brought my little brown, cardboard suitcase into our marriage and a very small bank account.

Lloyd was busy farming, haying, and tending cows. My days were long, and I had to learn to entertain myself through the lonely days when Lloyd was gone. I didn't have a sewing machine or any money to do hobbies. I do remember some sad days, but the joys in my life have been more than my trials. I have heard it said that: "Life turns out best for those who make the best out of the way things turn out."

I plunged into my unknown future and learned to bond with Lloyd. Both Lloyd and I value our vows, and we worked together to become a happy couple.

Each family is unique but different. I smile as I remember the little adjustments that we learned to make. Every family is woven together by their own traditions, and we pass our old traditions on to the next generation. Our traditions help us to stay connected to our family from the past. We lead the way to future family traditions, as we make memories with our family and create new activities.

I found some of Lloyd's family customs strange and other customs were comical to me. How funny it seems now that Lloyd needed a saucer to drink his morning coffee. He poured a little coffee into the saucer, let it cool, and sipped each swallow. His dad did the same thing to cool his coffee. I ate breakfast, but Lloyd never ate breakfast. He wanted a sandwich at 10 a.m. I found this very odd; at home we all ate breakfast about 8 a.m. and then we were expected to wait until noon before we ate again.

My family never had sauerkraut because Dad didn't like it. Lloyd's family made a large crock each year. Today Lloyd makes the crock half full for our own use. I enjoy sauerkraut too, and we have it once a month.

In our house, we waited until Mom had all the food on the table before we could start to eat. Lloyd will eat whatever is on the table, as soon as he gets to the table. I still rush to get the complete meal on at one time.

Mrs. Haase always had a tablecloth on her table. I liked a tablecloth on the table too. I put a tablecloth on our table, but Lloyd pulled it off and threw it on the floor. I have a closet with many new tablecloths today.

Our family looked at the Sears' and Eatons' catalogues until the pages were worn out. Lloyd refused to have a catalogue in the house. He said, "That catalogue belongs in the toilet."

Lloyd liked his toothpicks, and he chewed on one after each meal. After supper, he chewed that toothpick and when he was finished with it, he threw it behind the chesterfield. I told him to throw it on the floor where I could easily pick it up. After about a week of me complaining about picking up his toothpicks, he learned to throw them in the garbage himself.

I remember the first time I cooked macaroni for Lloyd and I. Mom always used her biggest kettle to cook pasta at home. I filled the kettle with water and added the macaroni. Lloyd and I ate macaroni for a week.

Marriage changed my life. I was used to a full house of people at home, now my house was empty when Lloyd was gone. I had breakfast, and Lloyd had his coffee. Lloyd went to Bill's each day to plan their workday together. If I was hanging up clothes on the line, I could hear Lloyd talking to Bill. (Bill was hard of hearing, and Lloyd spoke loudly. Lloyd's voice carried well.)

Nioma and I were together much of the time because our husbands shared the workload. Nioma had her son, Victor, to keep her busy, and Norman was on the way, but I was alone.

I also missed Judy. Her and I had worked together at the bakery and liked many of the same things. She came to stay with me on a few weekends; maybe she missed me too? We always had a joyous time when together. Lloyd often shook his head, and he went outdoors, as Judy and I got the "giggles". Judy's actions bring reactions and often in a joyful way. Judy and I still laugh at some childhood events where we made our own fun as we worked and played.

Lloyd's older sister, Eva Rolheiser lived in Edmonton, Alberta. Her son, Roland Rolheiser, was about twelve years old when we were married. Roland came to stay with Uncle Lloyd and spent most of that summer with us. He helped Lloyd in the hayfield, as he learned to rake hay with the John Deer M tractor. Roland also enjoyed horseback riding with his Uncle Lloyd, as they checked cows. There were many activities that I learned about later; like chasing a buffalo on horseback with my brothers. My brothers George and Lewis stayed with us and helped Lloyd too. They taught Roland, that city boy, all about country living before he had to return for school in the fall. I'm sure there are stories that I have never heard about too.

I struggled to find something constructive to do. I didn't have a sewing machine to sew. Mom gave me her old machine and what a headache that was. I fought with the settings, as I tried to make a useful blanket. Lloyd's sister, Mary, gave me some material scraps. I tore apart my sewing creations more than I sewed. When Nioma and I bought our new machines, I took a sewing course from Joan Kesenheimer. Joan is a dear friend today, and I visit her often. Thanks to Joan, I learned to enjoy my sewing. I make quilts today for a pastime and for pleasure. I give away many quilts to my family members. I made an orange-coloured quilt for Jillise, my granddaughter, but by the time I had it finished, she no longer liked the colour orange. I keep the quilt in my car.

I recall a hurtful incident after I was married and had two sons. The Gonie bunch attended a wedding and someone suggested that we all go to the bar before supper for a drink. I was not twenty-one, and I was not allowed in the local bar. My in-laws were older, and I was still a child by the alcohol standards. I was embarrassed and hurt.

The Gonie bunch went to a distant lake at the end of June. It was about a four-hour drive from Pierceland. They all had campers to stay in. The fishing was good, and they bragged about the good time they had. Lloyd and I never went, as our family was still in school, writing exams. Later, my kids were all teenagers, and I knew that Lloyd and I couldn't leave four teenagers if we went fishing.

It seemed to me that I would never be that perfect age to join in the Gonie group. By the time I experienced those awful "hot Flashes" and crabby days, my sisters in-law were long past that age. There still is the same amount of years between us, but now it's not a big deal to be younger. Today, I only have three who are alive. I learned to enjoy each day, as a good life has nothing to do with my age or anybody else's.

Chapter 55:
Granddad Gonie:

About 10 months after our wedding, Lloyd's dad remarried. He married Marian Plasko on April 29, 1967. Marian was a lady about twenty years younger than he was. I knew that Marian would care for Granddad in a great way. I had gone to school with her children and had spent some time at her house. Marian was a gentle and loving lady.

In 1981, we noticed that Granddad's health was failing.

Lloyd's dad was a leader, but when dementia set in, his wife Marian asked for help. Each of his kids took turns at having him in our homes. This was not a good idea as it made him more confused.

Granddad soon needed more care than any of us could provide; he was hospitalized. Later he was taken to Battleford, Saskatchewan, where he was placed in an extended care ward in a level 4 long-term facility. He lived out his last days there.

On September 27, 1983 William Gonie Sr. passed away. This was about a month before his 84th birthday. He raised a big family and helped his sons, as they bought their farmland. Granddad had lived a full life.

Marian and "Pa" had shared about 14 years of wedded bliss. Marian continued to live in her home and was always a pleasure to be around. She helped in the church and in the community with baking, cleaning, and her cheerful laugh, which was encouraging to all people.

In a few years, Marian suffered a stroke and needed extra care. Her children found a facility in Smoky Lake. When there was room in Cold Lake, Alberta, she moved into long-term care to live out her remaining days.

Marian's joyful smile and upbeat character will always be missed by all who knew her. She saw the good in all people and never had a harsh word toward anybody. Marian died in the Cold Lake hospital on June 8, 2003.

Chapter 56:
It's Just Me!

I married Lloyd, and moved nineteen kilometres to the east of Pierceland. I found it hard to be alone, and I shed many tears. It wasn't that far from my brothers and sisters, but now I didn't sit around a full table to share a meal each day and talk about the day's events at school or in the community. I had slept, ate, and enjoyed their company for eighteen years, and now I was often alone, as my husband was outdoors working on our farm. I struggled through many days with no one else to talk to, and I had a forlorn feeling that I had not experienced before. I learned to fill my days with a walk, planted a garden, and I did some reading that I didn't have time to do when I had worked. I longed for the weekend to come when I could return home for a visit and have Sunday supper with Mom, Dad, and my family. The evening passed quickly, and I was back in my lonely world when Monday morning came. I had to learn to move on in this new area of my life. Mom, I did experience your longing for your family, and I wasn't in another province like Mom was either.

When I married Lloyd Gonie, and I moved to his house, I felt, as Mom did when she left Edson — my heart would break without my family. Lloyd, my husband, drove the one vehicle that we owned. This old, black 1948 Dodge car was not reliable for me to drive; the brakes often failed and the gear shift was used to slow down the car, as Lloyd shifted to a lower gear. I was a new driver and could drive a standard car, but to shift gears to slow down or turn a corner fast was very frightening. This old car had other issues too. I recall riding with Lloyd and driving down the road in the dark. Lloyd went over a hill, and the lights went out. Lloyd pounded his foot on the floorboards to make the lights came back on. The dimmer switch was on the floor by his left foot; maybe there was a bare wire.

There was a round button on the dash, which was pushed to start the motor after the key was turned on. The back doors of this car opened the opposite way from the cars of today. I think Lloyd called these doors "suicide doors" because if the door opened and any one fell out, the back wheel of the car was sure to run them over.

My days seemed so long as I waited for my husband to return in the evening, and I wasn't a letter writer like Mom. July is haying time. Lloyd left in the morning and was gone all day long. I was not used to being alone. Nioma came each day to milk her cows, as there was not a barn at their new place where they had moved when Lloyd and I were married. Nioma's milk cows stayed at Lloyd's for the summer months until a fence and a barn was made at her place.

Nioma and I had planted a garden at our place in May, and Nioma came to pick garden vegetables too. The vegetables grew well, and there was enough for both of us to share. Nioma left and the days seemed endless; I was so lonely. How was I to fill this void? I had my driver's license, but I didn't have anything to drive. I walked to Nioma's each day at 3:30 to watch *Edge of Night*.

I went with Nioma to dig trees, and I planted trees in my yard, but my spruce became eye sores and needed to be removed; that was a make-work program for me. Nioma's trees thrived and became huge trees with branches that hide the windows. Celana enjoys the privacy today.

Nioma's second son, Norman, was born on July 29, 1966. Nioma asked Lloyd and I to be Norman's godparents. This made Norman special to us. Today we visit him and his wife, Shirley. Their home is in

Stony Plain, Alberta. I took care of Victor and Norman when Nioma came to milk her cows. That helped to fill about an hour of my day.

Nioma and Bill's house needed to be redone from top to bottom. The walls had been mudded and little slates covered the mud. Most of this was removed before it was moved to their farm, but there was much cleaning left. Nioma was thankful when Judy and I helped remove some missed slates and mud, one room at a time. Nioma cleaned and scrubbed that meagre house to make it a spotless home.

School was back in and my brothers went home, as did Roland. Our house had been full in the summer, but now I was alone. Lloyd was always on time for meals; dinner was at 12 p.m. and supper was at 6 p.m. One day he didn't come on time for dinner. I waited until 2 p.m. before I went to look for him. My mind ran wild; I thought that he had a heart attack or an accident, and I would find him dead. I found him alive and healthy on the road talking to a neighbour. I made a quick "U" turn on the road and went home. Lloyd followed me home and said, "Why were you upset? I'm a big boy." Lloyd can't understand why I get worried.

Two of Lloyd's brothers, John and Henry, had young kids when Lloyd and I were married. John and Marie lived about a kilometre to the south of us, and Henry and Rose lived about a kilometre to the north of us. Their kids were 8, 9, and 10 years old, and liked to play kick the can and any other games. In the evening of the summer months, Keith, Donna, Philip and Karen came to our house with their bikes. Lloyd and I took turns playing games with them. The boys often beat the girls. Everyone was a good sport. We finished the evening with hot chocolate before it was time for them to ride their bikes home. This was great fun for me; I felt like I was a kid again in our big family. (Keith is ten years younger than I am, and Philip is the age of my youngest brother.)

Lloyd and I did most things together, including repairing the fence. One day I drove the little John Deer "M" tractor along the fence line, and Lloyd walked along to tighten the wire on the pasture fence.

(There was no cab on this tractor.) A tree branch hung over the trail. Lloyd told me to watch carefully so that the branch wouldn't hit the tractor's radiator. I saw that it missed the front of the tractor, but that branch was aimed straight for me. I slid backward on the tractor seat to prevent the branch from hitting me. Soon I couldn't reach the clutch pedal to stop the tractor. I twisted myself on the tractor seat, and I fell off the back of the tractor seat. I landed on the hitch. My leg hit the gearshift, and I was able to knock it out of gear as I fell. The little John Deere came to a stop, and I picked myself up.

I can still see Lloyd just standing there frozen in fear and speechless. I was not hurt. I dusted myself off and got back on the tractor. Lloyd kept me safe, as he walked ahead on the fence line for the rest of the day.

Lloyd was a horseback rider, and he wanted me to saddle up and ride with him. I have never liked horses, but I agreed to take a ride. The horse I rode was supposed to be a well-broken horse. We were coming home from checking the cattle when my horse spooked. I pulled hard on the reins and pulled him into a squat position. I was able to jump off safely. Lloyd again felt helpless. He wanted me to mount up on his horse and ride home with him. I had enough of riding horses; I chose to lead my horse, as I walked that dusty trail home. Lloyd rode his horse slowly beside me.

Later on in our marriage, when the kids were in high school, I drove the grain truck for the harvest season. Rose Gonie, Henry's wife, helped me haul grain because Lloyd and Henry did the harvest together. Lloyd did the swathing and Henry did the combining. Rose and I got along well. I made lunch and supper and took her with me to the field when the guys were harvesting on our land, and Rose made lunch and supper when we were on their land. I went with her to the field too and enjoyed her company.

This was a learning experience, as I lined up to the granary to unload the grain. I placed marks on the ground that I could match the wheels with and a plank on the ground that I could back up to. Rose was there to guide me back. I often thought about the brakes failing, and not being able to stop. Most days I only had to make a load or maybe two if the grain was a good crop. The boys were home after school. Dan and Joe took over for me, and I prepared supper for the family. Supper was late in harvest time if the evenings were dry; the grain was too. I liked harvest time, but our schedule was thrown off because the days were long when the weather was perfect with a hot and dry wind to allow the combine to run into the night.

Harvest is different from the days I recall when I was growing up at home. I didn't have that large threshing crew to cook for like my mother did. Lloyd did the swathing first, and Henry drove the combine. When Lloyd finished cutting down the crop, he would haul the grain to the granary in the yard. An afternoon lunch was still required because the days were still long when the weather was cooperative.

Chapter 57:
New Life With A Family
(Dan, Joe, Angie, Bart)

In November, I went to check to see if the cow's water trough was full. There was a build-up of ice and I fell on the ice. I hurt my back. I went to the doctor. Dr. Wood said, "Your back is fine. You're pregnant." I was due on April 13, a week and nine months from our wedding day. I had a healthy pregnancy.

I was due in April, and I didn't want to stay alone. In March, I went with Lloyd to Primrose Lake for the Easter fishing season. There was one day of the fishing season left. Lloyd's sister, Bert, and her husband, Alfred Hewlett, were going home a day early. Bert stopped at our shack and asked me if I wanted to go home. I went home with them, as I didn't feel well. I had made a good decision.

Bert and I walked up the Martineau River hill because Alfred feared sliding back down the hill. He didn't want to put me in any danger. When we arrived home I went to bed, but about 8 p.m. I was in pain and drove to Nioma and Bill's. However, they were at Henry and Rose's for supper. I drove there, and Bill and Nioma took me to Cold Lake hospital.

I stayed in the hospital while my sister Nioma went home with Bill. This was a big ordeal for me; I was so afraid and full of pain. I didn't think that I would ever see Lloyd again. About midnight I was moved. I heard those double doors close behind me, as I was wheeled into the case room. I was sure that I was dying. I recalled the show *Dr. Ben Casey*. When those doors closed. many of his patients didn't come out alive. I know I have to die, but why was I chosen to die in so much pain? (I'm told most women think they are dying with that first baby.)

Daniel Lloyd was born on March 27, 1967 about two a.m. Our son arrived two weeks early. I was thankful we had waited for our wedding night to complete our love for each other. I was not prepared for a baby at this time. I had bought a dozen diapers, three nightgowns, and three little undershirts. Lloyd and I stopped at the co-op store and bought a few more diapers and other necessities for a baby. Nioma gave me some of Norman's clothes; he was eight months older and had outgrown the baby size.

To become a mother is surely the greatest event in a women's life. That first child has taught me so much; the trials, joys, and new ventures made me grow. The worries of this big responsibility can be overwhelming for a new mom. I never liked babies, and I had never bathed a baby. The first morning home, I undressed Dan for his bath. His arms and legs were flying about, and he was crying. I was afraid to place him in the basin with water. What could I do but put his clothes back on, wrap him in a blanket, and go for help? Nioma was the expert from her years of helping Mom. I took Dan to Nioma for his first bath. Nioma has helped me many times when I felt insecure about what to do as a mother. Thanks Nioma!

That year went by fast, and I was pregnant again. Lloyd had muskrat traps on Jeglum's Lake. In the morning, he asked me if I was okay before he left to check his traps. I felt different, but I didn't have any pains yet. Lloyd arrived home in about an hour. I was having a few small pains, and Lloyd took me to the hospital about noon. The doctor had told me to get to the hospital as soon as I felt different because he said that I had that first baby quickly; the next baby might come faster.

Our second son was born about one p.m. on Sunday. Joseph Mark was born on March 31, 1968. We now had two little boys, much like the two boys I babysat when I worked in Cold Lake (Sheldon and Eric Seager). Joe, the smaller one at birth, was one year and four days younger than his brother, Dan. I was more experienced now, but I was afraid of handling a small baby. How fragile he seemed. Joe was a thin baby, and he moved his small arms and legs when he was not wrapped in a blanket. The doctor said, "Set your alarm because a small baby needs to eat every three hours."

I struggled to get out of a warm bed to prepare a bottle for Joe. Three hours always came too soon. It was hard to have two babies. Dan was beginning to walk but still a baby. I understood when Mom said, "It's hard to bring a baby home when you have a baby at home." I remembered Mom saying that she was tired all the time; I was too. I learned to sleep when the boys slept; the dishes had to wait to be washed. Tone and Lorraine's kids are cousins to our kids. Their youngest child is the age of our oldest child. Lorraine gave me a great gift when Carolyn was over a year old; all of the diapers that she no longer needed. What a gift that was, as Dan was still in diapers, and Joe was a newborn baby. I didn't have a lot of diapers, and I didn't have an automatic washer or a dryer. When Dan was ready to start sitting up, I used a wooden chair that had no rungs left on it for a high chair. I turned it upside down, and stuffed pillows around Dan. Dan learned to sit up in that chair.

Carolyn and Dan went to school together. Carolyn is a fun girl with brown eyes, dark hair, and a body that is able to run a marathon today at almost fifty years old. She is married and has a family. Carolyn stayed at our place and joined in all the fun with the boys as they rode horses, drove motorbikes, and hiked in the woods. Carolyn fell from the bales stack; off limits for our kids, but the rules were broken. Lorraine came for Carolyn the next day and took her for an x-ray that showed a broken arm. I was distraught as Carolyn never cried or complained about her arm. How could I not have checked her out closer?

In August 1969, we installed the water and sewer at our farm. This was a great improvement to the work force. Lloyd could shower instead of splashing about in a basin of water that he had to carry out later. That tub was a joy to bathe the boys in. The toilet was even greater. I was expecting my third child in late August, and anything to make my life easier was appreciated. I was tired all the time. The doctor said I needed to rest or he would put me in the hospital where I could rest. I learned to lie down when the boys had their afternoon nap. How did Mom ever raise us with no conveniences or others to help her? Mom, enjoy your life now!

Chapter 58:
Time for Frills

It was September, and I had passed my due date of August 17. My twelve-year-old sister, Debbie, had stayed with me for the month of August, but now she had returned home to Mom and Dad's house. The day she went to junior high school in Pierceland, Saskatchewan was the day I went into labour.

It was September and Lloyd was in the field cutting the crop about five kilometres from home. The boys were having their afternoon nap, and I went to the garden to dig potatoes for supper. I experienced a few cramps. I sat down on my pail until they subsided. I dug my spuds, and I took my potatoes into the house before another pain hit me.

I needed to go to get Lloyd, who was out in the field. I woke up the boys and put them in our 1968 Dodge truck. Dan, the oldest boy, was two and a half years old, and Joe was one and a half years old. I was about a kilometre down the rough road when I had another pain, which made me stop until my contraction had passed. My mind began to run wild; what if I was in too much pain to drive? Would I need to lock the doors of the truck to keep the boys safe until help came?

My pains passed, and I continued to drive to the field. When I arrived at the field, Lloyd saw me coming and rushed to the truck. I stepped out of the truck to allow Lloyd to drive. As I walked around the truck I had another contraction. I needed to start timing how long it was between my pains.

My sister lived along the road on the way to the hospital. Lloyd drove into her yard so we could leave the boys with her. I prayed that she would be home; we didn't have any phones in the area yet. I saw her coming to the door, and I was relieved.

It seemed to take so long for Lloyd to take Dan and Joe into her house. The doctor had told me to rush to the hospital, as soon as I felt uncomfortable. I was more than uncomfortable; my pains had developed into hard labour pains that took my breath away. The Cold Lake hospital was still about 30 minutes away. With each contraction, Lloyd asked me if I was okay to which I answered, "Get me to the hospital."

A nurse met me at the door with a wheel chair and took me to my room. The nurse came to my room to get my paper work, as I gritted my teeth through another strong contraction. The nurse told me to try to relax; I was enraged at her and wondered if she had ever given birth. I am told that my labours are short, and birth is easy for me. I know I was not in labour for days, but to say that birth is easy was a big statement.

Lloyd went to his sister Sal's place in Grand Centre, as husbands were not allowed to stay with their wives back in the sixties. He didn't have long to wait; our beautiful daughter was born at 5 p.m. strong and healthy. Angela weighed 5 pounds and 10 ounces at birth.

Angela Marie was born on September 3, 1969. I felt so blessed to have a daughter. I have a good relationship with my mother, and knew that Angela and I would share many good times, as mothers and daughters grow together.

Angela was a good baby and not fussy like her brothers were. I could feed her, and she would sleep until her next feeding. I never woke Angie up to eat. The boys ate more often and required more attention because they were not as content. I guess I learned to be more relaxed too. I was a busy mom with three children under three years old.

I liked to dress Angela in dresses and keep her pretty like a little girl, but I soon discovered that pants were easier for her to crawl in, climb onto furniturem and ride her stick horse when she joined in with her brothers. Angie grew fast and was with her brothers in most of their adventures, as they raced around our house.

Angela brought joy to her brothers and to us, her parents. She grew with her brothers and joined in their fun with small metal Matchbox trucks. They wore out the knees of their pants, as they crawled about the room.

Stick horses were another well-used toy. The kids rode around the house and pretended to chase cows like their father did. McLeod's store sold these toys. The toys were made of wood, with a wooden horse head on a broomstick. The wooden horse head was painted with different colors. There was a plastic rein in the horse mouth, which was long enough to reach over the horse's ears, and the kids could hold onto that rein. The broomstick was placed between their legs, and they galloped about the house acting like a horse.

Lloyd was a good father; the kids would crawl upon his lap and cuddle close to his warm body. I was so pleased to see this great connection and felt that I had chosen the right person to be the father of my kids.

Lloyd played with the kids, and I had a little time to myself to take a walk, a bath, or to read. Our house was full of giggles, squeals, and fighting. We had a wide stripe of black pipeline tape down the middle of our floor. That wide tape held our linoleum together. That line of tape was used as a road, and it provided hours of joy for my kids, as they played with their Matchbox toys.

We had three small children, and our outings were to church on Sunday mornings. Lloyd carried Dan in one arm and Joe in the other arm while I carried Angie. I remember how hard and frustrating it was to get three kids and myself ready for church. Lloyd helped the boys to put on their shoes. One day he helped Angie too. I was sitting in church when I noticed that she had her pants on backwards.

Angela played and grew alongside of her brothers. She became a warm and loving person, who learned to share and help others.

Today she is there for her mother in-law, as she drives her to shop and doctors appointments.

In 1974, kindergarten was started in Pierceland, Saskatchewan. Angie's class was the first class in Pierceland to have the option of attending kindergarten. Angela didn't start school in the fall like her classmates because Joe had started grade one that year. I thought I couldn't handle two kids leaving at the same time. (I thought of Mom when her twins left together.) I sent Angie to kindergarten after Christmas. I never felt that she was behind her classmates.

Angie has grown to have strong opinions, but she has a positive attitude like her Dad. She makes things happen, as she stands up for what she feels is right and has spoken out when necessary. Angie is easy to please and happy with whatever life gives her. She has told me, "Mom, life is what you make it out to be, and I want to be happy. Happiness is a choice we all make."

Angie likes kids and volunteers at school. Her friends are numerous in both the church and in the community. As a young girl, Angela was involved in figure skating, volleyball, and also took piano lessons. Angela rode horses and was accepted among her brothers; whenever they found new activities she was included. She broke her arm when she fell from her pony because the saddle cinch broke. Her cousin Joseph was riding with her.

Angie also sings. I will be forever grateful for Margaret Maynard, who helped Angie with some voice lessons. I was so proud to attend a senior's luncheon and listen to Margaret play the piano, as Angie sang, "Thank you, Lord." Angie attended guitar camp and learned to play her guitar. She plays her guitar or the piano in church on Sundays. She makes our mass come alive and enjoyable too.

I too went to guitar camp under the direction of Sr. Anita Hartman. I did not pluck the guitar, but I helped cook for fifty people. The kitchen was well stocked, the church housed some bats, and the cabins were hot at night, but we had a ball!

Gail Foss, Chris Wild, and I were responsible for the meals.

Margaret Maynard said, "I often heard all of you laughing and sharing a lot of jokes, and I wished I was cooking and not strumming the guitar."

These were great times of learning, laughing, and growing in my faith with children and friends. We were isolated; only a phone reached across the lake. Storms were very frightening, as the wind blew hard; waves flapped against the rocks on the shore, and the sky appeared to roll with anger. The black clouds were filled with hailstones that bounced from the roof and splashed in the lake. God kept us safe; we gathered in the little church to pray.

In 1983, Angie had the opportunity to go to Disneyland with her cousin Paulette Stang and Paulette's husband Joe. Angie went to babysit their son, Tyler, as they attended a wedding. This was the start of Angela's travelling.

Today Angie and her husband, Dean, travel out of the country each year and enjoy the warm weather in Mexico or other tropical climates. Angie said that she feels better in the heat.

Angie drives a school bus each day and enjoys it very much. She has driven the bus for over twenty years.

Dean was Joe's best friend in their school years. Dean came for many adventure trips to the river. Dean and Angela went to school together in grade ten. During this year, they started dating; soon Dean was Angela's best friend. Dean came to visit Angie and not Joe. Joe and Angela have always been close and remain so today.

Nioma, my sister, was pregnant with her third child. She wanted to have a girl, and I also wanted her to have a girl so that Angela would have some girl fun and not always be with boys. My sister gave birth to her third son, Gordon Dale, on April 20, 1970. Gordon is seven months younger than our daughter, Angie, but he soon was bigger and stronger than our little princess. I am close to my sisters and felt that our daughter needed a sister too. Angela was still one girl with the five boys when Nioma and I were working together and travelling to the field. I was expecting in late April.

Chapter 59:
My Last Baby Boy

April passed and May rolled around. I felt like a whale; my baby was overdue. I awoke early in the morning of May 6th with pains. Lloyd took me to the hospital. My brother, Lewis Burge, was staying at our house after there was a confrontation at Mom and Dad's house. Lewis was asked to leave. Lewis came to stay with Lloyd and me. He rode the school bus and attended high school for a few months. On May 6th, Lewis was left in charge of our three small children until Lloyd returned from the hospital.

Barton Paul was born May 6, 1971. He's our last child. Lloyd took the boys to Rose Gonie's and Angie was taken to Nioma's house. When I came home with baby Bart from the hospital, the boy's were sleeping, and Rose said, "Go home and get settled in and I'll bring the boys later." That was such a treat. Nioma had kept Angie, and she also brought Angie home at a later time.

My days were full now. I recall putting the babies shoes on while I sat on the flush toilet. I had a long coat that covered my clothes when I attended mass. I didn't want to be late for mass, but time would run out before I was ready. My friend told me that she had pulled her coat over her pajamas a time or two, as she went to church. I never did go to church in my pajamas. I felt that I never had time to dress up myself; I just made sure that my hair was combed.

I was beginning to feel like my mother. There were periods when I thought that there was nothing beyond the family and home for me. It was too hard to go anywhere with four kids. I felt that nobody, except Kay and Lawrence, enjoyed a visit with four kids. I had a corner in my kitchen that was used for a time out if need be. It seemed that Dan used it the most.

Lloyd thought that I needed some time away from home. He took the kids to Rose or Marie, sister-in-laws, so that I could go along with him to Bonnyville or Meadow Lake when he went for repairs or took some cattle to the stockyards. I always enjoyed my time out, and often I had a short shopping trip to McLeod's or the Saan store.

Chapter 60:
Sunday Is For Rest

My religion has always been important to me. Going to mass with four kids was a challenge. That one hour of sitting still was a test, and there were times we came home early. One kid reached out and pinched, bit, or punched the other kids. I often thought that our family held the complete congregation's attention, as they focused on our family who put on a free show.

The Catholic Church was experiencing a shortage of priests. We shared a priest with the Goodsoil parish for a few years. When our parish managed to have our own priest living in Pierceland again, Lloyd and I took turns staying at home with these little monsters. The one that stayed home also did the chores. Mass was a pleasure again.

Each morning, Lloyd milked two cows, and I milked one cow and then took two pails of milk to the house and started the separator. Lloyd brought another pail of milk into the house before the separator was empty. The separator removed the cream from the whole milk and the skim milk was given to the pigs. I was able to sell two cans of cream each week to help buy the groceries.

When Lloyd was in the hayfield or doing spring farm work, I milked the cows and did the chores in the evening by myself. Sometimes it was a test, as I took four kids to the barn with me. I expected the kids to play in the manger until I was done milking. Bart was in the stroller by the door or I put him to bed. It took me about half an hour. One night, I ventured to the barn with all three kids; Bart was put in the crib for safekeeping. I placed the other kids in the manger while I milked two cows. I was milking the second cow when I heard Angela giggle. I looked around and saw her head by the cow's back feet. The cow switched her long dirty tail across Angie's hair.

I jumped up and spilled the milk. The boys had lifted Angie out of the manger. She was not hurt, but the boys were scolded and also confined to the manger.

Lloyd always came home at 6 o'clock for supper and returned to work after he ate until late in the evening. The kids were often in bed before Dad was home from work.

I recall a great gift — a clothes dryer. Lloyd went with Henry to Bonnyville. There was a hardware store called Marshall Wells. There was a big fall sale on appliances. Henry lent Lloyd the money to buy a dryer. I was overjoyed when the dryer was hooked up and working. Our kids were all preschoolers, and there were a lot of small laundry items to wash and dry. The dryer meant that I didn't need to hang my clothes outdoors; no more freezing my fingers and then bringing the frozen clothes indoors to place them over the backs of my kitchen chairs.

Lloyd and I took our family to the lake for a swim. I placed Bart, who was sleeping, on a blanket on the beach. I knew he wasn't going anywhere, and I was focused on the kids in the water. I feared that a wave might come and tip over their small bodies. Later when I checked on Bart, he was sun burnt. How terrible I felt because I hadn't provided any shade for my baby.

Bart was one year old when he developed bronchial pneumonia and spent a week in the Cold Lake Hospital. Nioma came to visit me and said, "Get that kid to a doctor."

I knew Bart was breathing hard but he didn't have a fever. Lloyd was working away, as he drove a Caterpillar for Lillico's construction. I took Bart to the hospital, and he was admitted. Bart was kept in the hospital for a week. I was told by the nurse that I shouldn't come to visit him because it was too hard for kids when the parents leave. My arms ached for my baby and I longed to hold him close to me. I went to the neighbours and phoned each day to inquire about Bart's recovery. The nurse told me that each day there was an improvement, but he needed a few more days. Bart stayed in the hospital for about a week.

Finally, Bart was ready to come home with me, but what a long week that was for me. Bart enjoyed his siblings, and soon he was able to join their fun. How happy we were to have him home again with his family. Lloyd worked away from home one winter and operated a dozer cat. He was home every night. He loaded enough square bales on the truck in the evening for the morning feeding. The boys and I rolled the bales off the truck for the cows to eat. If the truck started to spin, or I needed to back up again, the boys told me, "Goose the truck like Dad, then we will not get stuck."

Within seven years, my kids boarded the bus to school. I felt my heart "twinge" when my last baby, Bart, went to school. When I made a cake, Bart was always there to lick out the bowl, but my baby was gone to school too. This was the only time I felt the empty nest syndrome because I had grandchildren by the time Bart left home. The grandchildren lived close by, and I often had them spend the night or a weekend when their parents were away. Before long, my kids were in school; school days were a hassle. The morning rush of getting the books, shoes, and lunches together each day was a trial. We had one bathroom for a while; a big challenge, as each kid waited to take their turn. Angie was the first child to use the bathroom and then went to her room to do her hair. I felt that I refereed the boys more than I prepared breakfast.

Lloyd stayed in bed until the coast was settled. We enjoyed our coffee after the bus was gone. I still enjoy my quiet time with Lloyd. Today, Lloyd and I sit quietly together in the evenings; I guess whatever had to be said has been said after fifty years of marriage. It's a pleasure to know that love can be found in the silence of our hearts.

When Bart started school, there were 19 boys and two girls in his class. The teacher kept the boys in line and the girls partnered up for about three years when more girls entered their class.

Bart wanted to skate like his siblings, but when he fell he was disgusted. He crawled to the gate and wanted to take his skates off. I tried to encourage Bart, but he said, "Skating is just stupid. Why do I need to skate?" Most of the boys played hockey. Bart wanted to play too. I told Bart that he needed to skate to be a hockey player. His first position was in the goal. Later he became a right wing defenseman, and he skated backwards with ease.

There were too many boys for one hockey team. Names were drawn out of a hat, and two teams were made. If they played against each other, the boys got along fine; but it was the parents that "chirped" at each other.

Bart has always loved horses. When he was five years old, he had a horse named Buster. Buster allowed Bart to ride him in the morning. Bart led Buster up to the door step and crawled into the saddle, but in the afternoon, Buster would move so that Bart could not get in the saddle. When Bart went to school, Buster waited for him to come home from school. Buster would whiney and walk about the coral until Bart went and talked to him. Buster was over twenty-five years old when he died.

This was the same week that Bart's friend Brian Kesenheimer died in a vehicle accident. What a week that was for our family! I spent time with my friend Joan, Brian's mother.

Bart made his spending money by trapping muskrats, mink, and fox. He took his ski-doo to check his traps. Today he has a new ski-doo to travel with, and he has caught wolves too. He was excited and said to me, "That's a few less wolves to eat my calves."

One night, Bart went to Pierceland by ski-doo. I didn't know where he went until a girl's dad phoned me about 11:30 p.m. He wanted to know where his daughter Mary Ann was. Bart had taken her for a ride on the ski-doo. I was angry and wanted Lloyd to find him. Lloyd rolled over in bed and said, "Where would I go to find a ski-doo?" I stayed awake,— and stewed until Bart came home. I know it only made me tired. Mary Ann was a cute, little French girl that Bart liked; she had a brother Robin. Robin didn't get along with his step-dad. Robin stayed with us and shared Bart's room for about five months. The bunk beds were again full. Robin enjoyed homemade food and wasn't hard to please. He called my dumplings on the stew "fluffy clouds".

I wanted Robin to have a good self-image, and get an education. Robin was cooperative and rode the bus to school from our home. Robin wasn't afraid to try different things. He helped with the chores and other activities that we were doing. He went to Primrose Lake and helped us fish too. Robin was out with some boys one night and had too much alcohol to drink. The boys brought him home. The next morning, Robin was not able to eat breakfast, but Lloyd took Robin to set nets. The power auger was a lot of noise for Robin to endure. When Robin came in off the lake, he moved on to a friend's cabin. I felt for Robin and his hard life; he needed to make better choices. I should have been more understanding and taken the time to talk to him about misusing alcohol.

About six years later, Robin and a girlfriend stopped to visit us. I enjoyed seeing Robin and his friend. I felt that he was on the way to a better life.

Bart quit school after grade ten. He worked on the oilrigs, drank too much, and wasn't responsible. This was another hard time for me. I prayed for his safety and better use for his money. Bart would perform outstanding tricks with his quad to impress the crowd. He was a good driver, but there were times when he was intoxicated. I knew I couldn't control where he spent his money, but I am so against drinking alcohol. Bart was not responsible and caused me to fear for his actions.

Bart had a quad accident while he was at Dan's house. Dan and his wife Delilah had divorced by then, and the kids were at their mother's for the weekend. Dan called me and said, "Don't ask any questions, but go to the highway and meet the ambulance." Not knowing why an ambulance was needed was so hard.

It was about a half hour before I escorted the ambulance to Dan's house. Bart was in the bush and suffered from a sore knee and leg. Bart was put on a stretcher and transported by ambulance to the Cold Lake hospital.

Lloyd and I went to the hospital where Bart was treated. He was released and came home with us. I was angry, hurt, and so disappointed because it was Mother's Day. This was not how I wanted to spend my special day. Bart knew how sad I was. It was after this accident with a quad, that Bart quit drinking. Today, he is the son who helps his dad on the farm, as he is interested in taking it over. Bart told me that he has never had another drink since that day. He became responsible and bought a tractor and more machinery to manage our farm more effectively.

Bart has no children and is available to help us when we call with water problems, a broken garage door, or when I want to move furniture. Bart tells everybody that he is babysitting us. That's okay with me. Lloyd has no hobbies, but wants Bart to include him in all the farm activities. Lloyd helps drive machinery in the field, and he offers Bart advice too. Bart accepts Lloyd's years of experience and the wisdom he has. Lloyd and Bart work well together.

Chapter 61:
Our Kids Grow Together

Nioma was pregnant and wanted a girl; she had three boys. I wanted Nioma to have a girl too, so that Angie wouldn't be alone with six boys when Nioma and I were together. Nioma gave birth to her daughter at the Goodsoil hospital. Myrna Elizabeth was born on July 21, 1972. I was full of joy to have a girl for Angela to play with. The two girls are about three years apart, but they enjoyed some girl time with their dolls. Myrna liked to be a little princess. Many times the girls walked to each other's houses and played secretary; they used "walkie-talkies" from one room to another. They would put a crayon in their mouths for a cigarette. (Neither one smokes today.) They also tagged along with the boys and went on ventures to the river with the horses. The girls enjoyed bikes too. As Angie grew older, she bought a motorbike and followed the boys around, but her passion was to pretend she was Aunt Nioma driving a school bus. She would stop her bike, and say, "Good morning," and then drive away. Angie enjoys driving her bus in the Pierceland area today.

The years rolled along, and soon Nioma and I travelled together to the hay field with lunch for our husbands. All eight kids looked forward to lunch in the field where Dad had a short time to hold them and share some cookies. At times there were lost keys, no cream for Bill's coffee, and I missed packing cups. The thermos lid worked fine.

Other times a kid was uncooperative and cried most of the way. Each kid was responsible for their own shoes. If the shoes were forgotten, they couldn't run in the freshly cut hay. Nioma's oldest son, Victor, was the oldest of our eight children; he was eight years older than his sister Myrna. Together, Nioma and I had six boys and two girls.

Nioma and Bill's family intermingled with our family. When Norman got his driver's license, he often picked up Dan and Joe and went swimming or to the show.

Angie matured before Myrna, and they drifted apart through the teenage years, but returned to their friendship, as they grew older. Angie married and had a family while Myrna remained single and has a career as a teacher. Their lives are different and today they don't see much of one another. So too are the other children in our families, as they all are busy and scattered, but they remain close in their hearts and enjoy reminiscing at family reunions. Parents aren't told about all the events that their children take in. My adult kids laugh about keeping some of the more dangerous events from me. They enjoyed their mini skis, but I didn't know that they took turns pulling each other behind the snowmobile.

Lloyd loved his horses and wanted our kids to grow up with the knowledge of horse power. We bought five little ponies, four saddles, and a wagon for our kids to enjoy. They raced about the bushes on horseback and played the forest rangers. The walkie-talkie kept them in touch. The road was off limits for the horses, but friends told us some small horses dashed across the road right in front of their truck. Children often forget what they are told. I think that a guardian angel was overworked and needs a big thank you for all their safekeeping! We had friends with kids who came to visit. It was a treat to hitch the little team to the wagon and everybody had a ride, as Dan or Joe drove around the little field close by.

Sunday night we had a simple meal. Fried egg sandwiches and hot chocolate were served in front of the television set, as we watched *Walt Disney*. It was to bed early because Monday morning meant there was school. I felt like the zoo master many times, as I tried to control our little animals and get them ready for school.

Lloyd took Dan and Joe to fish in the river with the rod and reel when they were young. For their safety, Lloyd tied each boy to his belt; if they slipped on the riverbank, Lloyd could reel them in with that rope.

Our kids helped on the farm. Each child had some chores to do in the evening. Dan carried the separated milk to feed the pail bunters (young calves that are not nursing their mothers because we milked them) and some milk to the pigs too. Joe looked after the chickens and picked the eggs each night. Bart was the pig feeder. He gave them chop and a pail of water too. Angela was busy in the house, cooking and cleaning. She also practiced on her organ for 30 minutes each day. I enjoyed the garden, but if a kid got in trouble and needed an extra chore it was onions that got weeded. My kids also shelled peas and snipped beans. A garden is a lot of work, but it does provide a lot of good, fresh vegetables for the family.

Swimming lessons were held each summer at Howe Bay. I camped together with Doreen, Nelson's wife, and her kids, Wade and Zane. We both had gardens and chores at home. We took turns staying with the kids at the lake; Doreen stayed one day and one night, and then I took my turn. Our kids wanted Auntie Doreen to stay with them because she gave them treats at bedtime and allowed them to stay up later.

Another year, Judy and her girls, Meloney and Tracey, camped with me and the kids for swimming lessons. In the evening, Judy and I joined six adults for swimming lessons. It was great fun, as we laughed and splashed about. A few years later, the lessons were moved to Sandy Beach because there was not enough room for the many campers who came to camp so their kids could take swimming lessons. Lloyd took the tent trailer to Sandy Beach one year for me. The kids and I set it up alone; it was haying time and Lloyd wanted to get home to his work. I found it hard with not much help. Soon the kids were gone with their friends. I went inside, lay on the bed, and cried. I found it hard to be alone, but I wanted the kids to learn to swim. We live close to many lakes, and today each kid enjoys the water and takes their children to camp, water ski, and fish.

Chapter 62:
An Unforgettable Trip

Our family on Grandpa Hellekson's steps

Lloyd and I went to B. C. to see my Grandma Ruth Stahl in 1973 before any of the kids were in school. Dan was 6 years old, Joe was 5 years old, Angie was 3 and a half, and our baby Bart was two years old. We travelled with a tent trailer and camped at night. I had forgotten Bart's blanket that he always slept with. At night he cried for his "Blankley". I was also training him to use the potty. Why did I think that I wanted to go on a trip?

If the kids fell asleep, we travelled farther. Our first night was in Edmonton with Lloyd's sister, Eva, and Paul Rolheiser. The next night we went to my sister Judy in Calgary. She and her husband, Bud Bercier, went with us to Banff where we camped for two nights. We woke up to snow. We had a small stove in our tent trailer, and we all gathered in our tent trailer to have breakfast. Later we took a hike to some waterfall. I was terrified walking along the rough mountain trail with four small children. We went on a sky tram to see mountain goats. There was no room in the closed in tram for Lloyd and Bud; they took an open tram behind Judy and I with the kids. I looked back and saw Lloyd's pale face. Lloyd is afraid of heights. What a start to a holiday. I didn't know how to use a road map, and Lloyd had never been to B.C. We camped one night in Revelstoke, B.C. We finally arrived in Kamloops and went to see my Uncle Dean and his wife, Pat. They had two boys.

The next day we all went to see Grandma Ruth. Our four kids became overwhelming for me. I took the kids to the park while Lloyd visited with Blondie. Grandma was making supper in her small trailer. How can anyone keep four kids quiet and sitting down after they have been confined to a car for most of the week? Supper was almost ready when we all packed up and went back to Kamloops and had hot dogs for supper. I was sad because I never had a chance to visit with my Grandma Ruth.

We spent the night with Pat and Dean, and then started for home. After a day or two we arrived in Edmonton. We struggled to find our way through Edmonton. It was after supper when we decided to continue home. We were about three hours from home when the 1963 Dodge Monaco started to blow out oil. Lloyd put more oil into the motor and said, "We'll go until the car stops, and then we can camp." Our car did get us home late that night.

Need I say that the trip was not enjoyable for me? Lloyd and I never went on another family trip. Our travels were to Pierce Lake about 7 kilometres from home. There we all could have a swim and a have wiener roast later.

Another terrifying trip was in July a few years later. It was our tenth anniversary and Lloyd needed to take the 770 tractor south to get it repaired. I wanted to go along, as I didn't want to be alone on that special day. Lloyd had to take one side of the truck box off so that he could make the tractor fit into the truck box. We were up early to get the chores done and the four kids ready. When we reached the Beaver River, there was a ferry to cross. I do not like open water. Now we had to drive the truck with the tractor load onto the ferry to be taken to the other side. We all had to get out of the truck and stand on the deck of the ferry. I was shaking, as I instructed the kids to hold onto the rail. The crossing went well, but oh how I wished I had stayed home with the kids.

I still think that our anniversary is a special day, but I do not try so hard to spend it with Lloyd if he has places to go. Lloyd and I celebrated our 51st anniversary in July 2017. We had an ordinary day at home with one another.

Chapter 63:
I Fear For Lloyd's Health

In the spring of 1979, Lloyd experienced back problems. The local doctor sent him to Edmonton, Alberta. The specialist said, "Lloyd you have a herniated disk. I could book you for surgery, but if you learn not to try and move the world, it will heal." I was afraid that he would not be able to work again. Dan was twelve years old and too young to do the farming. I had a vision of leaving the farm that Lloyd loved. I thought that I was busy running the house and caring for the kids; I couldn't help much with the farm work. I have always been a petite lady, just under five feet tall and about 100 pounds. I wasn't built to work like a man. I worried that Lloyd would not be able to work on the farm, and I knew that I could not do the work. Lloyd's life was farming and he didn't have another career.

Lloyd was given painkillers and learned to rest more. He listened to the doctor and overcame the pain. He has learned when to rest and can manage his work fine.

My families living depended on mixed farming, but mostly it was the cattle cheque that paid the bills. One year we experienced sick cows. Lloyd didn't find any reason for their sickness. The local veterinarian was called and some blood samples were taken. This didn't give us any answers either. Animal health sent a team from Saskatoon to investigate. I recall a Dr. McLane who came into our house for dinner.

Our family had finished eating, but he welcomed the invitation. Before he started to eat, he said grace. I was so pleased to see an adult man, in a strange home, feel free to give thanks to God.

Later in the summer, we received a letter from the team of veterinarians who had come to our farm; they suggested that we may have had anthrax in our *deer* herd. We never had any deer. We were told that anthrax can be in the soil. I was thankful that our cattle herd was fine in the fall.

Another year, in 1993, we had another problem in our cattle herd. We had fed our cow's mineral block for the winter. In the spring, we add a selenium mix to their diet, which helps the calves to be healthier. I went to Pierceland veterinarian clinic for a pail of selenium. The vet suggested that we give each cow an injection to be sure that each cow received the exact amount. A lady vet came and gave the shots. The next day, some cows were sick, disorientated, had runny noses, rapid breathing, and were trembling. Three cows died. Lloyd was devastated. The vet came back to our farm and took blood samples, and again, we never got any satisfaction from the professionals. It seemed that our cows gradually managed to overcome the problem. I looked for some good in this bad situation, and said to Lloyd, "We can be thankful that it's our cows that are sick and not our children. Cows can be replaced."

The raising of cattle can be devastating.

Another year we experienced scours in our spring calves and lost 15 head. The calves soon became dehydrated and died no matter what we tried. I learned to give needles, feed sick calves, and haul away the dead calves. I could not save a calf that had a death wish. The vet suggested that we give the cows an injection before breeding time to eliminate the problem. This was the answer to the spring scours, and today our son still gives the cows a shot. Today we are battling the wolves. Our son is trying to keep their numbers down by trapping them. A pack of wolves can kill many calves, as they feed their pups.

Chapter 64:
Sickness Strikes (Cattle)

about 200 square bales on trailer

In 1976, Nioma's life changed. Bill, her husband, had a heart attack and could not work. Bill learned to slow down, but a few years later, Bill had a stroke and was left with a disability. Their oldest boy, Victor, was through school, had worked on the rigs, and now he wanted to take over the farm. Bill, Nioma, and the other three kids bought a house in Pierceland, Saskatchewan and moved to town.

I missed Nioma so much when she moved to Pierceland. She was no longer a short walk away for me to visit her. We had shared in our husbands' work, travelled in a crowded car, and settled some disputes with our children, as they hung out together. I felt that some rules were hard, but I knew that kids needed to obey and respect any older person. Nioma and I had listened to the complaints of our children, but we agreed that when they were at one of our places, they had to follow the rules or go home.

When we visit today, we shake our heads at the past events with our eight kids packed into a vehicle, as we journeyed to the field or to town. I can almost see the car with many heads looking out as Nioma drove her old Chevy car and I held my babies in the front seat. I think of the trips home to visit Mom with all the kids. I wonder if Mom was happier to see us come or if she was happier to see us leave. As a Grandma, I enjoy my grandchildren for a short time; but it's great to have peace and quiet too.

I helped Lloyd cut hay in the summer after Bill's heart attack. Sometimes we had a neighbour girl babysit. Nioma often kept the kids and at other times we took them to the hayfield with us. The truck had a covered cap on the back, and the kids played nearby. They could rest, ride bikes, or play out of the hot sun. I took a quick glance toward the truck, as we made each round in the field. If I didn't see one of the kids, we stopped to investigate. I didn't know of any fights, and I never witnessed a bloody nose or other signs of warfare.

I drove the tractor, as we made square bales. Lloyd needed about 3000 bales for the winter season. One sunny evening, as I drove the tractor, the sun was in the back window of the tractor, and I didn't see Lloyd lifting a bale up onto the pile. I shifted the tractor to another speed. When I looked back Lloyd was walking and carrying a bale in his hands. I had thrown him off the cart when I shifted the tractor. I stopped the tractor for him to catch up and get on the bale cart again; he just shook his head at me.

Another time when I was raking hay with an open-air tractor, I heard the tractor rev up. I turned around to check the rake; it was plugged with hay! The hay was piled up to the tractor wheel, and it hit me in the head, as I turned around to investigate. I stopped and began to pull the hay out, one hand full at a time. What a big job. I learned to pay better attention when I was raking the next time. I didn't want to work so hard at pulling out the hay from the rake wheels.

Chapter 65:
Fishing Day – The Next Generation

When I married Lloyd Gonie, commercial fishing was also a part of our family's income, and I became part of the fishing crew. I went to Primrose Lake, as I had with my dad. I fished on Primrose Lake for over thirty years. Fishing was a pleasure when the weather was cooperative. I have fished in rain, snow, fog, and forty-below-zero weather. Some years we made money, and other years were not so great, and we felt like we had spent two weeks washing the nets.

It was my job to take the nets out of the box, as another person pulled them into the water. The following day, we would tie a running line onto one end of the net and pull the net out of the water. We removed the fish from the nets, went back to the hole where we had tied the running line onto the net, and used the running line to pull the net back into the water for another catch. I learned to take out the fish like Lloyd did, just as fast too.

I always prepared for the fishing season by making buns, stew, and pies to freeze so when I came off the lake, I could make a fast meal. I was often cold, hungry, and my bladder was stretched very big; the toilet was the first stop. My days at the lake gave me a change from my routine at home, but I soaked in my bathtub when I returned home!

Primrose Lake had a small fish plant on the shores where the fishermen could unload their boxes of fish for the fish truck to haul to the

Beacon Hill plant where the fish were gilled, gutted, and packed in ice to be shipped to Chicago where they were sold. (It was about a three-hour drive on a poor road.) Eloise Gross was the manager at the lake plant, and he booked in the number of boxes that each fisherman brought in from the lake each day. A semi trailer truck with refrigeration came to haul the fish to Chicago.

When Mom's kids were old enough to stay alone, Mom worked the night shift at the Beacon Hill plant. Mom said, "Gutting those cold fish wasn't a nice job, but the money came in handy, and I felt that I was doing my part in rough surroundings although I wasn't at the lake."

The Gonie family had the fish-hauling contract from the Primrose Lake plant in the earlier years. My husband, Lloyd remembers some trips that were dangerous on the steep Martineau Hill with old, powerless trucks.

Each of our children learned to fish when they were twelve years old and could go to Primrose Lake. (The air base near Primrose Lake had a rule; anyone under twelve years old was not allowed in the air weapons range.)

I found it hard when the kids were too small to help. It became tradition to take our kids to Kay and Lawrence Tremblay's for the duration of the fishing season. Lloyd and I drove the kids to Mudie Lake the night before we went to the lake. We stopped at Nioma and Bill's for tea before we went home for a good night sleep.

That first day on the lake was a big race and Lloyd often was at the front of the line so that we would be the first couple of vehicles on the lake. Lloyd would take his truck to the lakeshore about an hour before everyone else did to get that first place. I thought that there were about 5 minutes from the first vehicle on the lake to the last vehicle on the lake.

Some years I came home from the lake for Christmas, but as the kids grew older, the boys were at the lake too. When my daughter Angie was a teenager, she babysat for a lady who worked at the fish plant. Later she went with Dean Gelowitz for Christmas day. I came home from the lake on Christmas Eve and attended mass. The next day I was alone; I did my chores, watched movies, cried, or slept. I went back to the lake early in the morning. Christmas was not a joy for me with my family at Primrose Lake. I learned that it was better if I stayed at the lake. I began to celebrate Christmas a week before the fishing season, and today we still have our Christmas a week earlier. That frees my kids to go to the "other" family for Christmas.

One year, my sister Judy and her husband Bud came to the lake on Boxing Day and brought a turkey and all the trimmings for supper. Another year, Nelson and Doreen brought perogies, and we fried fresh fish for all to enjoy. The families made me feel part of the Christmas season too, although I never made it for the Burge Christmas on the twenty-fourth of December. Back then I thought that Mom had many other children around her, and she wouldn't miss me. When my family grew up, and one of my children was missing at my Christmas meal I felt a hole in our family. It seems that experience is the best teacher, and I now understand the empty spot that Mom felt.

We set nets on the little lake for the first part of the fishing season to catch walleye fish. The nets are pulled two or three times, and then catching the fish is slower, as most the walleye are fished out. This little lake is over 35 metres deep in many places.

I remember a dramatic event during the 1980-81 fishing season. It was a warm fall, and the snow came early. The snow was like insulation, and there wasn't much wind to keep the water moving before it froze over. Most years there was about a half a metre of ice. The area that is referred to as "the big lake" is 12 metres long, and most of that lake has water that is from 2 metres to 6 metres deep. We set nets on the big lake to catch white fish. We needed to drive across the ice on the deeper area of the lake to get to the bigger part of the lake, known as the big lake. Our smaller nets were set in less water on the big lake where the white fish are found. A net is 90-metres long and is anchored at both ends.

I learned when I was a child that the ice would crack, as we travel across the lake. I was uncomfortable until we dug that first hole, and I could see there was about 30 centimetres of ice. There should be over 15 centimetres for a vehicle to travel safely on ice; however, Lloyd said, "Ice is never safe because it can vary from one place to another."

Lloyd decided to take the Bombardier to the lake and use it to go fishing, as the ice was thin. Lloyd said, "That machine is safer on thin ice, as it is spread over more area of the ice, and it won't break through."

The Bombardier is a machine with tracks, and the front end has big skis to allow it to travel on top of the snow. This was a good machine for fishing, as it is also closed-in like a bus. Lloyd bought the Bombardier from the south, around Lanigan, Saskatchewan, where it was once used to transport kids to school when the snow banks were too big for a vehicle to drive on the roads.

Henry and Dan helped us to fish, and they followed us with the ski-doo a few metres behind.

The motor is located in the rear end of the Bombardier, making the back end much heavier than the front end. We were getting closer to the shoreline of the island, and I felt relieved that we had crossed the deepest part of the lake. This lake is over 50 metres deep in some parts. The shoreline was only about a half a metre away, but I also know that in some places the water is 15 metres deep only a metre from the island's shoreline. We often set some nets about 3 metres from shore. I recalled a few trucks that had broken through the ice in other years, and the crew was able to get out of the truck, but the truck sank to the bottom of Primrose Lake. (The truck was removed after the fishing season.)

I did think that we were across the worst part of the lake, when suddenly, I heard a bleep, bubble, bubble, and the back end of the machine was immersed in water. In an instant, I knew that we had broken through the ice and were falling into the lake. In a split second, I opened the door. The water ran on my feet! With the door flung wide open against the side of the Bombardier, I instructed Joe to jump out toward the front of the Bombardier, and run toward the bush about 4 metres away. I jumped out, and followed Joe to the shore.

Lloyd appeared calm, and stepped out with a big chain in his hand. Lloyd always kept a lodging chain close to his seat. He wrapped the chain around the front bumper to ensure a safe hold on the Bombardier. What if this area was a spot where the water was deep? Lloyd wanted to keep the Bombardier on top of the ice; it would be easier to retrieve the machine than it would be if it went to the bottom of the lake in deep water.

Lloyd held on to the chain, and asked me to get a sink can with a rope on it to measure the water. I returned to the Bombardier, and I trusted Lloyd to hold that chain, as I climbed into the Bombardier and brought out the sink can to test how deep the water was. Lloyd dropped the sink can into the water. There was about 4 metres of water. When the ice was measured, Lloyd found only about twelve centimetres in the area where we broke through. That's only enough ice to walk on! A metre away there was close to 25 centimetres. We must have driven into a place where there was an undercurrent. Lloyd wanted to crawl into the machine and pass the nets out to be set. He would pass them to Henry and the boys.

I said to Lloyd, "I could not help you if the ice failed to stay as it is, but you could help to pull me to safety." He agreed with me. I crawled into the Bombardier and passed the fishing tools and nets out to be piled onto the safe ice. I had total trust in Lloyd if the ice broke any more; I knew I would be okay.

Joe remembered the Tupperware container that held some cherry tarts for our lunch was floating in the water inside the Bombardier.

It didn't take long to unload the nets, and the equipment that we needed to set nets. Lloyd decided that the Bombardier was touching the bottom of the lake, and that it would stay there until after the nets were set. We went to safe ice, and set our nets with the use of the ski-doo.

After our nets were in the water, and ready to catch fish, Lloyd and Henry froze some large poles into the ice close to the Bombardier.

They flooded the area around the Bombardier to make the ice stronger. When there was more ice, the Bombardier was lifted with a chain hoist and the water was drained from the machine. We used it for the duration of the fishing season. That Bombardier continues to run today, and the grandchildren used to enjoy a ride in the open field when the snow is deep.

In 2017, we sold our Bombardier. It was a hard decision for Lloyd to make, but he knew that his fishing days were over, and the boys weren't interested, as they all had jobs that prevented them from fishing through the Christmas season.

I trusted Lloyd when he told me that a Bombardier was a safer vehicle on thin ice, and I guess I can say that Lloyd was right about how safe it was because the skis were always afloat. Lloyd has been in many incidences where he has made good decisions.

Neither the lake nor the shack had the luxuries of home, but the kids always wanted to go to Primrose for the winter fishing season. Our grandkids were also excited about going to Primrose Lake. They recall cracking nuts on a big block of wood and eating them. The nutshells were thrown in the fire and burnt.

Everybody used the water from the lake to drink and cook with. This was a hard reality for the kids to overcome; they used the lake as a toilet when we were out pulling nets. Not one kid was going to drink that water, but after a day of working hard to set nets, they too "drank up." There was no bottled water to drink in the seventies.

In the evenings, there was a hot fire to dry the wet clothes for the next day. The top bunk was too hot, and at bedtime, the kids couldn't sleep until the door was opened for a while. The people on the bottom beds soon grabbed for the wool blankets.

There was a large sawdust pile to slide down with crazy carpets when I was a child. Now the sawdust pile wasn't as big as it was when I slid down with my brothers over twenty years earlier. Some years, the weather was cold and the hot fire was more intriguing in the evening, but our kids did slide down the sawdust pile too.

The Martineau Hill is still a big hill, but the trucks are much newer, and have more power. Lloyd and I commercial fished each year until Lloyd had hip surgery, and I thought it was too dangerous to be on the slippery ice. He didn't like to quit, but when Joe took him to the lake for a day, he must have decided that it was too dangerous because that ended our fishing season. I went one year with our son, Dan, to set nets. A year later, Lloyd and I went for one afternoon with Dean, our son in-law. Lloyd was able to bring some fish home for Dean, and he helped Angela with the fish sales. I stayed at the lake and helped the young boys take fish from the net. I enjoyed a shorter day, but my hands were not able to work as fast as they once did.

The nets needed to be straightened, put in box, and stored for the next year. The only warm place to straighten our nets was in our house. When our kids were young, they would take turns holding on to the bridle of the net and sliding on the floor, as Lloyd pulled them to the box that he was putting the net into. (The bridle of a net is a long line that is tied onto the net, and as the net is lowered into the water, the bridle allows the net to be spread open wide from the top to the bottom of the lake.)

After a few years when we had a little money, Lloyd built a garage, and the nets were no longer taken into the house. I remember that first year we were married, Lloyd fixed a transmission for the Bombardier on the kitchen floor, as it was too cold to work outdoors and there was not any building where he and Bill could work.

Our house had a wood stove in the basement, and we threw the wood down the basement window. I guess a young couple can handle less heat. The house didn't have much insulation, and it took a lot of wood. Lloyd and I went to saw wood almost every week. I liked the bush if there wasn't snow up to my knees. It was a big chore to carry a large block of wood and walk in deep snow. Lloyd helped me when he had all the long blocks sawed into smaller blocks. Our old truck often got stuck before we had enough wood on for weight so there was more traction.

A few years later, we had some insulation blown in the walls and in the ceiling of our house. The fuel bill was cut in half. What a good investment that insulation was!

Chapter 66:
Problems At The Lake

In 1988, while fishing on Primrose Lake, Lloyd became sick with abdominal pain. Our son, Joe brought us home from the fish camp. Lloyd was in pain, and I felt so helpless; the rough road made the pain worse, and we needed to stop, as Lloyd was sick to his stomach.

I took Lloyd to the Cold Lake hospital. The doctor said he wanted to keep Lloyd for the night for observation. I was worried about Lloyd, and I didn't sleep well. Lloyd had never been in the hospital before.

A call came from the hospital around 6 a.m. I was told that Lloyd would have surgery for appendicitis. His surgery went well, but this was the first time Lloyd was in the hospital. When Lloyd's blood pressure was taken by the doctor, he found a heart murmur. The doctor prescribed a drug called dioxin to make his heart beat slower and stronger. He was also put on warfarin, an anticoagulant drug to help prevent a stroke. Warfarin is a drug that Lloyd has now been on for 26 years without any side effects. He goes for a blood test every month to have his INR checked. (the clotting factor in blood)

Dioxin made his heart beat stronger, but slower. This drug made Lloyd very tired. He often needed to come to the house to lie down and sleep. I tried to control my worries, but Lloyd was not himself. Besides being tired, he was irritable and cranky.

In March I received a call from the lab in Saskatoon. Lloyd's heart was beating too slow from the dioxin. The lab wanted to talk to Lloyd. I said that he was in the bush getting wood. The voice on the other end went silent. I proceeded to ask what the problem was, as I sat down on my chair.

He asked me, "Are you his wife and is he alone?"

I replied, "Yes, I am his wife; our son is with him."

I was told that it was possible that Lloyd may not come home because his heart was beating slow enough to stop. Lloyd needed to see his doctor, as soon as possible.

I spent the next while in tears, as I prayed for Lloyd's safe return. I found that my mind carried me to a place where I might be alone, raising teenagers, making all the decisions, and I was so frightened that my body shook with fear. I needed to get control of myself. I lay on the floor, as I waited for Lloyd and Dan to arrive home. The time passed slowly. It was about an hour before I heard the Ford truck drive in the yard. I put my coat on, and I ran to Lloyd and asked how he felt. He said, "I'm fine and why do you get so worked up? It is what it is. We all have to die."

It was too late in the day for doctor hours. I had an uneasy night, and I thought that I heard him stop breathing a few times. Lloyd saw his family doctor in the morning. Lloyd was gradually taken off this drug, and he has continued to work without any farther problems. Lloyd remains under a doctor's care and is managing fine.

Later that year, my husband wanted to help me because I had day surgery, and I was to rest for a day or two. Lloyd wanted to make supper for me. He couldn't find the can opener or the knife to cut the bread. I complained to my daughter, Angie. She said, "Mom, you did everything for Dad so don't expect him to know where things are." Her statement was so true.

Chapter 67:
Facing My Trials

In April of 1985, I had a major surgery in Saskatoon. I had an upper and lower bladder repair along with a hysterectomy. Previously I had trouble with infections. For over two years, my cancer checks came back with the report that there was a potential for cancer cells to grow. I travelled to Saskatoon on April 19 with Mr. Ilnesky, a former teacher who was going to see a family member. This wasn't a perfect situation, but Lloyd needed to be with our four kids who were all teenagers. Lloyd had a nephew, Philip Gonie, living in Saskatoon. I spent the night with him and his wife. Philip drove to the city hospital in the morning. I registered and was put to bed. Later in the afternoon, I watched a video about my surgery, and how it would be easier to sit up and get out of bed. (There is no such thing as getting up easily after your stomach muscles have been cut.) I slept a lot because I was rundown from making extra bread, preparing casseroles, and having the laundry all clean before I left home. I wanted to make it as easy as I could for my family.

The doctor told me that I would be in the hospital for at least a week. I knew I would not be able to work for sometime after I was home from the hospital. The following day, I had some blood tests, and the IV was put into my hand to prepare me for my operation in the morning. I only knew my nephew and his wife, but they were busy with work and with their family. I felt so lonely. I prayed and told myself that this time would soon pass I would be home with my loved ones before too long. Lloyd would come in the morning and stay until my surgery was over. He was late. I was given a needle to relax me. I began to cry, and I was so afraid. I had only been in the hospital when I gave birth. The nurse asked if she could call someone for me. There was no one that I knew in Saskatoon that I could talk to. I prayed my way to the operating room and was wheeled into surgery, where soon I was asleep.

Lloyd was there when I woke up. I knew that I was alive because I hurt all over. I drifted in and out of reality for a few minutes until the anaesthetic wore off. When I woke up, and was more aware, Lloyd said, "You told him to go home and that you would call him when you were ready to go home." That first week was hard. Lloyd came to see me on the weekend. I was moving slowly and not able to eat; I had nausea. It was impossible to pick up a full cup of tea. I was weak, and my whole body ached, especially my shoulders. I was told that I was put upside down while in surgery. I felt that I would never again be able to achieve my housework or gardening. A nurse returned from a three-day weekend and told me I looked so much better than I did when she left. I spent two weeks in the hospital. Anyone who has had a major surgery knows how hard it is to get out of bed and walk. It was a big chore to get up and go to the bathroom that first week.

Lloyd managed to keep all four teenagers in line. Lloyd came for me, and before we were out of the city limits, I wished I was back in bed. We stopped in Battleford to buy Barton a watch, as his birthday was in four days. The door of the store was so heavy when I tried to open it. I needed time to rest and to heal. I still found it challenging to go to the bathroom. My days were spent lying on the couch. Lloyd wanted to go on the cattle drive. I told him that he should, as I was going to sleep. Dan came at noon, and warmed a can of soup for me. I was up long enough to eat. Thanks Dan!

I am thankful to my sisters who brought supper for Bart's birthday;

he had a good fourteenth birthday. My friend Chris came to visit me and brought a banana pudding. She asked if there was anything she could do for me. I had her put clean sheets on my bed for me. Debbie and Lillian planted my garden for me. I found it hard to watch others do my work. Debbie had her young daughter with her. Marcy asked her mother if she could touch me. I guess Debbie had told Marcy that she could not expect me to run and jump with her. I slowly began to do dishes, cook, and wash clothes. My kids were all robust teenagers and tested me often. Lloyd needed to discipline now. Would I ever be back to normal? It took so long to heal. I tired quickly when I tried to do anything. The jobs that were so easy before were now difficult. I rested most of the day. I found mixing bread one of the hardest jobs. I wanted Angie to mix bread for me; how hard that was to see her trying to mix the flour and water together. I tried to tell her that she needed to feel the texture of the bread. That blew her mind because she was not interested in learning to bake bread. Angie doesn't bake bread today either. She said, "Why do I need to? Mom and my mother in-law both bake if I want homemade bread."

Chapter 68:
Changes Come

guitar camp-lac des island

making porridge

Many of my friends had careers. I longed to feel fulfilled with a job away from home too. I didn't have time to do a lot of working before we were married. My kids were in school; I wanted to work outside the home. I never did work out because Lloyd said, "No wife of mine is going to work; I'll burn the place down."

I knew that he meant it. This was hard for me to accept. My need to work was filled by volunteering in the church. I helped with catering for over forty years. I taught catechism to the grade three classes for over ten years. I help with the R.C.I.A., an adult class in the Catholic faith too. I could see that it helped people to share with their friends, and I saw how religious studies improved the lives of all who live in the community.

I went to the O.M.I. Island camp under the direction of Fr. Luken in 1979. I taught the kids about God, and we enjoyed the great outdoors by swimming, canoeing, and having campfires.

My family matured and soon there were teens and high school to work through. I experienced issues with each child. I struggled through the difficult times, and we shared some joy in the good times. I prayed for good, trustworthy, and honest friends. As they developed, each of them found friends; some good, and some not so well behaved. Many kids stayed overnight. I knew where my kids were and with whom they were with. We all enjoyed horse rides, wiener roasts, and bush adventures.

In 1984, Dan's first job was away from home with his cousin Norman. My brother, George Burge, worked on a pipeline in Rimbey, Alberta about 5 hours away. I worried when the boys left. Would they find their way and would they drive safe? There was a canopy on the truck for sleeping. I said good-bye three times; they returned to get forgotten stuff. Were they a little hesitant about striking out on their own?

I went to visit a week later, and I was more at ease when I saw how the boys were able to manage. I found it so hard to let go of each child when they left my home. I thought of my mother and her twins; she often had two kids leave together when it was time to go to work.

Lillian, my sister, and her husband, Kirk Sharp, had a cattle ranch with summer pasture about fifteen kilometres from their home. The cows were fed at home in the yard for the winter. In the spring, after the cows had their calves, a cattle drive was held to take the herd to summer pasture. Help was needed and about twenty cowboys came for the big two-day drive. Lillian prepared breakfast and took lunch on the road for all the riders. This was a huge undertaking, as Lillian baked her own bread and made squares too. I know she didn't get much sleep for that week. The youngest rider was about five. He rode Bart's horse Buster. Lloyd and our kids rode horses with Kirk and his family; they kept the cattle on the move and safe from the traffic. I drove a truck ahead of the cattle with flashing light to warn motorists of the coming herd.

When young riders got tired, they rode in the truck. A truck and trailer were at the back to load any calves that were tired. If the young riders got tired of riding Buster, the horse was loaded in the trailer too. There was an overnight campout to give the cattle a rest at the halfway point. The young riders were ready to rest too. The kids got a taste of the old cowboy way in the dust, rain, and at times, it was cold. One night it was cold enough to make ice on the water pail. When it was time to start the day, all riders were expected to raise, feed their horse, and be ready to ride in about 30 minutes. Many shaking bodies left their sleeping bags, grumbled, and thought that they should have stayed home. After a cup of hot chocolate or hot coffee and some toast the sun began to rise. Soon everybody was ready to mount up on their horses and move the cattle again.

The cattle drive was a lot of work, but it was also enjoyable in the fresh air. Some people walking behind and visiting, as they kept the slower cows moving. This was a good time with family. I remember a night around the campfire. The boys were chasing one another around. Wade Burge thought it was a good idea to crawl under the truck and escape on the other side. Kirk Sharp jumped in the truck and started the motor. Wade scrabbled out from under that truck like a frightened squirrel. The cowboys all laughed at him. Another time a cow went into a slough for a drink of water and got stuck. Lloyd roped her to pull her out to the road. When she got on hard ground, she chased everyone that was close by. The rope needed to drag until it fell from her neck. The following day the cows were at the summer pasture. The helpers, saddles, and other necessities were loaded on the open-air wagon behind the tractor, and we were off for home. The bathtub was a welcome place to soak sore muscles and remove a couple of days dirt and grime. Lillian was an organized person, and when the fall round came, the cattle were brought home; then she rushed home and had a turkey supper ready for us. The cattle drive was on Thanksgiving weekend.

I liked to pick berries, and when my kids were small, I took them with me. My brother-in-law, Kirk Sharp, said it was like watching a mother partridge with her little chicks following her over a log. Each kid crawled over that log and stayed close to the old hen.

I listened for the crowing of the rooster to keep my bearings. One hour in the berry patch was enough for all of the kids and me too.

I recall a particular day, after the kids were all in school, I took my black dog to pick berries. As I picked, I saw a black form on the other side of the Saskatoon bush. I yelled at the dog. It was not the dog; it was a black bear. My dog had gone home. The bear quickly ran away, and I decided I had enough berries for the day. In 2015, the blueberries were plentiful and a good size too. I picked 35 ice cream pails of berries, and Nioma sold each pail for me at the farmers' market in Cold Lake; each pail getting forty dollars. Again in 2016, the blueberries were great. I picked 40 ice cream pails. I sold some and gave many away to Ashley, my granddaughter. Ashley's family enjoyed making slushies; what a healthy way for the kids to have a treat. Ashley's kids are busy and keep everyone around them busy too. (She has four children — two girls, and five years later, two boys were born about a year and half apart.)

Chapter 69:
My Family Is Split

I could feel tension between Mom and Dad when I went home to visit. I didn't stay long; as I was happy to return to my own fortress. My parents were no longer tied together with a big family. Josie, my youngest sister, was a teenager and had moved into Lillian's home to finish high school. Mom's family didn't require as much of her time as every child was a young adult. I helped Mom learn to drive and to get her driver's license too. Mom took her road test in Pierceland and was thrilled to have her license.

Mom went to Cold Lake to the air force base to work as a cleaner. "Swinging a mop was hard work," she said. Mom was able to pay off the store bill that was at the McClellan's store.

It took time, but Mom was able to buy a second-hand car, a Chevrolet Oldsmobile. Now she could go to some of the places that she had dreamed about when she was tied down with her family. I know Mom *never* had any extra money. Maybe she felt that if she made her own money, she could spend it the way she wanted. Mom never had a career. She said, "I wanted to achieve more than raising a family." Society used to believe that a homemaker is not a career. My siblings and I give Mom an "A PLUS" for a job well done. She taught us what was important and how to make our own way in a world filled with challenges. Thanks Mom!

Mom and Dad went their own ways and soon their marriage of about thirty-seven years ended. They were divorced in 1975. I learned of their divorce from a friend; how hard that was.

What a hard time for everyone, adult kids too. Our family was split; some children saw Dad as the culprit, and others blamed Mom for wanting to go to work. We all needed time to accept this change and realize that both Mom and Dad needed our support. We all needed to bury our feelings and reach out to both Mom and Dad's needs.

Divorce is a devastating event; each member in our family handled this "tearing apart" in a different way. I prayed that God would take one of them. I couldn't ask which one, but they couldn't seem to move on as a single person, and they continued to hurt each other. I found it so hard to hear one parent degrading another. At those special occasions like Christmas or Easter, the family was split, as some of my siblings went to Mom's to celebrate and others went to Dad's to be with him. There were about three or four of us who went to both places. I found that it was hard, as I was asked many questions about each parent. I tried to stay positive and answer in a loving way. I said, "I need both parents in my life, and I think that you too should make the time to help Mom and Dad through this rough time. Do you not know how much each one gave of their time and constant work to support you when your world seemed to be turned upside down?"

I felt overwhelmed, as my heart ached for each one of my parents. I returned home, and I had good cry. The next day it was a new day, and I moved on to help my family, as they were all young children who needed a mother who was healthy and able to help keep our family intact.

I will never understand why a couple called it quits after some thirty years of marriage. Mom and Dad gave endless efforts to keep me and my thirteen siblings healthy and together. Was there not that deep love that most married couples share? Maybe they too felt that life was slipping by, and they each wanted to achieve more than raising a family. I know that as I age, I realize how short our time on earth is.

Five Plus Five Makes Fifteen · 243

I am grateful that Mom and Dad found the courage and the need to stay together and raise us all as one family.

Mom moved to Cold Lake. I didn't see Mom for four months. I went to visit her and found her lonely and maybe a little remorseful. She was not able to share her hurt, but I felt it. Mom was undergoing a terrible time in her life. I have matured, and today I think I would have tried harder to share in Mom's deep pain. I ached for Mom. Mom had never had any luxuries in her life. I think she looked at some beautiful articles with hungry eyes, but she knew expensive things were out of her reach; her kids came first. Now, where were her kids to support her and spend a few minutes with her to chase away the loneliness?

I saw Dad more often; he lived in Pierceland, and he came to my house to visit. Mom has always remembered Lloyd's birthday, and she came to our house too. I had asked Dad to come but hadn't expected Mom. When Dad drove in the yard and saw Mom's car, he made a big circle and left. I was hurt and I felt like I was making a choice of which parent I wanted to come to my place. I saw Dad a week later, and he never mentioned a thing about being at our house. I was an adult and I struggled to be there for each parent. How do younger children manage to get through times like this in their life? I will be more sensitive to children from broken homes and take time to listen to their concerns.

Soon Dad became sick. I knew he had a bad heart, but he didn't dwell on it, and he did whatever he wanted to do. The stress of a divorce and insecure feelings led to a mental breakdown. I remember him saying to me that he had no reason to live. I told him that the grandchildren were young, and that he needed to be there for them so that they would remember him as a grandpa. (Bart was 5 years old.) Lewis, my brother, took Dad to Goodsoil, Saskatchewan, and the doctor admitted him. A few days later, Dad had a bed in another hospital. Bill, Nioma, and I took Dad where he could get help from the mental facility in the Saskatchewan Hospital.

This was a hard trip for me. When Dad saw the mental facility, he was not going to see any doctor there. I said to him, "The doctor works here and he sees all his patients at this facility. It's easier for the doctor to come to one place to see his patients." Dad soon told me that the former doctor had told him that he would need to stay for a few days. Nioma cried, and I prayed for guidance. I needed to receive the right words to say to him. I did convince Dad to go into the hospital. Nioma and I saw the doctor with Dad. Dad became angry, and the doctor was able to see how difficult Dad could be.

Dad was admitted, and he spent most of the summer in the Saskatchewan hospital in North Battleford, Saskatchewan. Most of us girls took turns, and went once a week to visit him; he cried because he thought that nobody would go to visit him. When the doctors told Dad he was ready to go home, he came home to an empty house and some uncompleted dreams. Dad was under the care of a therapist, and I went with Dad to Meadow Lake to his appointment each week. Did the loneliness and his insecurities take a toll? I think so, as Dad never learned to talk to others about his demons.

The end of July, my nephew Victor was with Lloyd on their way to see Tone, Lloyd's brother. Victor said to Lloyd, "Mom got a phone call to tell her Grandpa was sick." Nioma had a phone, and she knew that Dad was sick, but we did not have a phone yet.

I was hurt, angry, and disappointed that Nioma didn't let me know that Dad was sick. Our kids were back and forth many times; why didn't Nioma send a note to tell me about Dad being sick?

Lloyd and Victor stopped in to see Dad. He said, "I have chest pains, and nobody will take me to the hospital." I don't think that he had asked anybody, but Lloyd drove him to the Goodsoil hospital right away. Dad was admitted. After a week, Dad was discharged. Lillian and Josie went to bring Dad home from the Goodsoil hospital.

Dad had a massive heart attack in the parking lot of the hospital. The nurses took him back indoors, and the doctor worked on Dad, but his heart was too damaged. Dad died on August 4, 1977 from a massive heart attack. Our family gathered at Dad's empty house. Dad spent a lot of time in his chair, and I found it so hard to view that empty arm chair where Dad had read his paper every night after supper. Dad's funeral was four days later. All of his kids, except Nelson were present.

Nelson and Doreen were in Singapore where Nelson worked on the rigs. When Nelson got the word about Dad's death, they could not get a flight home. Later in the year, Nelson and his family came home. Nelson's siblings had gone to the funeral, and we all had time to grieve for our dad. How hard it was for Nelson when he came home and had to grieve alone. I ached for Nelson because he had not been there to share the pain of Dad's death with his siblings. Men try to show that hard face and make others believe that they are okay. Nelson had many questions about the care that Dad received all summer. I could not answer all the questions, and Nelson had to believe that everybody was there to help Dad. He could not have prevented Dad from struggling as he did because you can't help anyone who doesn't want your help. I never told any of my siblings about my prayer when I asked God to take one of my parents. I had to be satisfied with God's actions, although I cried.

A parent leaves many memories, some good, and a few that are not so great. Each one of Dad's kids tried to reach out to Dad, but it's hard to help a person who tells you they don't need anyone to help them. Dad was the next death after baby Leonard in 1953. Our family had a broken link, but we needed to carry on.

Chapter 70:
Mom Meets Albert

Mom started a new chapter in her life. Was she lonely after such a full house for many years? Did she want to go back to her teenage years that seemed to have been stolen from her? Mom met Albert Rowe, an oilrig worker, at a bar. I liked Albert when I first met him. Mom appeared happy. Would she have a good life? Soon I saw that Albert liked the bar life and wasn't in a hurry to go home. It didn't matter how long Mom waited for him to have another drink or two, *he* drove home. Mom offered to drive, but Albert said, "I can drive better drunk than any woman can drive sober."

This was just one of Albert's degrading comments. I soon saw that Albert was not that great person that I once thought he was. He disrespected Mom many times. I was so hurt by Albert's actions, but I tolerated Albert because he was Mom's husband, and I stayed out of their affairs. I should have done more to help Mom.

Mom and Albert travelled to B. C. to visit Albert's family. Mom said that Albert took her to a coin wash so that she could wash clothes. He was gone for hours; he had found a local bar, and he didn't think that he was gone very long. Albert was in control. He said when they left and when they came home. Mom had time for a short visit with her sister Irene in Kamloops before Albert said, "I'm leaving, are you ready?" Albert and Mom enjoyed an Alaskan bus tour and the North

Country. This time Albert was on a bus, and he had to be ready when the bus was. Mom said that it was a good trip.

Mom and Albert were married on March 21, 1979. I didn't attend the party that the neighbours put on for them. It was calving time, and Lloyd couldn't go with me. I didn't make it a priority to join Mom and Albert. Mom moved back to the farm with Albert, and they bought some cows. Mom did chores, as Albert worked on the oilrigs. I saw Albert, as a controller; Mom did what Albert wanted, and when he wanted her to. Mom didn't want to cause any drama, and she chose to comply with Albert's wishes and ignore his drinking.

Albert retired from the rigs in June of 2000. The cows were sold, and my brothers, Grant, George, and Graham Burge, bought the land. They have since sold it, and Dave Scott is the new owner. Mom and Albert moved into the Villa in Pierceland. They enjoyed floor curling and travelled together to tournaments. Mom never had time for sports before; but now she did. Mom said, "I won the first trophy in my life at curling. I am so proud of that trophy."

After a few years, Albert became sick and was diagnosed with esophagus cancer. He smoked and drank alcohol, which we were told added to his fate. Debbie, Lillian, and I took Albert for tests and then to surgery. Albert was not a good patient, and we felt that Mom needed support. Albert was ten years younger than Mom, but Mom has always been in good shape for her age. We stayed with Mom in a hotel and took her to visit Albert each day for about ten days until Albert was discharged. Healing was slow, and Albert never ate a good meal again; his food was pureed before he could swallow it. Albert never recuperated very well. Soon he was on a liquid diet. He lost weight, was tired, and lost interest in many things. It was about a year later when Albert became too weak to leave his bed much. Mom was tired, but Albert wanted her to stay by him.

The last week at home, I stayed with Mom and Albert to cook so that Mom could get a good meal and have the rest she needed. Albert never tired to control me, and he appeared thankful that I was there to help Mom. After a week, Albert was taken by ambulance to the Goodsoil Hospital. Debbie picked Mom up from the hospital at night, and took her home so that Mom could have a good night's sleep. Debbie lived about 10 kilometres from the hospital. I stayed at the hospital to be with Albert. I strongly believe that no one should be alone in their final days. How hard it was to see a man of 110 kilograms waste away to less than 40 kilograms.

Mom was present with Albert's daughter, Lena, and I as we sat by Albert's bedside on that last day. Mom felt guilty for not being able to help Albert with his problems. It had been a year; now Albert gave in to this disease. Albert died on March 1, 2004.

Mom made the hard move from her bigger place where she had lived with Albert into a one-bedroom place at the villa. She no longer could see the main road from her arm chair, another adjustment to make. Albert's chair was empty, as was her aching heart. Mom missed Albert. Mom loved to drive and came to my house often for many meals. Albert didn't like to eat away from home. In a couple of years, Mom slowed down. She wasn't cooking much and ate cereal or soup most of the time. Mom said to Debbie, "I'm not as able as I was, and I don't want to be a burden to my kids. I recall helping an elderly lady when I was young; it's a lot of work."

Debbie took Mom to show her the lodge in Cold Lake. A room was available. Mom moved into the Seniors Lodge in Cold Lake in April 2011. Mom enjoys all the services with no cooking or cleaning. Soon Mom sold her vehicle; she felt that Cold Lake was too busy for her to be driving in. Mom missed her wheels, but she said, "I don't need to drive; I have it all here. Living in the lodge is like a little piece of heaven."

Mom is the resident with the most company. Lloyd and I go every Sunday to visit her. Mom is always happy to see us and remarks, "Today must be Sunday—Barb and Lloyd are here." At times another one of Mom's kids show up to visit too, and we all share many laughs and have a good visit.

Chapter 71:
Dan

Our son, Dan Gonie, challenged us as parents. We were called to school when Dan was in a fight and were shocked when another time the R.C.M.P. drove Dan home after an altercation at school. Dan said to the teacher, "If you drive me home, I'll jump out." The principal called the police, and they brought Dan home. I recall another sleepless night when Dan didn't come home. (We didn't have a phone yet.) I asked Lloyd to drive past the police station on our way to church; I wanted to see if Dan's truck was there. It was not, and I went to church very uneasy. I know that I was not focused on the mass. When I came from church, there was a note on my steering wheel from Dan. I grabbed that paper and read it. Dan said that he and his friend Arnold were playing ball, and that he spent the night with him because they needed to leave early in the morning to go to the ball field.

Lloyd was right again; Dan was okay, and there was a reason he didn't come home. I tried to think positive. I wished that I could be like Lloyd and not let my mind run wild about the things that could have happened.

Dan graduated from high school on May 10, 1985. This was about a week after I was home from my surgery. I tried to dance with Dan, but I was too sore. I was so happy that Dan had achieved his first big goal and was enjoying the day. I struggled to keep him in school when some friends were out working, and he had a taste of making his own money and didn't think that school was important. Lloyd and I had managed to push and pull our first-born child through high school; a great accomplishment for us. Dan had set a good example for his siblings to follow. Dan loved hockey, played well, and dreamed of getting on a plane with his hockey bag to play in a big league. This was not to happen.

In July of 1985, Dan told us his girlfriend, Delilah Dayton, was pregnant. I thought that I had taught Dan life morals to help him grow into adulthood and prepare for his future. How hard life would be for him now.

I was so distraught, and my body was recuperating from surgery, but I saw pain in my son. To watch your child suffer is one of the hardest obstacles to get past. Why did this happen in our family? How would teenager parents manage to care for a child? Both of their young lives were filled with a task that lasts for a lifetime. A parent's love and care is forever. So many questions arose in my mind. I was 19 when Dan was born, and I found it hard. This was a tough time for me. My tangled mind was hurt and full of disappointment, as I knew how hard it can be to make a relationship work. Now there would be a baby to add to the mix. This young couple would be parents forever. I wrestled with becoming a Grandma so young. I was not yet forty years old. I managed to process this event in stages, a day at a time. It was hard, but I matured and realized that my thoughts were trivial. I needed to dwell on helping my son and my grandson.

I feel that a man thinks that sex can fix everything. Lloyd hurt too, but he wanted to have sex. I refused. I said, "How can you think of sex; it's because of sex that I'm hurting so much." Lloyd replied, "I had nothing to do with Delilah getting pregnant. Dan and Delilah made that choice." I cried myself to sleep in Lloyd's arms.

I was able to talk to my family, as I sobbed my way through this suffering. I realized that I was not being judged. I learned from this incident and felt more compassion toward other kids who faced similar trials. Caring for a baby is constant and, as a parent, it becomes a career that is long-term and takes much dedicated labour. Parenthood is gratifying, and it is our greatest gain —but when we are mature and ready to give it all our energy. As I prayed and cried, my mind drifted to the lady in Saskatoon. Phyllis was pregnant with her second child. I remember her being happy, as she cared for her son.

Our first grandson, Bradley James, was born February 2, 1986. Dan placed Bradley in my arms, and I was able to focus on the joy of a grandson, no matter what the circumstance. Bradley soon fit into our family, and we wondered how we ever lived without him. He added renewal to our family, as each of us watched him learn to sit, walk, and talk. Dan helped Bradley to learn to skate on the frozen pond. Brad soon enjoyed hockey with Dan, and they stopped at our place often. Delilah was a good mom and was devoted to Bradley's care.

Dan went to work, and Delilah missed her school friends. I wanted her to continue with school, but she didn't feel that she fit in any more. I longed to make her see that Bradley wouldn't be a baby forever, and her life had to continue. A good education was necessary to make it easier to raise a child. What if this relationship doesn't work? It takes a lot of building from both sides before a couple can bond together. Dan and Delilah played house for a while. When that didn't work out, Dan asked if he could come home and live with us. Dan said to me, "I don't deserve to live in your house, but could I live in the garage?" (The parable of the prodigal son is real for me: Luke 15; 11:31 in the American bible.) I found it so hard to say to him, "You can live with us in the house but the rules remain the same."

Their relationship continued off and on. In less than two years, a girl, Ashley Nicole, our beautiful granddaughter was born to these young parents. Ashley also brought joy to our family. Delilah dressed her like a little princess. Dan phoned me and said he and Delilah were getting married. I asked when. He said, "On Friday." I guess Dan heard my astonishment. He said, "Not this Friday but next Friday." Dan married Delilah Dayton on April 21, 1989.

Their wedding day was a hot day. We took pictures in front of a row of spruce trees in Delilah's auntie's yard. We went to Cold Lake for supper. Lunch was served at the dance. A friend of Delilah's brought Bradley and Ashley to the wedding dance. Lots of attention was given to them; they were in the spotlight. They both were adorable.

Dan and Delilah moved to the farm, about a kilometre from our place. I enjoyed walking with the kids from our house to theirs. Delilah was afraid to be alone when Dan was gone working. She said, "I can't even see lights from other people's places." One night, Delilah phoned me and said that someone was breaking in. Lloyd went down to Dan's place. He discovered a porcupine in the corner of their step. The porcupine swished his tail, and it hit the door. Soon Dan and Delilah moved to town. I guess it wasn't the location that was important because they bought a mobile home and moved back to the farm.

Dan and Delilah's third child, Lyndon Ray, was born on October 22, 1989. He too is a blessing for us.

After a couple of years, Delilah wanted to live in town again. The mobile home was sold, and they moved back into Pierceland. Dan moved with Delilah into a low rental house. After about a year, Dan and Delilah bought a house in Pierceland. Dan tried to please Delilah, but she was not happy; they had a rocky marriage.

Dan worked on the pipeline and was gone much of the summer. Delilah was young, and she felt alone, as she cared for their children. Her friends were graduating from high school; she was a mother, and tied down to her home and family. How hard that was. I helped Delilah learn to drive. Lloyd kept the kids when I went driving with Delilah. She was a determined person, and I often told her to get out and see for herself what I had told her about being too close to a parked car. She got her license and bought an old car. I was worried when she came in the wintertime without any socks on Bradley's feet. I had her call me when she got home. She always did, and I went to bed, and I was able to sleep.

This couple struggled for a few more years and tried to make a

Five Plus Five Makes Fifteen · 253

happy home, but in 1999, after eleven years of marriage, they were divorced. How lonely their former yard appeared when I walked through it to pick berries. Bradley went to live with his mother, in Marshal, Saskatchewan, but before long, he too was with Dan and attending school in Pierceland. This didn't last long for Bradley, and he went back to live with his mother. The change was hard for Bradley, as he attended school and met new friends. Bradley struggled until grade ten. School was not for him, and he quit at a young age.

We didn't see much of Bradley. When he came to Pierceland, he stayed with Grandpa and Grandma Dayton. Bradley continues to work for a pipeline as an operator. He's not married and has no children.

Ashley lived with Dan and Lyndon for a year. When the next school year started, she moved with Delilah and lived in Marshal. Lyndon missed her. Ashley came back to Pierceland for the last half of the school year. She was a teenager and didn't like Dad's rules. When the school year ended, she moved to Lloydminster with a girl friend. Ashley went to school and worked at Seven Eleven until she graduated. She learned how to fill every minute of the day. Ashley now lives on acreage with her boyfriend Joe in Hillmond. Ashley has four children: Kianna, Kaelynn, Grayden, and Jameson. Joe works on the rigs.

Ashley works for an oil company as a dozer operator. She found that she could make more money, but she works long hours and often drives a long distance to work. Ashley is kept busy with her girls in dance. The girls go to Lloydminster school. Dance lessons are after school. Kianna and Kaelynn attended a competition in Seattle in May of 2015 with 400 participants. Kianna placed in the top 10; then placed first to receive a diamond award trophy. WOW Kianna! I am so proud of you! I pray that you will continue to excel in all your endeavours.

After Dan and Delilah divorced, Lyndon lived with Dan in a holiday trailer for that first winter. They showered and had supper with Lloyd and me.

Lyndon said to me, "I don't want to camp anymore. Dad and I camped all winter long. It was cold in the camper." Lyndon got himself out of bed and to school in the morning after Dan went to work. Lloyd phoned Lyndon each morning to be sure his alarm never failed him. Lloyd picked up Lyndon from the bus and brought him to our place after school.

In the summer of 2001, Dan bought a house trailer and moved it into the yard site; about half a kilometre from us. Now Lyndon and Dan were more comfortable and cooked and showered at home.

Dan met Lorraine Weir at a dance. This was a boost for me to see Dan with some happiness. Lyndon said me, "I think my Dad has a girl friend because I smelt perfume in the house." Lyndon was right. This relationship lasted for about eight years. Lorraine's kids, Holly and Jason, became close to Dan, and they come to visit Dan and join us for Christmas, Easter, and Thanksgiving celebrations. Holly told a co-worker, "Lloyd and Barb are like my grandparents."

A broken home is devastating, and all members are hurt. I watched my grandchildren undergo what they could not understand. Each child wondered why this was happening in their family. I witnessed everybody suffer, and I wanted to support each child, as I remained open to their needs. I tried to give assurance and help each child find joy, as they struggled to discover their place in this world. I gave hugs and listened, as a grandmother can. This was a difficult time in my life. I felt so helpless.

I never felt that I was able to fill the "family" void. A family needs a mom and dad to function well.

Lyndon lived with Dan, and he saw his Mom when there was a school break. I drove him to Marshal or met his mother part way. Lyndon then spent the weekend with his mother; if there was no school for a week, he went to see her, and they shared time together.

After living with Dan for two years, Lyndon decided to live with his mother. I asked Lyndon if he was unhappy. He said, "Dad had me for two years, now its Mom's turn for me." That statement broke my heart; a child should not feel that it's their place to please their parents. I prayed for all members of Dan's family that each one would fine peace. Dan missed Lyndon when he went to Marshal; so did I. Dan said, "My work is the only reason to live. Lorraine has her kids with her, but mine are all gone."

Dan was alone; my heart ached to watch him go through a failure phase. Was he in danger of giving up and not wanting to face another day? A mother should be able to comfort her child, but I wasn't able to bring any joy into Dan's life. Sure, I could invite him for supper, but he felt that he was able to look after himself and should not run home to Mommy. I said to Dan, "Your kids will be back when they mature and realize how precious you are to them."

Lyndon returned in about 6 months to live at Dan's place. Lyndon was a farm boy, and enjoyed the freedom on the farm. I like to think that he missed his grandparents too. Dan found a new purpose with Lyndon in his home. Lyndon was fourteen and needed his Dad around him.

Lyndon always loved trucks and mud. His favourite toy was a big monster truck. He crawled on his knees and splashed in mud puddles, pretending to make it through all terrains when he was a preschool child. Lyndon was a shy lad who didn't join in school sports. He seemed to think that he could not achieve what other kids did. He felt like he was a year behind from when he went to his mother's. He soon hated school, and he quit in grade ten. Dan said, "If you don't go to school, then you need to go to work." Lyndon went to his mother's and started to work as a labourer in Battleford, then in Lloydminster. Soon he went north to work for a welder.

Dan began a new chapter in his life on July 9, 2016. He met Tracey, a schoolteacher from Two Hills, Alberta in 2015. This developed into a new start for Dan. Tracey has a son, Ryan, from a former marriage. Dan and Tracey's kids are all adults and now the two of them can make a life together.

Lloyd and I travelled to be with Tracey Gilbert and Dan as they exchanged their marriage vows. The weather was hot, but there was a cool breeze from the rushing rapids behind them. Dan and Tracey were married on July 9, 2016. Congratulations Dan and Tracey!

I enjoyed visiting with Ryan and his girl friend in Jasper Alberta, as we waited for the marriage ceremony to begin. I enjoyed this small wedding of about 20 guests. I also enjoyed that no one drank too much alcohol. There was a D.J. to dance the night away; it was a good time.

Lloyd and I celebrated our 50th wedding anniversary on July 6, 2016. This was three days before Dan's 2nd wedding. We had supper with Grant and Cleo, as we were on our way to Jasper to share in Tracey and Dan's wedding. We took a trip to North Dakota in the fall to celebrate our anniversary.

Joe, our second son, was born one year and four days after his brother, Dan. He was smaller and needed to eat every three hours. He has always been a good child with few problems; maybe he saw how Dan's dramatic life brought him many trials. Joe started to rack hay for his dad when he was about ten years old. I was concerned for his safety, as Joe was a small child and needed to slide down and place his back against the bottom of the seat of the little John Deer to be able to push in the clutch pedal. That little John Deer M had a breakdown in the hayfield. The motor on the tractor was burnt out. Lloyd came home for supper and said, "Joe blew up the John Deer." Later that night we were going to the drive-in show, and we drove past the field where the tractor was. Bart looked over to the field and said, "Dad, Joe didn't blow up the tractor. I can see it in the field."

Chapter 72:
We Have A Son in-law

Angela and her boyfriend Dean graduated in 1987. Angie was accepted at Camrose College to take early childhood development. That summer she went with Dean to Saskatoon where Dean was enrolled for college for business management. Angie phoned me from Saskatoon. The news she had for me was agonizing. She said that she was not coming home or going to college in Camrose. She wanted to stay with Dean.

Parents often are wounded by their kids' actions as they learn to let go and allow each child to choose their path in life. I was deeply hurt, as I never had an opportunity to go to college or get a career; but this wasn't about me. This was another difficult time for me.

I poured out my heart to God and found comfort. Our little princess was grown and was making her own choices. I missed her and didn't see her until Christmas time. I longed for her, but I knew that I must allow her to choose her own way. I do wonder if Angie later missed her daughters, Jennifer and Jillise, the way I missed her when she left home to make a life for herself. Dean and Angie came home after Dean received his diploma. They co-habitated in Pierceland. I found that arrangement hard, but I wanted to support our daughter and help her to be happy. They both worked in Cold Lake, Alberta for minimum wage—Angie at a grocery store and Dean at a hardware store.

Angela married Dean Gelowitz on May 20, 1989. I wrestled with many emotions because marriage is a lifetime commitment. Lloyd struggled with his daughter leaving too. Lloyd complained about all things to do with their wedding. Dean and Angie were close to Dean's family. I asked Angie to come home to dress; I wanted to be close to her before she started this new chapter with the man she chose. Now we can see what a great choice it was. Angela chose the song, "Daddy's Hands", as she danced with her Dad. They both had tears of joy.

I know that Angie and Dean struggled for the first while to make ends meet. Dean was paying back a college loan, buying a house, and they had a car payment. Not once did they complain about money matters. I told them we could help, but they never accepted the offer. I knew that I had to honour their choice. I understood, as I too wanted to make my own way in life.

Angie and Dean have a strong marriage. They celebrated their twenty-fifth wedding anniversary on May 20, 2014. When they renewed their vows, our priest congratulated them and said, "You are a good, but rare example of married commitment."

Dean and Angie's place has an atmosphere that all people enjoy and they have a lot of company.

Today Dean is an electrician with a prosperous and viable business—D.N.A. Electrical. He is able to be home each night. Angie and Dean have three children: Jennifer, Jamie, and Jillise. All three kids graduated from Pierceland High School. They all enjoy time with Mom and Dad.

Jennifer Rosann was born February 14, 1990. Jen was very petite when she was born and remains small today. Jen loves to play cards. She learned her numbers before she attended school. Jennifer played cards with Aunt Kay; she walked about three blocks to Aunt Kay's house. They both had a good time.

Jennifer was in gymnastics when she was young. I held my breath, as she flung from the high bar and landed on the gym mat. Jennifer also loved soccer. She would run until the coach called her off the field.

She was a small girl, but wasn't afraid of the bigger girls. She was in figure skating too. Jennifer also likes kids, and kids flock around her like a hen with little chicks.

When she graduated, she left home to babysit for her cousin Ashley in Lloydminster. In a few months, Jennifer started waitressing, then worked at a pool, a men's clothing shop, and a sign shop. Jennifer moved to in B.C. with her aunt and uncle in July 2014. She got a diploma in Early Childhood and works at a daycare where she enjoys all the kids. She is not married, and she has no children.

Jamie Dean was born on May 4, 1993 — a son for Angie and Dean. He is a loving person and can open up to all people. Jamie loved to visit at the farm. He didn't like the animals, but the shop tools held his attention. Uncle Joe was working on his truck when Jamie crawled under the truck and tried to tell Uncle Joe where the problem was. Jamie is a delightful child to be around, has a sense of humour, and can tell a big story. Jamie enjoyed trips to the river with horses or the quads. He played hockey, but the crowd interested him more than scoring a goal.

Jamie liked to ride his motorbike. He rode to our farm to feed my chickens and gather the eggs if we were gone; but there were no more chickens after Jamie graduated from high school. Jamie has the gift of the gab and can make a conversation with most every person he meets. Many people know Jamie and have talked to him.

Today Jamie apprentices for an electrician in the D.N.A. Company. He has received his first year in electrical, but has plans to get his journeymen's in electrical.

Jillise Marie joined the family on January 17, 1995. Jillise is a positive person and shows her affection to her family and friends. Jillise fits in the family to a "T." She is affectionate and gives everyone hugs. She enjoyed all the adventures that the family did, as long as there wasn't too much walking. Grandpa and Jillise liked to use the quad to go where they wanted to go.

Sports event were not held high in Jillise's life, but she figure skated to be part of her friends' crowd. Jillise liked school and enjoyed her whole class. She has many friends and is a compassionate person. The teachers all commented on her ability to love everyone.

Jillise attended North West College in Edmonton for one year in pharmacy. The next year she changed into nursing. Now she has a diploma, as an L.P.N. I'm sure she will be a ray of sunshine in a dreary world of the sick and aged folks that she cares for. Jillise likes fashion and buys clothes at Lululemon. I'm told that is an expensive shop. Keep on working girl!

Chapter 73:
Lloyd's Siblings

(Gonie family at our wedding) 1966

Lloyd's family from the oldest to the youngest:
- Mary was born 1920.
- Eva was born 1921.
- Bert was born 1922.
- Kay was born 1924.
- Bill was born 1926.
- Rosa was born 1927.
- Tone was born 1930.

John was born 1932.
Sal was born 1933.
Lloyd was born 1934.
Henry was born 1936.

Mary was the first child born to Lloyd's parents. She had a round face, straight hair, and dark eyes. Mary was outspoken, always wanted to be right, and often told people how they should do things. Mary was married to Alfred Jelinek, and they lived on a farm near Mary's parents. They had four daughters: Annie, Yvonne, Charlotte, and Kathleen.

Mary had a sore left arm and shoulder. Alfred took her to Goodsoil to see the doctor. She was kept for the night for observation. On February 8, 1988, Mary passed away in the Goodsoil Hospital due to a blood clot.

Eva married Paul Rolheiser, they had three children; Marie, Paulette, and Roland.

Eva was a slim lady and her father called her skin.

Bertha Hewlett was another sister of Lloyd's. She was the mother of that special baby, Rob, that Mom babysat years earlier while she had to go through cancer treatments. She seemed to have won her fight with thyroid cancer. Bert and her grandson, Dwayne, went to bingo in Pierceland. Bert won a jackpot and came home excited. Many of the Gonies had just gotten home from playing cards at John Gonie's birthday, February 23. Dwayne watched TV as Bert made herself a cup of coffee and sat down in her chair to relax. In a few minutes, Dwayne heard her fall from her chair. Bert had suffered a fatal heart attack. Bert passed away February 24, 1998.

Kay married Lawrence Tremblay, they have no children. They lived on a farm in Mudie lake about 20 kms south of Pierceland.

Bill was Lloyd's oldest brother. His hair was dark and wavy, his eyes were blue, and he was a great dancer; everyone wanted to dance with him. Bill suffered a heart attack in 1977. Bill slowed down, but the family moved to town, and 11 years later he had fatal heart attack. Bill Gonie passed away on October 30, 1989.

Rosa, Lloyd's sister, was married to George Gurski. George became ill in August 1991. George was taken to Saskatoon and was told that his kidneys were failing. George was sent to the local hospital in Goodsoil. I drove Rosa to Goodsoil to see George for the last few days. George didn't want Rose to stay at the hospital. He said, "Go home and get some rest." I took Rose home. George passed away on August 30, 1991.

Lloyd had not said good bye to any of his family since his sister, Mary passed away on February 8, 1988 and his brother Bill in 1989.

Tone married lorrianne and they have six children, Rosanneette, Lori, Steve, Bill, Harvey, Carolyn.

Tone was the great neighbour that all the Burge's loved.

John married Marie and they have three children, Philip, Karen and Trish. Their farm was 3 km west of ours.

Sal married Clarence Hickie and they have five children, Eva, Koreen, Allan, Patricia and Mark. They live in cold lake south, formally known as Grand Centre.

Lloyd is the tenth child.

Henry married Rose and they have three children, Keith, Donna and Russell.

Their farm is 3 km north of ours. Henry is the brother that Lloyd often worked with.

Chapter 74:
Life Continues

My sister Nioma remarried on November 6, 1999. Marvin Hatch and Nioma were married in a small ceremony in a country house with Nioma's twin brother Nelson by her side. Marvin is a good man and cares for Nioma, as a husband should. They both like to dance and go to jamborees.

Marvin, and his two daughters, Danielle and Donna, moved to White Court, Alberta, This was the first time Nioma moved away from Pierceland. Marvin worked as a millwright. Marvin had lost his former wife, the girl's mother, to cancer. The girls expected their family to return to the former life they once had with their mother.

Nioma was challenged with two girls in the house. Danielle was a teenager and Nioma was the step-mom. This was a tense situation, and I felt for both Danielle and Nioma. Danielle was a slim, beautiful girl with dark hair; she was a teenager who struggled to find her place in the world. She felt that Marvin, her dad, had less time for her. Danielle was unhappy and didn't want to obey Nioma's rules. Marvin would not come between his wife and his daughter. It was just easier to walk away and he did.

Nioma has always been a leader and a worker, and she was not patient with Marvin's girls. She expected Danielle to help with the housework and make school a priority. I pined for Nioma and her extended family. I knew I had to stay out of her drama, but how hard it was to see Nioma wanting to control Danielle. Every family has different rules and family traits; Nioma was let down when she couldn't keep peace in her new home.

Danielle made the choice to move from the home and in with a friend where she finished high school. The family lived there for three years before Marvin retired from his job. Marvin, Nioma, and Donna, the youngest girl, moved back to Pierceland, closer to Nioma's family.

Donna was a young girl who was less outspoken than her sister was. Donna was behind in her reading, and Nioma helped her to catch up to the standard level for her age. Donna is also a beautiful girl with dark hair, a soft voice, and she has the ability to please others.

Nioma, Donna, and Marvin lived in Pierceland for awhile, but soon they moved west of Pierceland to their acreage. Donna graduated from high school with good marks. She went to Edmonton to work. At the present time, Donna is working in the north on a fire watch. She likes the bush and the loneliness she can handle.

Nioma and Marvin continue to live on their acreage and enjoy their greenhouse. They attend the farmers' market in Cold Lake Alberta and sell bedding plants and fresh vegetables every week. Nioma said, "It's good to be the first to sell vegetables." The green house is a lot of work, but Nioma has never been afraid of work. Nioma ate fresh radishes for Easter!

Marvin and Nioma bought horses to drive. This proved to be a good thing for Marvin, as it kept him busy when Nioma was in the kitchen baking bread for the farmers' market.

Nioma likes to be busy and when she sits down, she has a ball of yarn that she keeps her from being idle. I think she doesn't know how to relax. I remember going with Nioma in the winter months to paint quilt blocks with Aertex paints. I started a quilt the next year. My quilt took me two years to complete. Nioma works on a project until it is complete.

Chapter 75:
We Lose A Brother-In-law (Paul)

Lloyd's family was older than my family was. I knew that it was important to spend time visiting his family.

Lloyd and I went to St. Walburg to visit Eva and Paul Rolheiser, another sister of Lloyd's (parents of Roland). Eva was a schoolteacher who taught for 30 years. She was well liked, got along with all the teachers, and made time to help any child who needed it. Eva was tall and slim and always cared about her appearance. A priest remarked how Eva made sure she wore her Sunday best when she took her turn to read at mass.

Paul, Eva's husband, always treated Eva like a queen. Paul was a handy man, and he was patient and willing to do the things that Eva demanded. He changed many cupboards to suit Eva. Paul worked at the university as a custodian when they lived in Edmonton. Eva retired from teaching, and they moved to Saskatchewan to Bright Sand, a resort with a beautiful lake for fishing and swimming in. The grandchildren spent many of their summers with Grandma and Grandpa at this paradise.

Paul began experiencing lung problems. They had an auction sale and moved into St. Walburg, Saskatchewan. This arrangement worked for a year or two, and Paul was put on oxygen to help him breathe easier. In a few years, Paul was hospitalized. The doctor said, "Paul, you have a serious lung problem, and there is nothing I can do." Paul returned to his local hospital without any talk of a recovery. Eva was brave; I stayed with her and drove her to visit Paul for the last five days of his life. Eva was strong and managed to spend most of the day with Paul. I witnessed her sobbing through the night; she and Paul were married 54 years, and now she had to accept that he would soon pass on. I yearned for a way to share her pain and make it easier for her to say good-bye. I wasn't able to come up with a thing. I hope that my presence was enough. How helpless I felt.

I had taken a few courses to help me deal with death and bereavement. I was so glad that I had learned not to fear death but to accept it as a way of life. One day, Paul tried to tell Eva something when we arrived in the morning. Paul said, "I can't" and he was out of breath. Eva was annoyed and didn't understand what her husband was trying to tell her.

I said to Eva, "Yesterday you said that you hoped to have Paul for one more Christmas. I think Paul wants to tell you that he cannot be here for one more Christmas." I looked at Paul and he said, "Yes." I told Paul that he had taught Eva how to care for herself, and that she was a tough lady. I said, "I will stay with Eva for as long as she needs me."

I then told Eva that she needed to tell Paul that she didn't expect him to stay for her for another Christmas. Eva stood up straight, took a deep breath, and said to Paul, "You don't need to stay for me; I'll be okay."

A few minutes later after she finished speaking, Eva and I prayed by Paul's side, and Paul took that last breath. Paul appeared to be brave and ready to meet his maker. He didn't fight any longer when Eva told him she would be fine on her own. Paul Rolheiser passed away peacefully on December 22, 2001. Paul's funeral was held on December 24th, as the funeral director said, "I feel that it is easier to say good bye before Christmas day; Christmas day is a day to celebrate."

The Rolheiser family presented me with a ring. It was their way of saying thanks for being by Eva's side at Paul's passing. The ring is my birthstone and has a few small diamonds surrounding the turquoise stone. I have it on my finger every day. Eva told me to go home with Lloyd after the funeral because she could manage with the many friends she had to help her. Eva attended mass each day and often went with her friends for lunch. Eva said, "When I watched the evening news I often spoke to Paul about all the events in the news. I turned to speak to him, but there was no answer. It was so hard to see the empty chair." The tears of healing flowed freely, and Eva longed for her former days with Paul.

Chapter 76:
Time For Changes

Winter came upon us with a blast. More time was spent indoors to quilt, read, or watch television. I bought a laptop computer and learned to type. I enjoyed writing about events from my past. A large family has much to write about and many events to share with others.

I know life becomes slower with age; but the snail's pace is not for me; or so I thought. I helped to cater with a group of younger ladies and realized that I should step aside. Each lady filled my shoes in a great way. The ladies were kind and thanked me for my knowledge in the kitchen.

Life moved quickly and soon the road faded behind me. One morning I looked in the mirror and said, "When did I become my mother? My youth has vanished." I was not fond of those streaks of grey hair and my saggy body. At this time, I had a friend with cancer, and she was in chemotherapy treatment. I learned to give thanks for any hair. My friend's head is bald after her cancer treatment, and she was able to accept it. Why would I fret about my grey locks? I fit in with my in-laws who are ten and twenty years older. My school friends are my same age under their glamorous dark hair. If that makes them feel good, that's what they need to do. I like the natural look. I wanted to rock, but I wasn't ready for Grandma's rocking chair. Now our family had grown, and I felt that it was time for us. I had some places I wanted to visit and experience some different life styles; maybe travel.

In May 2004, we bought Rose and Henry Gonie's holiday trailer. It is a 5-metre Travel Air and fits us well. We went to jamborees in the summer and spent time in the great outdoors as we heard music from the past.

We didn't travel far from home that first summer as Lloyd was waiting for his call for surgery.

Lloyd was experiencing pain in his right hip. He suffered much before he agreed to see the local doctor. Lloyd moved slowly, and he found it hard to stand. He was sent to Edmonton to see a specialist doctor. The doctor said, "The x-rays show that there is bone rubbing on bone. You need to have a hip replacement."

I could see fear in Lloyd's eyes, but the pain was severe and he agreed to surgery. Pain changes a person's character and Lloyd wasn't able to enjoy the outdoors. He was awake much of the night. I wrapped a tea towel around my head to lessen the smell, and I rubbed A535, a muscle relaxant, to help relieve his pain; sometimes it was three times a night. I could see Lloyd was frustrated, as he lost movement and could no longer do the work he wanted to. He felt he was useless and a burden to me. I told him, "I will be there for you whatever lies ahead, and I will help you to be healthy again."

On September 22, 2004, Lloyd had a total hip replacement at the university hospital in Edmonton. Lloyd never complained, but this was a big deal for me. I thought of his heart condition and prayed that he would be strong enough for surgery. Lloyd was taken into surgery and I returned to my room to sleep. The nurse told me it would take about 4 hours, and that I would be called when Lloyd was out of surgery. I went to my room to sleep, but I could not sleep. After 4 hours of waiting, I went to check to see if Lloyd was out of surgery. I learned that he had not had surgery because his blood was too thin. He was given vitamin K to thicken his blood. By the time Lloyd was able to have surgery my kids were with me.

The kids took me to dinner and that helped to pass the time. The surgery went well; we spent ten days in Edmonton. I stayed by his side watching for swelling and listening for a change in his breathing (any sign of complications). I was able to stay at the hospital in a day ward that was for patients who were having cancer treatments. I needed to check in each morning to see if my room was available for the night. I stayed for the duration, but some days I needed to change rooms.

Ben Kesenheimer and Bart came to see Lloyd the day before Lloyd was discharged, and Bart drove our truck home. Lloyd and I came back to Cold Lake with the ambulance. He stayed for two more days. He needed to walk up the stairs before he was released. Lloyd's replacement hip healed well, but now his right knee was causing him pain.

In May 2005, Lloyd had a total knee replacement. Lloyd needed care through both surgeries. I was thankful that I was given good health and was able to be Lloyd's caregiver.

I was nervous about city driving as we needed to drive to Edmonton for his check-ups. I made out fine, but I will let others drive in the city if I can. I drove to Cold Lake for therapy as the doctor asked Lloyd not to drive for two months. Lloyd was a good passenger and allowed me to drive my way. Sometimes he asked why I went the way I did.

I call Lloyd my bionic man, as he has a ceramic and steel hip and a titanium knee. Lloyd recuperated well; we went to the mall in Cold Lake to walk as the outdoors was not as safe; before long he left the cane behind too. Lloyd's pain was gone, and Lloyd was his old self again. I thanked the doctor for giving me my husband back.

Life was back to normal with Lloyd.

We went to visit the Haases, our long time friends and my former employer. Lloyd has rented Art's land for fifty years. This was a good arrangement for Lloyd as it is close to our place, and Art was happy to have a renter that was honest and trustworthy.

The Haases were both in their nineties and showed signs of aging; their health was failing too. Mrs. Haase had trouble remembering how to cook and where things were, and she didn't like to leave her home. In the fall, she fell and broke her hip. She was in the hospital for months until a place was available in long-term care in Goodsoil.. About a year later, Art moved to a seniors' residence in Goodsoil, where he could walk one block to have dinner with his wife, Annie. This arrangement lasted for about a year; then Art also fell. He spent time in the hospital and eventually was placed near his wife in long-term care in Goodsoil; they were together again.

Lloyd and I checked Art's place each week until he was able to sell it. Lloyd and I went to visit them once a month. The first while when we spent time with them, we played that marble game as we had played when they lived on the farm. Mrs. Haase started to make mistakes, and she was frustrated. The game was put away, and we tried to talk about the events in our town where she and Art had lived. Art's mind remained intact, but she often drifted off.

I longed to support this couple as their three sons didn't live close by. This was another time that I felt unable to fill the loneliness that overtakes a person who no longer feels that they are of any use in this world. My heart ached to see my elderly friends lose their mobility and their health. I decided that all I could do was to be there and support them in their last days. Mrs. Haase passed away on April 28, 2010. Her husband Art passed away on September 28 in the same year. My longtime friends had a good life.

When the family went through the things that needed to be passed on, they remembered Lloyd and I. The special marble game was passed onto us, and we now enjoy it with our grandchildren.

Chapter 77:
Losing a Sibling (Lloyd Burge)

In 2010, my family met with some new challenges. There had not been a death in the Burge family since my dad's funeral in August of 1977. A former brother, baby Leonard, had passed away in 1953, a few hours after he was born. My large family was blessed with good health, happiness, and there had not been any other of Mom and Dad's children who passed away. There were some accidents, but a not one life was lost.

Lloyd Burge, my brother who was about two years older than I am, was always near with his witty ways as I grew into adulthood. He found fun in most everything. I had not seen much of Lloyd after we grew up, as he worked away most of his life, and I was busy with my family. I missed his big smile and his positive ways. I have good memories of him. Lloyd, my brother, passed away on March 19, 2010.

Rita, his wife always got up early, before Lloyd. Lloyd liked to sleep in when he wasn't working. She went to call him in the morning and found him motionless in bed. Lloyd had a fatal heart attack and never suffered. I thought of Rita and how she would struggle to make a new life. Rita had just recovered from cancer. She was determined and with her daughters to help her, Rita moved on in her life.

Lloyd's funeral was held in Innisfail, Alberta. When I walked with my family into the service, my heart felt that empty spot where Lloyd should have been walking ahead of me. I always stood next to him at family pictures and other functions. I was full of empathy, but I knew that I had my memories to cherish.

In August 2010, my doctor diagnosed a spot on my face as a pre-skin cancer spot. Cancer is a dreaded word and nobody wants to hear it. Many thoughts ran through my head, and I recalled that my brother Lloyd had skin cancer. His cancer was successfully removed, and he never had any more concerns about skin cancer. I did wonder if I was going to follow in Lloyd's footsteps.

Lloyd and I had shared part of our lives together and joined in work and play, as we were only about fourteen months apart in age. I decided that if I was to leave this world, going to bed and never waking up was a good way to depart.

The couple of spots were treated with no further problems. I could continue to live the good life with all my family and friends around me. I did learn to appreciate life a little more and enjoy each day.

Chapter 78:
The Open Road

Lloyd my husband had worked all his life and wasn't sure if he wanted to travel, but I had dreamed of seeing faraway places from the time I was a child. A big family doesn't have the money or the means to leave their garden, chores, or their home. I needed to talk to Lloyd and persuade him to travel. Time has a way of moving quickly, and I wanted to see more of Canada. Lloyd was willing, but work was all he had ever done, and travelling was not part of his life. It didn't take much persuading to get him onboard. Lloyd and I now had time for us. Our kids were happy and making their own memories with their kids.

On August 4 of 1998, there was a Burge family reunion in Prince Edward Island. Lloyd agreed to go to the Maritimes. Nine members of the Burge family travelled together to meet the eastern Burge families. We found that the pace in the East was much slower and more relaxed than what we were used to here out in the West. While we were there, we booked a mini tour of the Maritimes. More time should have been allotted to see all the amazing places like Anne of Green Gables, the Bay of Fundy, and Lunenburg with the famous Bluenose boat. Peggy's Cove lured us to the lighthouse with the vast ocean water near. What a wonderful tour it was! It was a few years before Lloyd and I went on another trip.

In July 2000, my sister, Judy and I travelled by bus to Drumheller to watch the passion play. I was so thrilled with the acting and the setting for the play. It was a hot day, and sun burnt my lips. I went to the drug store and bought a lip balm that froze my lips. Soon all was well. The tour also took us to the Tyrell Dinosaur Museum. It was nice to see, but I'm not interested in dinosaurs.

I had dreamed of visiting some different parts of this beautiful country we call Canada. When I was growing up, we never went any farther than about 30 kilometres from home. (My family was too large and money and a good vehicle were factors.) Lloyd and I took our first bus tour to British Columbia on September 2, 2010. We travelled eight days by motor coach to the inside passage up to Prince Rupert. Lloyd's sister, Rose Gurski, went with us. Lloyd and I both agreed that a bus tour was the way to travel as no one had to drive and no road map was needed. I was never told that I took us on a different or wrong highway. I didn't enjoy the ferry when I couldn't see the shore line; it was a 15-hour scenic voyage on water. The coast of British Columbia was okay, but when there was only water to be seen, I lay on the floor of the ferry and had a sleep until we were near Prince Rupert. I did enjoy the rest of the trip with good scenery and good food, mostly the fresh fish. The eight days passed quickly.

In 2013, I travelled with a church group to Mexico City. The weather was hot everyday, and I enjoyed our tour guide as he showed us many churches that had so much gold in them. I missed Lloyd, but I knew that there would be too much walking and religious sites for him to handle well.

Day one: We drove from home in the snow until Ashmot, Alberta. The road to Edmonton was good after that.

Day two: We boarded a plane with six members from our church (Gail Foss, Sharon Rawlake, Collette Rawlake, Dauphine Vicko, Theresia Grundner, and Barb Gonie).

I sit by the window on the United Airlines plane. The highway below was like a snake winding along on its way.

Day three: We visited Juan Diego church and the Aztecs people;

then to the pyramids at Teotihuacan.

Day three: We saw the parliament buildings; I'm uneasy as there was a truck with men carrying guns. We walk to one more church, where someone was preparing for a simple funeral.

Day four: We travelled away from the city. The land is poor, with just a few goats and sheep; the flowers are beautiful with red, yellow, pink and orange colours. Karen and I sat in the hot tub while others enjoy a drink before supper.

Day five: We saw the statue of Christ the King on the mountaintop. The road was narrow and steep. We visited the cobble stone street; dogs were everywhere.

Day six: We toured a narrow street. There is a large cross that is lit up, and the downtown square is full of activities. This reminded me of Saturday night in our hometown of Pierceland when the farmers went to town.

Day seven: We celebrated mass in the courtyard; it's beautiful. We had a steak supper with a baked potato. This was the first potato I had. Mexican food has a lot of tortillas. The band was loud and the T.V had a sex show playing. Karen asked the waiter to turn channels or shut off the TV. He did.

Day eight: We arrived at the airport and said good bye to our tour guide. The flight was late, and we waited 4 hours. We arrived in Edmonton; it's -32. We left when it was plus 32. It was amazing to think that the temperature could be so different after a few hours' flight. Theresia stayed in Edmonton with her husband, Tony, and their daughter Melisa drove us back to Pierceland. I was happy to be home.

In February 2015, Lloyd and I travelled by motor coach to Texas, Louisiana. and the Deep South. This was a 24-day trip, but the time passed quickly as each day we experienced new areas with interesting attractions. This trip was very enjoyable; for me, I think it was the best trip we took. The weather was cold; we only had one day when we didn't need a jacket. I needed to buy another sweatshirt and jeans, as my shorts were never worn.

We saw Kansas City, Oklahoma City, Fort Worth, and the John F. Kennedy Center. Then we went on to San Antonio, Corpus Christi, Houston, and Lafayette. I liked the Oak Ally plantations and the swamp visit in Lafayette. We went to New Orleans; I didn't like all the partying that went on there. I experienced many drunks and my shoes stuck to the sidewalks, as we walked to see the jazz band. I did enjoy the steamboat cruise.

The wind was cold as we entered Memphis and Graceland, but Elvis was worth it all. In South Dakota, I enjoyed Mount Rushmore and Black Hills National Forest. It was great to return to Canada and spend the night in Swift Current, Saskatchewan. Lloyd and I were gone two days longer because we needed to travel four hours to Edmonton to start the tour and back home from Edmonton.

It was 2016 when my sister Judy went on a bus tour with Lloyd and me to Minot, North Dakota for a Host Fest. Daniel O'Donnell was my favourite singer. His love of music and good family life was revealed in his songs.

On September 20, 2017 Lloyd and I travelled by train from Edmonton to Toronto, Ontario. What a great way to travel! After a day in Toronto, we took the bus to Niagara Falls to see one of the Seven Wonders of the World. We returned to Toronto and took the plane home. This was the first time we had travelled alone without a tour guide; we made out fine.

Chapter 79:
My Grandson's Accident

Lyndon with protective helmet

The phone rang in the early morning with a call that no parent or grandparent wants to receive: "Lyndon was in an accident and taken to the Cold Lake Hospital. He has many broken bones, but the most serious injury is his head injury. Lyndon's skull was broken, and there is tissue oozing from his head. If you want to see him, you need to be at the hospital within the hour because Lyndon is going to go by air to Edmonton where a team of surgeons are waiting to operate." It was December 19, 2010 when our son Dan made that call. The evening before Lyndon had told Dan, "I'll be late getting home because it's my friend's 21st birthday." How was he to know that it would be many months before he would return to his home?

Lyndon, our grandson, was at death's door. My eyes popped wide opened before Dan finished talking. I was aware that accidents happen often, and sometimes the family managed to arrive at the hospital in time to say good bye to their loved one. Would this be the case with Lyndon? I dressed, washed my face, and tried to build myself up so that I would be able to support my son through this horrible ordeal. In a few minutes, Dan stopped by to pick up Lloyd and me. Dan drove us to the Cold Lake Hospital on icy pavement, as it had rained through the night. Dan was devastated as he said, "Mom, I knew Lyndon was going to celebrate with his friends; this was the last boy in his class to turn twenty-one years old. I should have said more than, 'Do not drive home when you are drinking.'"

Lyndon told Dan that he didn't know how he would get home, but he knew better than to drive when he had been drinking. I prayed and tried to help Dan to see that this accident was not his fault. Lyndon was an adult and could make his own choices.

The drive to the hospital was about 30 minutes long. The road was so long. When we arrived at the hospital, Dan and I hastened to each side of Lyndon's bed. Lyndon's head was wrapped up in white gauze so he looked like "Sinbad the Sailor". My mind was foggy as I viewed Lyndon's head and saw the machines on both sides of the bed to monitor his vital signs. One screen showed small ripples on the brain activity. The constant tick of those machines would go on for weeks. The doctor told us that Lyndon had many broken bones, and he would need many surgeries, but his head injury was severe. Tissue oozed out of a broken skull; he needed surgery soon. The doctor stressed how serious his head injury was and that Lyndon might not survive his injuries. I asked how long Lyndon had to live. The doctor said, "I think he'll make Edmonton, but maybe ten hours." Lloyd stood back by the door, and I heard the nurse ask him often if he was okay. Lloyd has a heart condition, and I was concerned about him too, but I trusted the nurses to watch him. Right now, I needed to be with Dan and Lyndon.

The doctor told us things that I didn't want to hear. Lyndon brain injury was so severe, if he did live, he would not be able to function as he had; maybe he would never leave his bed. The lady doctor said, "The team of doctor who are waiting to do this very serious operation in Edmonton will tell you more. This surgery is serious, but Lyndon is strong, and he is young."

Dan had not heard what she said. The doctor looked at me and said, "Dan should not drive." I didn't want Lloyd to drive, and I was not comfortable driving on icy roads. How hard it was to crawl into the back seat of the truck with Dan behind the wheel. My heart was breaking, but I had faith that the Lord would keep us safe as we drove. God's hand guided us, as we travelled the four hours to Edmonton. Our trip was made in safety.

Dan and Lyndon's mother, Delilah, are divorced. Dan called Ashley, his daughter and she called her mother. They arrived in Edmonton before we did, as their drive was shorter. Ashley phoned Dan on his cell phone, which is connected by blue tooth in the truck. I witnessed my granddaughter fight her way through all the hard words that the Edmonton doctor had told her and her mother. "Lyndon will be in surgery for about four hours. Brain surgery is very serious, and the doctor said that they needed to trim away part of his brain to try and prevent blood clots."

We arrived at the university hospital in Edmonton when Lyndon's surgery was close to being over. The staff was good; they told us where we could park and how to find our way to the ICU ward where Lyndon would go after his surgery. The nurse gave us a small room with a chesterfield, a big chair, and a table with a lamp and some books. No one wanted to read; our eyes were cloudy and we fought to find ways to get through this drama. I was numb as I waited. It was about 10 to 15 minutes before Lyndon was out of surgery and rolled into the ICU ward. We were escorted to see him. He looked much the same as he did in Cold Lake but his head was bigger.

Dan and Delilah controlled themselves well as we all talked and waited for the doctor to come and talk to us.

The doctor's words were hard to grasp as he said, "The surgery went well, but don't get your hopes up. We trimmed away as much of the tissue as we felt was safe, but he may not come out of his coma. There are three factors to get past: blood clots that cause a stroke, bleeding, and infection. The first 10 hours are critical, and then if he lives, we will go for 24 hours, then 72 hours. These are the milestones to get past. Now we wait, but don't expect any good news for about 14 days. It's going to be a roller coaster ride with all the ups and downs. If he can make it through the entire trauma, I don't think Lyndon will be the same person you once knew; prepare yourselves for the worst. If he bleeds, and we can't stop it, he's gone. If he has a stroke, there will be more brain damage, and he will be left a vegetable. Then there is infection to get past."

I was quick to ask how he could get an infection in a clean hospital. The doctor told me that Lyndon's immune system was gone; now he had nothing to fight against infection. The doctor's favourite words were, "Now we wait. Lyndon is in serious condition; you need to prepare yourselves for the worst. It's going to be a long and rough road ahead. If he does live, he will not know you, have any emotion, or ever leave this bed.

It was heart wrenching to hear. I pined for Dan, my son, who wouldn't accept that Lyndon might die. The doctor said, "If Lyndon lives for 48 hours, the chances go up a little. When he makes 10 days, the chances are better." After two weeks, I was hopeful, but the doctor said, "Don't get your hopes up. Lyndon's head could swell for three weeks or more."

Lyndon's head was already as big as a soccer ball! I felt like I had been kicked when I was down; would there never be any good news to give us hope? How would I have the strength to hold everybody together? I went to the chapel to pray, but I could only cry and plead to my God to be with me through every minute as I carried this burden. I said every prayer that I know, but then I spoke to the Lord from my heart: "Please Lord, stay by my side and give me the strength I need to help everyone that is involved." Would I be able to support both Dan and Delilah?

None of Delilah's family was there except Ashley, her daughter. She is a strong, young lady, but I know how close she is to her brother. "Please Lord, be near her and give her the strength to endure whatever is ahead." Will her visits be a support for Lyndon? She had a young family at home who also needed her.

Each of us was allowed in for a few minutes, but we were told that the best thing for Lyndon was to rest. That constant click of the machines and the little ripples of brain activities were hard to digest. I wanted to see those ripples become large waves, but that didn't happen.

This was the biggest trial that I have ever faced. I know I needed to care for myself if I was to help others. I tried to eat healthy; it was a challenge. The minutes seemed to pass like hours and the hours became days and then months. About 10 hours later, Lyndon suffered a stroke, and we were told that there would be more damage. Lyndon might be in a vegetable state for the rest of his life if he could pull through. The stroke left Lyndon with a weak right side.

Lyndon was put on blood thinners, which caused another problem; he had a bleed in his brain. Dan and I stood over him in the ICU. Dan said to me, "Do you think Lyndon's colour is different? I did see Lyndon's grey colour, with a yellow nose and blue lips. We were asked to leave and soon the doctor came to talk to us. He said, "Lyndon needs another surgery. He has a bled. If we cannot stop the bleed, Lyndon will be gone in a few minutes."

Dan told the doctor to do whatever it took to save his son's life. I talked to Dan and told him that these doctors face this drama every day, and they usually know what the best outcome is for their patient. I asked, "Dan, do you know who holds Lyndon's life in his hands?"

Dan said, "Yes Mother, I do, but I know Lyndon is going to be okay." Dan asked me to pray; I had not stopped praying. Angela and her family arrived. I hugged her and cried like I never had before. She said she came for me, and she wasn't able to go into Lyndon's room.

We gathered in a little room, about fifteen of us; we all joined hands to make our prayer complete. I ask the Lord to be with Lyndon, and us too, as we wait for good news. "Please Lord, do whatever is best for Lyndon, and please give each of us the strength and the courage to accept your will. Help each of us to acknowledge whatever the outcome will be. Please Lord, touch us all, and assist us to consent to your will. Give me hope and courage to be there for my family, as we are forced to accept what we cannot understand. Make us aware of your constant love. Amen."

Lyndon came out of surgery once again, and I stood by the side; would he be a vegetable? How could I rationalize with Dan and help him to see that this is not what Lyndon would want. Could he endure this new Lyndon in this state? The nurse came closer to Lyndon and took his vitals. I asked Dan if I could baptize Lyndon. He questioned me, and I told him, "If Lyndon cannot be with me in this world, then I want to know that he will be in the next world." Dan told me that Lyndon was an adult, and he should make that call. I had to accept that hard, cold fact.

I took turns going in with Dan and then with Delilah to see Lyndon. Delilah accepted my help, and a nurse asked Delilah if I was her mother. She replied, "Barb has been there more than my mother was." I hugged Delilah, and we sobbed together. I told her, "We are going to be here every day for Lyndon." (Delilah's parents did not come to the hospital.)

I know that real happiness comes from thinking of others and giving of oneself, but I needed a shower of God's grace. I was given courage to stand by Lyndon's parents. His parents and I spent many days by his side, as he was not expected to live; any day could have been his last day. The medical team told us if Lyndon lived, he would not leave his bed. "Don't get your hopes up."

Dan insisted that Lyndon would be fine. I struggled with Dan and his inability to listen to the doctors. I said to Dan, "You need to listen to the doctors. They see these cases every day. They know what they are talking about." Dan responded, "Mother I know that Lyndon is going to be okay. They just need to save him today. I know who holds the keys to life; Lyndon will survive and leave his bed." Lyndon was in the ICU, and after 10 days, he was still in a comatose state to allow his brain to heal.

Christmas Day was approaching, and I heard voices say "Merry Christmas" to each other. This wasn't a joyous time for me; I almost felt angry at a Merry Christmas wish. Lyndon was moved to a private room; he had a lung infection. Lyndon had managed to get through a stroke and a bleed and now he had to fight this infection. The doctor said, "He is young and he is strong, he *may* get past this too." Lyndon did!

His lungs were pumped twice a day. The doctors found the right medication to treat him, and gradually he got past this too. Little by little, there was a glimmer of hope. Lyndon's lungs were clear and he started to open his eyes when the doctor or nurse told him to. Following a command was a big improvement. Lyndon showed little signs — like a blink of an eye or a soft squeeze of my hand, which was a big deal for me.

In time, Lyndon was put in a sling and moved from his bed into a wheel chair to be pushed around. Lyndon had no control, and he rolled about in the sling like a bowl of jelly. His eyes were full of fear too. How would he ever learn to sit or get any control of his body? I went home on Christmas Eve with Christine Urlacher, Dan's friend. Dan phoned me at home on Christmas day and told me that Lyndon had cracked his eyes open.

Judy, my sister, and her daughter, Meloney, stopped in on their way home from the Urlacher farm. (Judy's daughter is married to Andy Urlacher.) Meloney said to me, "I will explain to you how serious Lyndon's injury is if you want me to."

Meloney, my niece, is an E.M.T. and flies north to work. I was annoyed and responded with: "I know that the brain is like a motherboard in a computer. It runs the whole body. Nothing will work without those brain messages." Meloney agreed and didn't offer any more advice.

Dan was there each day, and I told him he should take a break from this hospital crisis. Dan went home to do some year-end paper work. I know how hard that was; Lyndon was still knocking at death's door. Dan returned in two days; not much had changed for Lyndon.

The doctor needed to know if Lyndon would ever breathe on his own. He removed the tube for a short time. Lyndon turned blue, his blood pressure went over 200, and I gasped. The doctor said, "It's okay, he's young, and this is only for a second." This was repeated three times when Lyndon reacted. Each day the tube was closed for a longer time until Lyndon was able to breathe on his own.

There was talk about sending Lyndon to the University of Saskatoon Hospital, as Lyndon was a Saskatchewan resident. Dan was against this, but there's nothing he could do to prevent it. After a month in the University of Edmonton Hospital, Lyndon was taken by air to the university hospital in Saskatoon, Saskatchewan. Edmonton had saved him, but now Saskatoon would help him to move on with rehab.

Dan called me each day, and kept me informed about Lyndon's improvements. I was overjoyed when Dan told me that Lyndon had cracked his eyes about half open when the nurse asked him to; he had followed a command. Each small task was an accomplishment and a major step for Lyndon. That first blink was encouraging; he needed time, and I was happy to accept any small improvements.

I didn't see my grandson for about two weeks. We went to Saskatoon to see him; his eyes were open wider, but they were dull and full of fear. Lyndon began to recognize his dad. Lyndon was elevated in his bed and his eyes followed Dan when Dan spoke. He looked much better as his eyes were opened and following Dan about the room.

In about three weeks, we returned to see Lyndon. The tracheostomy tube was taken out of Lyndon's throat, and Dan said that he had spoken. I know that Dan wanted Lyndon to be okay, and Dan never wavered about Lyndon's healing. I said to Dan, "You need to take a break; you can't help your son if you are sick." Dan told me he would not leave his son. I said to Dan, "You are my son, and I my heart aches to see you not caring for yourself. You cannot help anyone if you become sick."

I think I struck a chord in Dan. Dan and Delilah, Lyndon's mother, started to take turns at the hospital. Each stayed for a week.

I returned to visit Lyndon in about a month. I asked him if he knew the names of his nieces. It took awhile for him to answer, but he answered correctly. Gradually the tubes were taken away, one at a time. It was hard each time, as his body found it hard to re-adjust without the tubes or the machines. He had so far to go to be an active soul again! He threshed with his left hand and tried to pull out the IV tubes and any other tube he found. Lyndon's hands were tied down and he fought to get them free. Dan asked for permission to have Lyndon's hand untied when he is by his bed. The doctor agreed.

Lyndon learned to sit, and Dan took him in a wheelchair to therapy. I saw Lyndon at one of the first therapy sessions in Saskatoon; he was sitting, but when the therapist asked him to reach for her hand, Lyndon toppled over like a young baby. He didn't have any control of his upper body. Therapy taught Lyndon to build up his core muscles so that he could sit. Lyndon continued with the ups and downs for a long time. Lyndon's improvement was so slow.

A month later, I went to Saskatoon to visit Lyndon. In two weeks, Lloyd and I visited Lyndon again. There was an improvement, but he had to learn all things over again. All Lyndon's accomplishments were slow. That first walk between the bars was more like a push and a pull movement. Two therapists helped Lyndon move along between the bars. He worked hard each day and grew stronger. Dan spent five months in the hospital with Lyndon; he did not work because he wanted to be near Lyndon. Slowly Lyndon did respond and was determined to leave his bed.

With much hard work and determination, Lyndon was released from the Saskatoon hospital. He came home on May 12, 2011. He was in a wheel chair until he got in the house. That chair was used to go outdoors, but not in the house. Lyndon flopped about; Dan supported him with a transfer belt. Lyndon had poor balance, but he was able to move, a jerky walk at first, but his weak side became more muscular, and each day he walked better. Lyndon's job was to work on his exercises.

Lyndon needed to be cautious as his neck wasn't healed; he wore a neck collar for about six months. The first time we took Lyndon to Cold Lake for therapy after he had his collar removed, he was too dizzy to do his exercises. We were told that the rough road was hard on his neck. Each time we drove over the rough road, I was worried about his neck, but in time the muscles grew strong enough to hold his head. He had a helmet to protect his brain because there was no bone flap; it had been removed in Edmonton for surgery. The helmet was gone after he had another surgery and a titanium plate was put into his skull almost a year later.

Dan wanted to go to work, as he has not worked in five months. Dan had a homecare lady come to his place to care for Lyndon. Lyndon didn't like her and said that he could stay alone. We all knew that this wasn't possible. I also knew that people heal faster if they are happy. Dan asked me if I could be Lyndon's caregiver.

I didn't feel that I was qualified to care for someone with so many problems. Lyndon still needed to wear a helmet as he had no bone flap and a neck collar to protect his 3rd and 4th vertebra in his neck. There was a screw in his neck, but it was holding by about a half a turn. I wondered would I be strong enough to hold Lyndon upright if he started to fall. I was terrified to be in full control of Lyndon's life.

What if I failed to do the right thing and Lyndon ended up back in the hospital? I had no training in health care. I said to Dan, "I want to be a grandmother and not a caregiver for Lyndon, but I will try for one week."

Lyndon was happy at my house, and I learned to get past my fears of the neck collar and the helmet. Dan stopped for supper, and then he and Lyndon went home for the night. Dan went to work early; I waited for Lyndon to call me in the morning then I went to tighten his collar and put on his helmet, transfer belt, and his shoes. I helped Lyndon to become stronger, and he learned all things over again. Lyndon started therapy two weeks after he was home from Saskatoon; therapy was every weekday.

Highway 55 was under construction and that was a challenge as Lloyd and I drove him to Cold Lake for his therapies. Lyndon did speech, physiotherapy, and occupational therapy for a year and a half. Some days he had two therapies and came home tired. Many days I slept in the afternoon with Lyndon; I was blessed with good health and was not sick on any days as I cared for Lyndon.

Lyndon was devoted and did his exercises. He had to learn everything over again; we practiced synonyms, signing with his left hand, getting up and down to sit, and walking too. Some days I was tired, and I felt that I could not do enough to help Lyndon to recover. After a good cry, my mind was able to move on and be thankful for Lyndon's state as I recalled all the doctors who had told us he would never leave an institution.

Lyndon and I walked about the house, and he graduated to the outdoors; I was always close by. The dog walked with us, but not by Lyndon's weak side. Did the dog know something was wrong with Lyndon's right side? I was able to give Lyndon the care he needed throughout the day and Lyndon was happy to be at my home. I helped Lyndon to say new words and to comprehend their meanings. It was not hard to care for Lyndon; I found it rewarding to see improvements in his small steps, as he learned to walk better.

After a few months in therapy, Lyndon's core muscles were built up. Lyndon learned to stand up alone as he pushed himself in an upward motion with the aid of the chair arms. He also was shown how to roll when he fell and to slide to a place where he could pull himself up. He also had to learn to sign his initials with his left hand.

Lyndon was devoted to his therapy for about a year and a half, and he wanted a break. Lyndon seemed to have reached his goal, and his therapist said that he could take a break; but he never resumed his classes after that. Todd, his therapist left his file open, and Lyndon did stop into Todd's office for help aids and to hear a reassuring word. In a few months, Lyndon was fitted with a leg stimulator, which is worn on his leg muscle. Often it's hard to place it right so that he can lift his foot; a small shock is sent to the muscle to tell the brain that he should step ahead. He wears this today to help him walk, but now the little box is placed around the calf of his leg. That first aid had a small box placed around Lyndon's waist with a wire that ran down his leg. I often had trouble placing that stimulator in the right place. He wasn't always patient with me, and I learned to let Lyndon play with it to get it right.

Lyndon didn't like to be living at Dan's place. Lyndon wanted his independence, and I found it so hard when he left to do his own thing. Dan was heartbroken when Lyndon moved out from his house to live with a friend, about four kilometres away. He lived there for about three months.

I knew Lyndon needed to be guided, but he also needed to be happy. Lyndon drove his side-by-side and came to visit me about once a week. I filled Dan in on Lyndon's progress.

I worried about Lyndon not getting the care that he needed, and I couldn't help him when he was away from my area. I prayed that Lyndon would want to return, but I knew it had to be his idea. My days were filled with anguish, and I felt that Lyndon had not made a good decision. There were many hard days as I tried to understand my son and my grandson too as they struggled to listen to one another.

After a few months, Lyndon did decide to buy a mobile home and move close to Dan's yard. I was glad about his decision, and I took him to the local bank so that he could get a mortgage. Lyndon had an insurance policy so he receives a part of his wage from when he worked. He has enough money to manage comfortably.

I struggled and found myself being over protective as I dwelled on every move that Lyndon made. Lyndon was the one that helped me to move ahead and live my own life as a grandmother. He had his own home, and he was closer now. Lyndon said, "I am an adult, Grandma. I can do it myself." I wrote the following poem:

My Grandson

Oh where, oh where has my grandson gone?
He grew so fast and became so strong.
His legs were short, and his eyes were blue,
His short blond hair had a cow lick too.
He played with toys in the mud when small;
He never was ready if his mother should call.
The years passed by and too soon he's grown,
Ski-doos, quads, and fast trucks he's known.
We warned him and suggested, "Slow down."
Then he went out for a night on the town.
In the early morning of the Christmas rush,
The hospital called; we were all so crushed.
We saw him lying there, so swollen and still,
Then away to the city to doctors with skill.
Slowly and gradually, there's a glimmer of hope,
He's able to get through a day without dope.
The hours and days, then the weeks go past;
We comfort each other and pray it won't last.
The road to recovery was agony and pain,
We asked for patience to keep us all sane.
The winter and snow gave way to the grass,

He learned to walk, and it was a great task.
Each day he moved his right hand with joy,
The hard work made us so proud of our boy.
The teenager who was once stressed by a mole,
Must learn to exercise to reach a big goal.
Forced to leave fun and games behind,
The struggles of life are of a new kind.
Healing means rest as you try to sleep,
These are the rules he learned to keep.
Days and months often turn into years,
I want to reach out to all who have ears.
Never forgetting the decisions you make,
Will help you in the direction you take.
He often told people, "I can do it myself,
I'm not a flower you can put on a shelf.
His life has been altered, but not come to an end,
This heart-breaking message I surely must send
I've struggled through changes; I want you to know,
But don't ever think that he's unable to grow.
Life is a journey and rewards can be found,
Let's have the courage to kneel to the ground.
Praise and thanksgiving we all want to say,
To all who have helped us along the way.

Lyndon had surpassed all expectations that the doctors said he would. Lyndon accepted his new changed life. I gave thanks to God; I knew God gave me the grace to carry out my every action as a grandmother and a caregiver.

Time passed quickly, and his friends spent less time with him. Lyndon said to me, "I have no friends anymore." I remind Lyndon that life has changed for them too. They have women and babies to care for. I think he understood.

Today Lyndon is able to manage his personal needs and drives his side-by-side to our house to play cards with us.

Lyndon's right side is weak; he is disabled and unable to work, but he brings joy to me when he comes to play cards with us, his grandparents. Thanks to all who helped me along this journey!

I learned to face whatever would be and give thanks for waking up healthy each day. Yes, there were days when I was tested, but this was the most rewarding work in my life, and I would do it again in a heartbeat. It took a lot of my energy as Lyndon improved, but the reward was gratifying.

I am available to give Lyndon help when needed. Lyndon appears to be happy, and he can manage with a little help, like being driven to the doctor or for groceries. He is not married and he has no children. Lyndon has had a few girlfriends, but he's often hard to endure when he is having a bad day. However, Lyndon met Chantal in May 2017. She has a one-year-old daughter. Maiah is a joy to be around. I do hope this relationship will grow into a lasting bond.

Chapter 80:
Family Fun

In 2014, I had a sunroom built onto the south side of our living room. I love to sit in the sunshine and feel the sun's rays as it shines through all the glass windows. It's a great place for houseplants too. In the summer, I need window blinds because it is too hot for sitting in and the plants wilt too. This new addition needed to be painted. In 2016, I had a neighbour help me paint the outside of our house. My house is no longer white in colour; it's a two-tone brown. Painting was a big job, but I am very happy with the outcome and the sunroom is the same colour too.

Mom had her ninetieth birthday on October 29, 2014. A celebration was held in her honour. Mom had five generations in attendance. (Mom, Me, Dan, Ashley, and Kianna.) There was a family supper, an open house, and a dance followed. A good time was had by all who attended.

Mom went home a little worn out, but with great memories. The night of her birthday, I think that the flower Mom received wilted before she did. Thanks Mom, you kept us all safe and gave us memories to cherish. All my siblings have grown into adults and no longer seek to impress others. We accept each other for who they are and are thankful to spend time with each other. We are all unique; no one can do what another one can, but each of us has learned to use our talents and make a mark in this world. We have learned to keep open minds and hearts, as we flow in the river of life.

We didn't pull down the shades, but rose up to the challenges when they appeared. Thanks Mom for ruling with an iron hand.

We also have fun at family reunions. At one of our reunions, the Burge girls asked our brothers to sit away from the group as we planned a re-enactment of a dramatic storm, full of rain. A large country map was drawn up. My brother, Grant was asked to explain the weather system in detail as it moved in this area. (Grant can tell a good story.)

Debbie instructed the boys to pay close attention because there was a question period to follow. Five of us girls waited in the kitchen with pails of water and when Grant said that the storm would be much like a tsunami, we ran out and threw the pails of water at the boys. Not one of the boys had expected a thing.

My family played simple games of dress up and appeared to be like a famous movie star. All of our guests were to guess who we were pretending to be. The grandchildren didn't know the older stars, and we didn't know some of the younger stars that they mentioned.

We all are grandparents and a little slower; maybe in a "pokey" mode. Many thrilling stories were kept from Mom when they happened. We sat by the glowing fire, and the boys shared dramatic stories of trips to the drunk tank or about having those cold, hard hand cuffs strapped to them. The stories were a hit, but the girls stories were not as vivid. Our kids roared with laughter at our action-packed past.

Mom declared with a smile, "Those guardian angels must have worked over time to keep my family safe. I did receive many blessings. God never sent a thorn without sending a rose to bloom. I have been truly blessed."

Mom's 91st birthday was a little smaller as 16 members of her family joined her at a restaurant for supper. For Mom's 92nd birthday we gathered at my sister Nioma's for supper.

Mom is in good health, and she enjoys the choice she made to move to the senior's lodge in cold lake. Mom sleeps a lot.

I said to Mom, "Why are you so tired?" Mom was quick to reply, "I missed out on a lot of sleep with the babies and then with teenagers." Lloyd and I visit each week.

At another of our family reunions, my family showed young people how to enjoy some simple events that didn't include cell phones. The cell phones were shut off for a day. Some kids rolled their eyes, and walked away. The adults thought they couldn't do such a thing as they needed to stay connected.

I challenge you at your next reunion to stash all the cell phones for one day and allow kids to enjoy each other's company. The older folks will also take pleasure in "talking to" the younger folks. So go ahead and dare to try something different; let the kids chatter to everyone and see the sparkling eyes and maybe tears of Grandma and aunts and uncles when they tell you stories of days gone by. I became a senior on the 12th day of the 12th month of 2012.

One summer, Lloyd and I went to Mallaig, Alberta for a cancer fundraiser — Haying in the Thirties it was called. There were many activities from the days gone by: haying with horses, threshing, a sawmill, and a stagecoach . I had my first and only ride in a stagecoach. I heard one man say, "This is like visiting a museum in action."

The campsite was a short drive to the town of Mallaig. We enjoyed camping, music, and good food for the weekend. The highlight for me was a trip to Sunday mass with a tractor and wagon. There were about 15 people who arrived with windblown hair, some dust, and a heart full of joy. This brought back memories of my childhood and my First Communion in Pierceland. My family too must have been covered with dust and had windblown hair.

Chapter 81:
Reaching Out to In-Laws

Lloyd's brother, Tone, was that great neighbour that we enjoyed as kids. Tone had a stroke in 2004 and was left speechless and confined to a wheel chair. He never left the care centre for more than a day or two. Tone's family was very good with him. His daughters, Carolyn and Rose Annette, always had him at the local gymkhanas in Pierceland. Tone loved to watch the grandchildren ride their horses in the many events of the gymkhana. Tony didn't feel well, but he wanted to stay and watch the last grandkid ride.

Tone's two daughters, Carolyn and Rose Annette were by his side, as he gently gave up his life. Tone passed away September 1, 2013 in Pierceland. Lorraine, Tone's wife. was diagnosed with cancer in 2017. She enjoyed two of her grandchildren's graduations and a trip to the health spa where her aunt and her daughter came to join them. On June 16, Lorraine celebrated her 85th birthday with family and friends. It was a great party!

Kay Tremblay was another one of Lloyd's sisters. She was about 10 years older than Lloyd, but she and Lloyd were close to each other. Kay would work to help anyone who needed her help. She had a strong body, rough hands, and blue eyes. Her hair had a reddish tinge in it, and it was wavy when she was younger. As she aged, Kay had wave clips that she put in her hair before she went to town.

Kay was an outdoor person who liked to shoot gophers, trap rats, and milk her cows. I soon became close to Kay, and we shared many good times together as we enjoyed many of the same things like the outdoors.

Kay and Lawrence Tremblay were a big part of our family. Lloyd and I were able to give back to Kay and Lawrence when Lawrence became sick. We drove them to Battleford and to Saskatoon for doctor appointments when Lawrence needed attention for health problems. Cancer was diagnosed. After two years and two surgeries, Lawrence lost his fight with cancer. Kay was with him through it all. I went to Pierceland on Monday nights to stay with Lawrence. Kay went to her bingo; she needed time away from all the stress of a terminally sick husband. Lawrence died November 14, 1996.

Kay and Lawrence had always been close to each other and went everywhere together. Now Kay was alone. Kay was determined to make the best out of her single role. I stayed with Kay a night or two after the funeral until she felt she was able to adjust to being alone. She said to me, "You can't stay with me all the time. I will be okay by myself."

I called Kay each day. If she didn't sound good, I went to visit her. Kay never turned down a chance to travel, and she went with me to many places. A day away from home seemed to help Kay.

She said, "Sundays are the worst days, as everybody is with their family; nobody comes to visit me." Kay came home with us after Sunday mass. Kay liked pancakes, and each Sunday, I made pancakes before we played cards. We visited and had supper together. If Lloyd and I were going to visit somebody, she came along with us, as she knew all my family too. Lloyd and I drove her home in the evening. I saw how it helped Kay to be away from her home on Sundays. This lasted for 14 years, until Kay couldn't live alone because her health was failing.

I knew that it was hard news for Kay, and I longed to help her with her decision to leave Pierceland, her friends, and her home. She felt

Five Plus Five Makes Fifteen

that she could still manage fine by herself. Many memories were made there with her husband Lawrence. Why would she want to leave? The future did not look bright for Kay. Mom and Kay were born the same year, in 1924. Mom had a large family; Kay didn't have any children. This separated their understanding of a family, and the how the children are willing to help and support you in all your struggles.

Kay was 85 years old and had never been in the hospital in all her years. Her feet were sore, and she had no energy. I took Kay to her doctor. He said, "Kay your kidneys are failing, and you are getting over pneumonia. You should not live alone." I felt helpless, as I tried to reach out to Kay. I stayed a few days with Kay to cook and support her in any way I could. Lloyd and I were going to see Lyndon in Saskatoon. We drove Kay to her sister, Sal Hickie, in Cold Lake. Kay stayed in Cold Lake with Sal for about a week. We picked her up and brought her back to Pierceland and her home. I stayed with her and cared for her needs. Lloyd and I were going to be gone, and I told Rose Gonie that Kay was sick.

In January of 2011, Henry and Rose took Kay to the hospital. Lloyd and Henry helped Kay to see that another home with people around her for company, bingo, and card playing wasn't so bad. Kay moved to the Cold Lake Lodge in Alberta on February 15, 2011. This was a hard move for Kay, but she struggled through the changes. Lloyd and I visited the lodge, and Lloyd went to see Kay and I went to see Mom and then to see Kay. I missed Kay on Sundays, when she moved. I never seemed to have much time to spend with her at the lodge; when I came from visiting Mom it was time to go home.

Kay lived at the lodge for two years without cooking and other household chores. She made new friends and enjoyed bingo and card playing, but it wasn't home. Kay was hospitalized in July and then again in October. She spent her last three weeks in hospital care. Linette, our daughter in-law, spent the last few nights with Kay.

I offered to stay with Kay, but she said she didn't need me. I was hurt. I had stayed with her and her husband Lawrence in his last days, and I said that I would be there for her too. I guess she thought I was too busy helping Lyndon, and Kay didn't want to take me away from his care.

Kay passed away October 27, 2013 due to kidney failure. Her ashes are placed next to her husband Lawrence in St. Antoninus cemetery, in Pierceland. Kay and Lawrence are at peace.

Soon the months rolled by, and it was time to prepare for Christmas. December is a month filled with joy for many people, as Christmas is a time for family and friends to join in celebrations for the birth of Jesus and to give thanks for all the blessings of the past year. I look back each year and see the many blessings that I have received, as I anticipate the surprises of the year to come.

December 12, 2016, I received a phone call that told me that Lloyd's brother, John, was experienced breathing problems. A lung test revealed an advanced cancer of the lungs and a few months left to live.

John is our daughter, Angie's, godfather. On January 12, we went with Angie and Dean to visit John and Marie. He was in the St. Paul hospital in Saskatoon. John said to Lloyd, "The road is getting narrow."

On January 14, 2017, God called John Gonie home to eternity with his family members at his bedside. At John's request, there was not a funeral service.

Chapter 82:
Looking Forward To A Celebration

My brother, Nelson and his wife Doreen were planning their fiftieth wedding anniversary on January 29, 2016. This was not to take place. On May 13, 2015, the paramedics called me from Nelson's house in Pierceland. Doreen was able to give them my number when she found Nelson under her kitchen window.

The paramedic's words were, "Come to Doreen Burge's place. There's an emergency at Nelson's house."

When I arrived, I met my sister, Lillian, on the doorstep. She often stopped in to see how things were going. Her face was drained, and she said to me, "Nelson is gone; a heart attack has claimed his life."

This was a sad time for our family, as we supported Doreen. Nelson's sisters took charge of his funeral lunch. Each one of us knew how important it was to Nelson to present a good lunch and to be sure there was enough food for everyone present. Judy said, "If I would die suddenly like Nelson, I do not want to be the first to face my brother if we run out of lunch."

Nelson's large funeral was held in Cherry Grove, Alberta. He was laid to rest in that community cemetery. Nelson often spoke his mind, sometimes in ways that were not in loving ways. He had strong opinions and didn't listen to another's way of seeing the situation.

The following months were devastating for Mom, as a child is the hardest death to accept. Nelson had always been a part of Mom's life, and now he would no longer visit her at the lodge. Mom said, "Nelson worked hard and he contributed to the Burge family's wellbeing too."

Mom struggled to see why her son left before she did. Mom kept Nelson's picture close; on her stand by the TV. Mom's kids focussed on her pain and helped her to be restored to her old self, as best she could. Life is a big treasure that cannot be bought or sold. I heard a statement that said, "It isn't the assets that we acquired that make us great, but the relationships that we take time to shape." Nelson had many friends with whom he shared his love for sport fishing, hunting, and visiting. I have heard it said, "If you want friends, you must also be a friend." Nelson was a friend who helped others. Doreen, Nelson's wife, found it hard to be alone. Her boys tried to support her, but it seemed that Doreen needed more help than either of them could give her.

A year after Nelson's death, Doreen looked for Nelson, and called Lillian to help her find him. Doreen struggled to accept that Nelson was not coming home. Kirk and Lillian went in to town to help Doreen understand that Nelson was not going to come home. Debbie, Lillian, and I visited Doreen each week while she was at home; she didn't want to leave her home. Doreen soon was hallucinating and didn't trust anyone. She accused people of stealing her money and her goods.

Lillian and I took Doreen shopping, as she was not reliable to drive herself. Lillian was excellent with Doreen, and Doreen listened to Lillian. Lillian made two and three trips to town to keep Doreen safe and took her food that she could eat without using the stove range. This care lasted for about one year before the health system was able to test her. Doreen was broken; she needed more care.

How hard it was to find a place for Doreen when she refused to believe that all was not well with her. "I am managing okay by myself," she said.

We took Doreen into the hospital in Goodsoil so that she could have blood work done. Doreen was tested while she in that facility. The health professionals agreed that Doreen should not be alone in her house.

I'm haunted by the little white lies that I had to tell her to get her to agree to enter into that facility. I could not say hospital or old folk's home; she wanted no part of those places. Doreen's sons thanked us; it was not a call that they could make. They wanted her to be safe and told us that they couldn't take her from her home.

In June of 2017, Doreen was accepted in the Goodsoil facility. I know Doreen will be well cared for, but how it hurts to see her longing to return to her home. I put myself in her place, and I know that I wouldn't want to leave my home either. I will support her with a visit.

The seasons moved along and I found myself another year older and a little bit wiser. Summer is a pleasure with the full sun, a warm rain to keep all of creation growing, and visits from new and old acquaintances. Each passing year takes me to another age, and I feel my body not wanting to do all the activities that I once did. I am thankful to be healthy, mobile, and able to enjoy my writing. I have made a life of memories to share with my family too. I want to use my talents, as I flow in the river of life. I want to prepare for more occasions when my big family gathers. Coffee is always ready at all of the Burge families' homes.

Chapter 83:
My Sisters And Brothers

My story wouldn't be complete without more information about my siblings. Below is a short version about each of their unique characters and a few events that I recall sharing with them.

Nioma Irene Burge was the first twin born on November 23rd of 1943. She entered the world at the Edson hospital three months early. Nioma weighed in at 3 pounds, 10 ounces. She and her twin spent the first three months in the hospital.

Nioma was the stronger of the twins and soon took the leading role in all matters. Her twin was content to follow after her and learn from her example. Mom said, "From a young age, Nioma was responsible. When I became sick with yellow jaundice, Nioma was ten years old. I was too weak to get up and Nioma bathed and cared for George, as he lay beside me on my bed."

When Nioma and her twin, Nelson, started school, they walked about 2 miles to the little country school house. It was a one-classroom school with one teacher who taught grades one through eight. Mom said, "Nelson and Nioma held hands as they walked."

Nioma had her brother Nelson close to her; what else would she need. Today all the twins share a special bond. Nioma is a strong lady.

Sometimes she uses harsh words that often offend people, but maybe she is hurting and doesn't know the impact that her words have on another person. Nioma is emotional and caring; she volunteers in the community, in church, and at the seniors' functions.

Mom was afraid of Nioma maturing too fast and leaving the nest; Mom's reliable help would be gone. Nioma is four years older than me and able to run the household. I learned many things from Nioma; she was the one who told me about the birds and the bees. I doubted many of the things that she said to me. Nioma found school hard and quit in grade ten. Was it because she was too tired, as the eldest in this big family? Nioma said, "I don't ever remember having fun. I always had to work."

When Nioma was eighteen years old, she went to care for three children whose mother was at summer school. Nioma kept in touch with this family, as Bill was the teacher's brother. Nioma and Bill started to date and were married two years later.

Nioma was not afraid to try new things. One day she wanted an old cupboard to fit into a smaller space. She asked Bill to help her. Bill said, "I will cut off the cupboard when I have time." Nioma became impatient with the wait. She got the handsaw from the shop, and she cut the cupboard to make it fit. Bill said, "Woman, I was going to do that."

Nioma and Bill had four children: Victor, Norman, Gordon, and Myrna. Nioma and Bill worked together on the farm until Bill's heart attack in May 1977. After some time, Nioma and Bill bought a house in town and moved with three children. Her son, Victor was now 19 years old took over all the responsibilities on the farm.

Bill had a stroke in 1983. Nioma was determined to raise her son Gordon and her daughter Myrna. Nioma worked at many jobs to pay the bills. Nioma worked at school as an aid for disabled children. She also worked at the post office. She knit sheep wool socks to sell too.

Bill passed away on October 30, 1989. Bill was tired of lying around. One day he refused to take his pills. Bill passed away at home. Nioma went to call him for supper, and found him deceased.

Nioma was alone for about ten years, then Nioma met Marvin Hatch, and they were married on November 5, 1999. Marvin and Nioma moved to White Court, Alberta for a short time. They bought a quilting machine, and when they returned to Pierceland, they bought a quilting shop and Nioma gave quilting lessons. Marvin and Nioma bought a café and served people for about 2 years. Nioma bought a house for resale. This worked out well and she purchased another and another. Nioma helped with the remodelling, did the painting, and some landscaping. Nioma has worked hard, a talent she learned at an early age. (Mom never allowed anyone to be idle.)

Nioma also kept her kids busy. Her children said to her, "If you were the Prime Minister there would be no unemployment. You can find work for everyone."

Today, Nioma and her husband live west of Pierceland. They enjoy their acreage with a big green house and sell bedding plants and vegetables too.

Their dog and horses also enjoy Nioma's attention. Nioma does crafts, bakes, and quilts. This is when Marvin hitches his team and goes for a drive around the block.

Nioma has six grandchildren that are the best!

Victor, Nioma's oldest son, married Celana Pikowicz, his high school sweetheart in 1986. They have three children: Tifarah Rose, born in 1988; Jake, born in 1990; and Briar, born in 1994. Victor and Celana's girls were involved in the high school rodeos and won many awards. Both girls won scholarships that took them to the States too.

Tifarah was the high school Canadian champion in barrel racing. Tifarah married Ryan Monteith, and they make their home on acreage in Cold Lake, Alberta. Their daughter, Leah Rose was born in August 2016, making Nioma a great-grandmother.

Jake, Victor's son, enjoyed dog racing that took him to northern British Columbia and to Manitoba. He too was a winner many times. Jake has his carpenter's papers. He is kept busy building and repairing all sorts of buildings. Jake also has a cement business, making concrete look like old planks. Both businesses keep him working. Jake makes his home in Pierceland. He is not married.

Briar is studying in the United States; she is interested in the environment and will be a biologist when her schooling is done.

Briar also loved her barrel racing horse and won the barrel racing at many rodeos.

Nioma's second son is Norman William. He works in the oil field and is married to Shirley. They do not have any children, but Norman enjoys Shirley's kids from a former marriage. They both enjoy their grandchildren.

Gordon Dale, Nioma's third son, is a professional roofer in Edmonton. He married Darla Eistetter, a local girl. Darla is an accountant and works in the city. Their home is in Edmonton, Alberta. They have three children: Ben was born in 2003; Kamryn Patricia was born in 2005; and Jayda Rose was born in 2008.

Myrna is Nioma's daughter. She is a school teacher and lives in Pierceland. She is not married and does not have children. Myrna is active in the Catholic Women's League and organizes many caterings and church functions and teaches religion to preschooler kids, as their parents attend mass.

Nelson Joseph Burge is Nioma's twin and also premature by three months and born in Edson. Nelson was 3 pounds, seven ounces. Nelson struggled to survive at birth. Nelson was watched over constantly by a nun, as he threatened to stop breathing. Mom went to the hospital every day to see her twins and bond with them. When Mom took Nelson home in January, he weighed almost five pounds. Later, Nelson took convulsions; Mom was told to keep his body warm and his head cold. When he was about four years old, he got severe ringworm, and he was kept in the hospital for three weeks. He had many shots of penicillin, and after this, he never had another convulsion.

Mom remembers how Nelson would wait for Nioma to try new things before he tackled them. As the oldest boy in a large family, Nelson worked hard at an early age. He was seven years old when the family moved to Charlie Larson's place for the winter months. It was Nelson's job to carry snow indoors to melt for water, and Nelson cleaned the stalls each day too. Nelson went with Dad for firewood, forked loose hay onto the hayrack, and fed the cows, pigs, and horses.

He struggled in school, and when the teacher said that school was not for him, he quit. He was 15 years old. He went to Fort Kent, Alberta to work for a pig farmer, cleaning barns. He worked two years for two pure-bred cows. Nelson went to work, and Dad sold these cows because he was not there to help look after them. Nelson said, "I didn't receive any money for my cows. Dad kept the money."

Nelson also went to Primrose Lake fishing with Dad. These days were not good days for Nelson, and he didn't like the cold weather. Nelson once said, "Driving in the cold was the easy part of fishing. Working with the old man who screamed and yelled all day long was not going to happen again. A person must be out of their mind to work in the cold all day and fall into bed to prepare for the next dreadful day."

The short winter days were too long on the dreadful lake. Nelson went to work and didn't come home to go fishing.

Nelson wanted perfection in whatever task he did; his image was important to him. This made it hard to work with Nelson, as he was hard to please. He said, "If I do it myself, it is done right." Nelson was outspoken and often voiced his opinion when it wasn't called for. His opinions weren't always accepted, but he was always ready to help others with a job and would do more than his share of the work.

Nelson was very responsible and loved to work. Nelson was about seventeen years old when he and Peter Toma went to Eston, Saskatchewan to work for the fall harvest. The big combines were so much better than the old threshing machine that came to our farm to do the harvest for Dad. Nelson returned for the harvest for about three years. Nelson stayed with Uncle Len for about a month, and he worked for awhile in the grain elevator too.

Nelson bought his first car in the south; a green 1952 Ford. I thought it was the best car I had ever ridden in. Dad was not so happy. As an adult, I know the worry of your child with wheels is a big change. Dad knew that his son was growing up and would soon leave the family unit. Nelson took Doreen, his girlfriend and me to the outdoor drive-in show.

When Nelson came home from the south, he worked at the grain elevator in Grand Centre for eight months. He also worked on the golf course at the air base as a grass cutter for one summer. Doreen's cousin, Daryl Ayres, works on the rigs and he said to Nelson, "If you want to make more money, you need to go to the oilrigs." Nelson went with Daryl and started to work on the oilrigs. In 1965, Nelson and his family went to Singapore, and he worked on the oilrigs there. He worked on the rigs and moved up the ladder until he became consultant with his own business. He retired in 2012. Nelson enjoyed his work.

Nelson and Doreen were married in January 1966. Their first home was in Edson, Alberta. Most of Nelson's work was in that area. Later in 1975, they bought some land in Cherry Grove and moved in a trailer. The oil business took them too many towns; their biggest move was to Singapore for two years in 1977. In 1981, he returned from Singapore and built a big cedar home in Cherry Grove where their trailer was; it was beautiful. Their home was a joy to both of them, and they often had family gatherings in their large house. Lloyd and I and our family often went to Doreen and Nelson's home to visit as Lloyd and Nelson played pool.

Nelson bought a new car too. His car was a 1982 Dodge which was the top of the line. He was proud of his new car.

Nelson and Doreen have two boys: Wade Nelson Burge and Zane Walter Burge. Their boys enjoyed the farm with horses and quads to ride about and chase anything that moved. Wade works on the oilrigs. He has one daughter, Brandi Dawn. She graduated from the Cold

Lake high school in 2014.

Zane and Debbie have two sons: Jesse and Marshal. Both of Zane's boys live in British Columbia with their mother, Debbie. Zane doesn't see his boys any longer. Zane is a quiet and reserved lad who sticks to himself. He worked in Winnipeg, Manitoba where he met Jody Kuivenhoven.

On September 29, 2007, Zane married Jody. They moved to Pierceland after a few years of living in Manitoba. Zane and Jody were often at Doreen's to help her after Nelson passed away in May 2015.

Nelson's yard was well kept, and he had many comments by all who passed by. His Christmas display was the envy of many folks, as Santa and his sleigh seemed to fly between the house and garage. The many lights glittered throughout the crispy Christmas season. Nelson and Doreen sold their house in Cherry Grove, Alberta and moved to Pierceland in 2003.

Nelson had a positive attitude. He said, "Life is what you want it to be, and it's up to you to make it so."

Nelson was close to Mom and never forgot her birthday or Mother's Day, often taking her flowers. Mom has the orchard plant that Nelson brought to her a few days before he passed away. Nelson had a fatal heart attack on May 13, 2015. He rests in the Cherry Grove cemetery.

Lloyd Raymond Burge was born on February 5, 1946. He was the third child and not as responsible as Nelson. It was fine with Lloyd if another person made the decisions. Lloyd often found trouble but could wiggle his way out of it or talk another person into taking the heat for him.

Mom said, "As a baby, Lloyd was cute and chubby." Maybe she had more time to dwell on him, as there was only one baby. Lloyd soon learned to make this distinct character work for him. His big blue eyes and broad smile were a real clincher. Lloyd was not shy and could warm up to all people. Mom and Dad were easy on him. He could always talk his way out of trouble and turn any situation into a joke.

Lloyd threw the shovel down the basin hole while we were fishing. It was Nelson who went to tell Dad that the snow shovel fell down the hole. Dad never did know that it was Lloyd who threw the shovel down the hole to show Barb how the wooden handle would float. Nelson was the one who needed to use his feet to clean the ice from the basin hole, as we continued to fish.

Lloyd went to school in that little country school at Black Raven. He walked with the twins, and wanted them to carry him because he was tired. I'm thinking that Nioma or Nelson often did.

At school, Lloyd soon learned that he could get his way with a good story or a joke. He did love to laugh and was often the life of the party. Work was not a priority for him and often found a way out of work.

Lloyd was the one that bought vogue tobacco and thin papers to roll cigarettes. I was Lloyd's helper, and I stood in the barn door and watched to be sure nobody was coming to the barn. He also showed me how to roll cigarettes.

Lloyd was a crafty person; he would be sick until Dad and Nelson left the yard to get wood. Mom saw through this and sent Lloyd to carry water. The pail was only half full when he got to the house. He seemed to know that Nelson would carry the rest when he came home.

Lloyd got along well at school and had many friends, but soon he wanted to have money and buy a car like Nelson. Lloyd was 16 when he quit school and went to Edson, Alberta to work on the rigs. Lloyd worked the oilrigs all his life.

Lloyd met Rita and they had 36 years together. Rita was a pretty, outgoing, and strong lady. She was like a queen to Lloyd. They went overseas to the Baltic Sea, Libya, Scotland, and England. Dad and Lewis flew to Scotland to visit Lloyd and Rita at Easter time in March 1977. Dad enjoyed this trip with Lewis. Dad was amazed at the Amsterdam airport. It was so large!

Lloyd returned to Canada and became interested in horse racing. The track was a joy for him. Soon he bought thoroughbred horses and tried to raise a winner. Lloyd did win a few smaller races, but the stakes soon became too large to play in. His dream of winning the Kentucky Derby never happened, but his love for his horses never changed. Lloyd and Rita lived in Innisfail, Alberta on forty beautiful acres. Rita was Lloyd's chore boy, and she was also a caregiver when Lloyd fell and broke both wrists. She helped him do everything. She put on her bathing suit and helped him shower. Lloyd was not a good patient and didn't thank Rita for her help. What a big heart Rita must have had, as she waited on Lloyd and tried to please him.

Lloyd went back to work away from home and felt that it was too costly to have a hired hand. Rita watched the clock and did the chores on time, as Lloyd demanded. Rita was diagnosed with cancer, went for treatments, and won her battle. Lloyd struggled to keep the horses while Rita struggled to live.

On March 19, 2010, Rita called Lloyd for breakfast. There was no answer, so she went to wake him. Lloyd had passed away in his sleep. Lloyd was resting peacefully. His heart could no longer handle his stress that he kept so well hidden. Lloyd had no children.

Barbara Ann Burge: I am the fourth child in the family. I am less than five feet tall, have shabby hair, and brown eyes. I now weigh about 115 pounds, but as I grow older, I seem to gain about a pound a year. My weight is important to me, and I refuse to be a person who "waddles" when they move from one place to another. I walk 1.5 kilometres each morning, say my rosary, and enjoy my dog by my side. I plant a garden and give many vegetables away to my family. I pick blueberries on most afternoons in August. I too am a strong-willed being and worked to make a good marriage with my husband Lloyd.

We learned what is important and accepted each other; no longer wanting to change a thing about the other. We celebrated our fifty-first wedding anniversary in July 2017. I have four children, six grandchildren and four great-grand children. I enjoy all my family members. I am devoted to my Catholic faith and attend mass each Sunday to give thanks for the past week and to ask for blessing for all family members in the coming week.

I'm thinking that my writing gives you many of my heartfelt actions, and I won't repeat anything more.

Judy Evelyn Burge is the next in line in my family. Judy and I were born 14 months apart. Judy and I have shared many events; what one could do, the other could also. I know that everyone grows at a different pace.

I recall that I was upset when Mom bought Judy a brassiere before she bought me one. I was older and should have been more mature. How foolish this sounds now.

Judy loved sports, horses, and the outdoors. We spent many days romping about the cool meadow grass with the Hewlett kids. Their parents were haying in the nearby meadow. We played among the willows and pretended to have little rooms near the willow roots where the ground had bare patches.

Our old horse Pal took us on adventures to Janice Seland's house. All three of us girls would ride Pal; Judy was in charge of the reins.

Judy is a strong-willed person and this led her to many rivalries. She never backed down and earned her place in the pecking order. Judy was able to express her opinion to all people; a trait she never lost. Judy is a caring person and is willing to help others in need, but she also insists that they need to make things better for themselves. Judy said, "There are jobs out there, and you need to start at the bottom and work your way up." Judy had many boyfriends and went to dances and rodeos often. I chose only one; Lloyd, the man I later married.

Judy left school early to go to hairdressing school in Calgary. Dad took Judy to Calgary where she boarded with Dad's sister, Mary; an old aunt that was not known to her. Aunt Mary worked the night shift, and Judy went to school in the daytime. Judy never saw much of Aunt Mary.

Nelson and Doreen moved to Calgary a few months later, and Judy stayed with Nelson and Doreen. Judy worked at a bus depot, at a drug store, and helped with kids too. It was her determination to succeed that led her to become a good hair stylist. Her hairdressing certificate was earned in 1967 and is displayed in her shop. While Judy was in Calgary, she met Bud Bercier, an electrician. Judy and Bud enjoyed each other for about 2 years. They married in November 1968 and made their home in Calgary. Bud worked in Calgary and later in Fort McMurray at an oil well plant as an electrician. Judy and Bud have two daughters: Meloney Bercier and Tracy Bercier.

In 1972, their family moved to Fort Kent, Alberta on a quarter of land. Bud bought a few cows, and Judy soon managed her own hairdressing shop in Bonnyville, Alberta.

Ostriches became part of their workload. This was a new venture, and they learned a lot about those big birds. Some of the large eggs that were not fertile were drained and painted on to be sold for display in arts and crafts shows. Caring for the ostriches was constant work, and it tied Judy and Bud down each day. The ostriches were sold after a few years. Judy and Bud's girls went to school in Bonnyville. Both girls were involved in synchronized swimming. Judy became a coach, and they travelled to many competitions.

Both girls graduated and pursued careers.

Judy and Bud had a rocky marriage, and in 1993, they were divorced. Judy moved to Cold Lake, where she continued to work as a hairdresser—a job she held for forty years. Judy enjoys dancing, crafts, gymkhanas, and travelling.

Meloney, her first daughter, is a paramedic, and works in the north. She married Dean Mans but later divorced. Meloney lives in Cold Lake, Alberta. She loves to travel. She met Randy Cross, and they were married in Jamaica with family and friends present. They do not have children. Meloney said, "I'll enjoy my sister's kids, and I don't have to discipline them." This sounds like Grandma's words.

Tracy went to secretarial school. She returned home and found a job in the Cold Lake area. Tracy was our typist for our family cookbook. She married Jim Gagnon. This marriage failed, and Jim and Tracy divorced. There were no children.

Tracy has always loved horses and farm life. She competed at the local gymkhanas and won often. Tracey ran for the rodeo queen for the "Little Britches" rodeo in Cherry Grove, Alberta. She won this competition.

Tracy met Andy Urlacher at a gymkhana. They both like horses, and soon they enjoyed one another. Today Andy and Tracy live on a farm near Goodsoil, Saskatchewan. Tracy and Andy have two children: Cheyanne and Rhett.

Judy likes to spend time with them on their farm near Goodsoil. Andy works for a local contractor. Judy, Tracy, and the girls saddle up, pack a lunch, and ride about the pasture on trail rides. The roasted wieners are always delicious and a highlight for the kids. The kids attend the Pierceland School. Both children love the outdoors and sports. In winter, they are busy at the rink as they both play hockey.

Judy likes to travel and has a winter holiday each year. The warm climate of Mexico is often her destination.

Graham Harold Burge is Grant's twin. Mom told me that, as a baby, Graham was content to sit back and watch Grant try new stuff. Mom said, "Graham sat back and looked out through the bars of the crib and giggled as the cat rubbed her tail along the crib. Grant was the one who would try to catch the cat through the rails."

Graham was about three years old when the Cold Lake air base began to fly their planes over our house. Graham often screamed in fear and jumped around in a circle when he heard loud noises. Were the jets and planes to blame for these panic traumas?

Graham was observant. A neighbour man came each year to do our fall threshing. He was a Romanian who enjoyed his whiskey, and he spoke with an accent. Graham asked him why he talked funny and why he had a big red nose. The man said to Graham, "Why do you have a big mouth and ask so many questions?"

Graham is not a person who can see what needs to be done; his selfish ways often leave his wife, Earla, carrying all the groceries, the luggage, and their kids too. Graham often does his own thing and others are dumbfounded.

Graham dreamed of being rich. As a young boy he collected the paper coverings of tin cans and stored them away in his dresser drawer. That was his pile of money bills. I know Mom never cooked out of cans, and Graham never found much money while he lived at home.

Graham worked for the neighbours and saved his money until he could buy a motorbike. He spent his free time riding about the countryside. His shinny black bike was stored in the barn in the winter. His brothers gazed at that bike with longing but didn't dare touch Graham's prize possession. Graham still enjoys his bike and goes biking with his buddies. He now has a bigger and better bike.

Graham's longing for money grew. He dropped out of school in grade nine and ventured to the oilrigs. He worked his way up and became a consultant for the oil company. Graham married Earla Marcellus in 1975. Earla has short blonde hair, greenish eyes, and an amazing laugh. She was the lady who organized that wonderful trip to the Eastern provinces in 1998 for the Burge reunion. I enjoy her laugh, as she is able to laugh as loud as the rest of her in-laws. Earla is a determined girl who finished high school by correspondence after she was married. She took up bookkeeping and works around the Bonnyville area. She volunteers for the abuse shelter and finds time to bowl each week. She and Graham make their home on a large acreage in Cold Lake, Alberta.

Graham is an avid golfer. Now as a semi-retired person, he hits the park early in the morning when the birds are singing and enjoys a few rounds of gulf.

Graham bought a house in Arizona to enjoy the sun. After a few years, he sold that house, as there was a lot of maintenance to do, and

Earla wasn't ready to move there.

Graham and Earla's two children are Kim and Petrina. Both children graduated from the Cold Lake High School and moved on to careers.

Kim played soccer as a goalkeeper at the provincial level. Kim went to be a pipefitter and works in the Cold Lake area. He married Nicole. Nicole works as a teacher's aide for the Cold Lake School division. They have two children: Payton and Joshua.

Petrina finished school and went to business management at Mount Royal College in Calgary. She has always worked, but she makes time for her family too. Petrina is married to Larry Johnson. He is a good father and a husband. Larry works in the construction area. They have two children: Kerris and Jacey. They make their home in St. Albert, Alberta.

Grant Malcolm Burge is Graham's twin. Grant was the leader in most of the twins' encounters. It was Grant that wanted to go to the lake for a boat ride. Graham didn't like water much, but he soon helped with the launching of the old boat. The boys twisted and turned the vessel until it was in the water. The old wooden boat was not in good shape. The twins climbed aboard and used a stick to push themselves out into the slough. They drifted a few metres from shore when the boat tipped over. Grant panicked when he landed in the cold water. Grant thrashed and wailed about in terror. Graham's fear of water didn't stop him now. He stood up and sternly grabbed his twin. "Stand up," he said. The water was about a half a metre deep.

Grandma Timmoth focused on Grant and marked him as the "bad one". Grandma said to Mom, "Evelyn, that boy is going to be a handful. You need to step on him now." Mom was too busy to worry about Grandma's little comments. Grant heard this statement and often did little things like gently stepping on Grandma's toe when he passed by her. Grant likes to challenge many things and is verbal too. He is often in a debate over his strong feelings.

Grant is a thinker. He claimed he could figure out any problem. He was a headstrong teenager, who thought he knew everything. Dad tried to discipline him. Dad said, "Get out and see how hard it is to make it in this world." Grant looked at Dad and said, "You told all my brothers to leave; I think it your turn to leave." This was not a good scene. Grant went down the road mumbling. He did learn to respect and admit that there is always a person in authority. This lesson helped him all through his life. Grant is Mom's only son that finished high school. He attended college and became an accountant. Grant could make his few cents reach; he rode the bus a few times for 10 cents because he used a lot of pennies, and he said they made a lot of noise as they were put into the dish, and nobody was going to stop to count the money.

It was in Calgary that he met and married Cleo Baker. Grant brought Cleo to meet the family. Cleo had dark hair, a round face with a big smile, and joined in all the fun. Grant and Cleo were married in 1975. Grant and Cleo like curling in the winter and camping in the summer. Grant and Cleo lived in Grand Prairie while the children were in school. Grant worked as secretary treasurer of the Catholic school District for over twenty years. He and his wife attended mass each week and helped with the parish functions; raising money to help the church support a soup kitchen and children's activities.

They have three children: Corey, Bryce, and Brandi.

Corey married Emma Laver, and they had three children: Brian, who lived just a few weeks, and Jacob and Adrianna, who are busy people and a joy to be around. Corey's marriage ended in divorce. He is married now to Veronica.

Bryce has not married. His love is music — namely his guitar and saxophone. He works as a butcher. Brandi went to college and is a registered nurse. She now works at teaching other nurses. Brandi and Bill have three children: Bailey, Brody, and Brieanne. Their home is in Sylvan Lake Alberta.

George Earl Burge is also a twin. Mom had two sets of twin boys in just over a year (four babies in thirteen months). When George was born, his twin Leonard was born with collapsed lungs and only lived a short while. George was a strong baby and grew fast.

George wanted to do whatever Grant and Graham did. At a young age, he was the same size as they were. George is easygoing and tries to make people happy. If there is work to do, he is right there doing his share. George is over six feet tall and has broad shoulders. His blue eyes sparkle when he can help others work. George is kind and helpful to all people. George passed his grade nine and started to work. He went to the pipeline. George worked for the pipeline for over forty years. He enjoys his work and didn't let his sixtieth birthday slow him down. He said, "I want to work until I can no longer move and as long as people are willing to put up with me." He's referred to as "the old man" on the job. He works as an inspector.

George wakes up early and is in bed by 8 p.m. George married Rozalyn Pylypiw, and they have one daughter, Jolene Burge. Rozalyn was a good mother to Jolene. She liked her jewels. She was a slim lady, had painted nails, and liked to turn the heads of all men. This came to be a problem, and their marriage ended in divorce. Rozalyn passed away in July 1995. George did his part to raise his daughter with the help of Rita, Lloyd's wife. Jolene went to college and now has a job as an environmentalist. She lives and works in the south and enjoys the outdoor work.

George has always loved to work in the outdoors. George's second marriage was to Kathryn in 1994. She was raising four daughters. This marriage also ended in divorce. Was it the girls who played a part, or was his work a priority and did Kathryn feel that she was alone much of the time?

George had a quadruple bypass in 2000. He lost weight by going to the gym and exercising. It was hard for him to slow down and allow himself to heal. He is healthy again. George now lives with Wendy. Wendy is a nature person and spends hours watching the wild life that visits their acreage. Each spring, a deer comes and has her two fawns in the little clearing by the fence. Wendy is compatible with George. They live in Rocky Mountain House, Alberta. Wendy is a plain, down-to-earth lady, who is happy with their home — a log cabin nestled in the spruce trees. The furniture is handmade from the trees that were grown in that area. Their acreage is home to moose, deer, and noisy squirrels. George is proud to display his dream home, as he should be. George is a great person who will help anyone with a problem. He wants all people to feel that they are here to make this world a better place to live in. George goes to the coffee shop each day, as Wendy likes to sleep in late.

Lillian Rose Burge is a twin to Lewis. Lorraine Gonie worked at the hospital when these twins were born. Lorraine said, "I enjoyed caring for two babies that were so cute." Lillian became the leader in this duo. At school, she defended her brother many times. The twins are still close. Lillian isn't afraid to give her opinion as she tries to lead her family members. Lillian is a loving and compassionate lady, always ready to help others. She was a big help when Doreen Burge struggled in her home. Lillian went to check on Doreen two and three times a day. Lillian is the one who likes the mirror. Her hair always appears like she has come from the hairdresser's shop. She has a wit about her that helps anyone who is feeling down to see a brighter side of things. She has the ability to respond with a phrase or a story that makes us all laugh and move on to a better place.

Lillian met Kirk Sharp, and they were married in 1972. Kirk is a small man in stature, but his heart is big as he worked for his family. He has a full head of hair and not any grey ones, as a senior. Kirk listens before he speaks, and he and Lillian support one another in all matters. Lillian and Kirk continues to draw people and many folks drop in for a cup of coffee and her hospitality. She takes pride in her house, cooking, and gardening. Kirk and Lillian live on a ranch in the

Pierceland area. At one time they had pasture land about 40 kilometres from home. In the spring and in the fall about twenty cowboys helped move the cattle to greener pastures.

Kirk and Lillian have three children: Kirk, Michelle, and Christie. Kirk Jr. finished high school and now works as a welder. He loves horses as his dad and grandfather did. Kirk races pony chariots and pony chuck wagons. Kirk won many races too. I recall taking his grandma, Violet Sharp, and Kay to watch Kirk in the chuck wagon and chariot races. Kirk also played hockey, meeting Shauna at the rink. Kirk and Shauna were together for a few years. They have three children: Tristan, Keisha, and Bronwyn. This relationship came to an end, and the children went with their mother. Kirk is now with Mallory and they have a daughter Paisley.

Michelle was married to Robin Todd; they had Caitlyn Rose Lee Todd. That marriage ended in divorce. She is now married to Maurice Bernier. They have two children: Colton and Chaelyn. Michelle works as a secretary for a large company.

Christie married Kyle Gross; they had two children: Dharma and Myah. That marriage ended in divorce. Christie is now married to Darcy Ford, and they have one child, Jackson Ford. Jackson is a joy to be around.

Christie is now an aid at the local school. She volunteers for many of the children's activities. She is kept busy as she takes her girls to dance each week. The girls went to Las Vegas with their dance and had a good time.

Lillian enjoys her grandchildren and is often involved in their activities. She has travelled to Disneyland with her daughter and some of her grandchildren.

Lillian spends time visiting at the lodge where Mom lives. All the ladies gather around to share coffee and a laugh. Lillian is never bored and helps where she is needed. Lillian is in charge of Mom's pills and has the prescriptions filled when Mom's pills are low.

Lewis Robert Burge is an adventurous character. His childhood was not boring. Lewis was the youngest of Grant, Graham, and George. Maybe this was the reason Lewis was always in trouble. He couldn't run as fast, so he was often caught, and he didn't know how to put the blame on others. When the boys helped Dad cut the potato eyes from planting, it was Lewis who thought Dad was too fussy about the size. Lewis jabbed the knife into the potato and said, "You can cut your own dam potatoes." Lewis stood to leave, but when Dad stood up, Dad blocked the door. Lewis soon sat down and cut the potatoes the size that Dad wanted.

When Lewis was a teenager; Dad helped Lewis hitch our old horse to the stone boat to get some straw bales for the next day's feeding. The square bales were loaded, and Lewis took the reins to drive home. The horse lunged through the deep snow and toward the road. A big Co-op truck was coming down the highway. Lewis was not able to stop the horse. The big semi could not stop either. The driver of the truck laid on the horn. Lewis pulled on the reins, and yelled "whoa" for the horse to stop. The old grey horse was stronger than Lewis and was able to jerk the lines out from his hands. Dad yelled and Lewis took a head dive into the ditch. Old King was out of control and sped across the highway. The truck drove over the stone boat and the bales. The bales were scattered all over the road. The horse went home without Lewis.

When Dad got afraid, he also got angry. Dad arrived home and gave Lewis a tongue lashing for being so stupid. Lewis removed the horse's harness and spent the evening in his room to think about all the dangers he had experienced.

Lewis had a good imagination and used it to make our play more fun. In the summer, a popular game was Cowboys and Indians. Lewis decided that the cowboys needed ropes to swing, and the Indians needed tomahawks. Lewis never planned on getting caught by the cowboys. He was caught, and the other boys decided to string him up. The rope was around his neck and getting tight, when my sister ran to his rescue. Lewis was truly a captured Indian. He was always in the centre of the all action.

I recall running to retrieve the small hatchet from George when he was chasing Grant. That brought an end to playing a game with real weapons.

Many near death experiences are part of Lewis's life. He has rolled a quad and broke his pelvis, was in many different vehicle accidents, and slid away from a tractor wheel just in time, as that large back tire rolled into the spot where he had been. He has had encounters with wild life too, including once when the gun jammed and another person shot the charging moose. Lewis also outran the cops and drove through their roadblocks. He said, "Those boys in blue dove for the ditch, as I pealed rubber and went through their barricade." Do angels work overtime? Life was never dull where Lewis was. He still can bring people running to his house. Now it's for a gathering of the clan, as his yard and large fire pit is attractive. Lewis has worked many jobs, including on pipelines, rigs, trucks, and in construction and as a grounds keeper. Today he is the shop manager for a local company and is home each night.

He married Dawn Nault, when he was just out of high school. This marriage didn't last. There were no children.

In 1979, Lewis married Lavinia Sharp. They live in the Cold Lake area. Lavinia always has goodies to enjoy. She is a short lady, carries a full body, and is willing to help at all functions. She is involved in the farmers' market and attends with her fresh honey from their bees and makes pickles and jams to sell. Lavinia is a giving person. When I visit, I often come home with some article she bought on sale or something she found at the market. Thanks Lavinia.

Lewis' passion is fishing. He has a big boat and each summer he and Lavinia travel to the West Coast to salmon fish. I often say to his wife, "What kind of a holiday do you have sitting in a boat, as Lewis fishes?" Lavinia is an easygoing person and waits on Lewis in all things. Her big smile and her open arms are there to pick Lewis up when needed.

They have two children: Joseph and Cody. Joseph is the eldest son; he is married to Stacey White. He works in construction and as a truck driver and now has his picker license too. Stacey, his wife, works in an office at the health care centre in Cold Lake. They live in Cherry Grove, Alberta on a small farm. Joseph and Stacey have two children: Carter William Lewis and Ciara Lena Marie.

Cody is the second son. He is a pipe fitter and lives in the Cold Lake area. He married Brandi. They have one daughter Aura.

Debra Mary Burge was a shy little girl. The first day of school she wanted to follow Lillian into her class room. Was it because there was always someone by her side at home, as she worked and played indoors or outdoors? Her teachers helped her to gradually overcome her shyness. Now she is able to speak in front of a group of people.

Debbie has always loved her sports. She was on the high school soft ball team, curling team, and tried her hand at hockey too. Debra graduated from high school and went to Edmonton to work in an office. Later she received her diploma in office administration. Debbie married Larry Hempel in 1976. Larry is a big, strong man with light hair, big lips, and big hands. He is a hard worker and can fix whatever needs to be fixed. This is an asset on his cattle ranch. They have two children: Carson and Marcy

Debbie soon learned to drive all the machinery and worked alongside of her husband when the kids were in school. In the summer, when it was time to put up the winter's feed for the cattle, Debbie was in the field too, as she drove the swather ahead of the silage cutter.

It was a big event as Larry, Deb, and Larry's Dad calved out about 400 head of cows. These calves sometimes got sick and need attention. Anyone who has worked on a farm will know that the hours of sleep are short in the spring time. Debra learned to spot sick calves, and she kept a list of which calf belonged to what cow.

Debbie isn't afraid to work hard. She likes gardening and can grow many tomatoes and cucumbers; she gives many vegetables away to others. I have received many tomatoes.

Debbie and Larry are both sports minded, and they like to curl in the winter time, winning many tournaments.

After the family was grown, Debbie worked at the Health Centre in Goodsoil until 2011. When they sold their ranch, Larry's parents moved to Cold Lake, Alberta. Debbie and Larry built a new house in the Bonnyville, Alberta area and moved there. Today Debbie is employed by Notre Dame High School in Bonnyville, a job that she loves.

Larry and Deb like to camp and do water sports. They have property at the lake and have built a beautiful cabin for future days. Their two children, Carson and Marcy, also have property at that lake.

Carson married Alana Journault from St Paul, Alberta. They have two daughters, Brooklyn Jayda and Kyra Mae. Carson is an electrician, and they live in Edmonton Alberta. Alana works for the city of Edmonton, a job she's had since high school. The Hempel families all like their sports and enjoy attending games.

Marcy is a physical therapist and works in Bonnyville, Alberta. She married Chad Bordeleau. Chad is a plumber. They have two children: Haily Jae and Cali Bryn. Their home is in Bonnyville, Alberta, near Debbie and Larry's home.

Lance James Burge was the last boy born into this large family. He and Laura are the last set of twins. Lance, as the youngest boy, has always been babied and given more than any of the other boys. As a young lad, his brothers bought him a bike. He only had to share with his twin sister and a younger sister, Josie. They rode his bike when and if Lance said they could ride.

When Lance and Laura were two years old, our family moved about five kilometres closer to the highway. They boarded the school bus below the hill. They never experienced that 1.5 kilometre walk in the rain or the cold weather.

Laura has always looked out for Lance. At school she would carry his lunch box and do his home work too. Lance and Laura were always close to one another; they married cousins in Cherry Grove, Alberta. Today they live about five kilometres apart. Lance married Susan Somers of Cherry Grove, and they live in Susan's old stomping grounds. Susan works at the Cold Lake air base and is a manager of the cleaners there. She goes to work early each weekday. Susan is a great person who often hosts the Burge reunions. Her blue eyes, pinkish skin, and her gentle voice is an asset. She supports my brother, Lance in all their endeavours. They live on their small farm in Cherry Grove. Susan and Lance are a joy to visit.

As a teenager, Lance liked to ride his bike to town. He went to town and met up with some friends. We know how kids can bring out the worst in each other. The town had poured some concrete sidewalks in front of the credit union. This appeared to be the perfect place to leave a mark. Each boy ran across the wet cement. The next morning the policemen came to our house. They asked if Lance had been in town. Lance said, "Yes I was."

The officer asked to see his shoes. Lance eagerly showed his shoes to the officer to be checked for concrete. Lance was confident that they would not find any concrete on his shoes. The officer was surprised, but there was not any evidence of Lance being guilty. The officer left without any further questions.

Mom asked Lance, "Are you guilty of leaving your footsteps in the concrete?"

Lance knew better than to lie to Mom and admitted that he was guilty. Lance showed Mom *her* shoes. They were heavy with cement. Lance needed to remove that dried on cement.

It seemed that Lance often wiggled his way out of trouble.

Lance helped my husband, Lloyd in haying time. Lance caught his finger in the sickle mower and cut the end of his finger off. I remember driving Lance and his finger to the hospital in Goodsoil. The highway was under construction and so rough. It seemed to take a long time to get to the hospital. The doctor sewed the finger back on, but the finger never reattached and the doctor took it off at the first knuckle.

Lance quit school at a young age. He said that he didn't need to know anything more about ancient history or outer space; anyway, the government isn't going to let anybody in Canada starve. Lance has made his way too. Lance has worked at many jobs, including on the rigs and pipeline and operating heavy equipment. He owns his backhoe today, and he digs in sewers around his area. The local people count on him to help plan the "Little Britches" Rodeo in Cherry Grove.

Fun often comes before work for Lance. It's often at Lance's house that we have a potluck supper in the summer time when friends or family show up on short notice. His yard is big and beautiful. Lance and Susan are accommodating to us all.

They have one disabled child named Randy. Randy has a muscle disease that is destroying his ability to walk. He lives in their basement. Randy loves to go fishing and spends some time on the computer. Randy has a girl friend.

Laura Kathleen Burge is Lance's twin sister. Laura is soft spoken and often is not heard among our family gatherings because of it. Laura was a happy child and covered for Lance when he was in trouble. Laura is always there for her kids.

Mom's diary told me this about the two-year-old twins: Laura was just talking when she came into the house and said, "Baby town." Mom looked for Lance and understood what Laura was telling her. Lance was in the cart when Dad left to go to town. Mom ran after the tractor, but couldn't catch Dad. She crossed the meadow and ran down the highway. A car stopped for her, and when he heard Mom's story, he picked her up and they were able to catch the tractor and stop Dad. Lance was still bouncing in the cart. Dad looked embarrassed, as Mom retrieved Lance. He was not hurt. Mom didn't remember how her and Lance got home.

Laura is easygoing and able to sleep anywhere. One day, Laura was lost. Nioma ran to tell Mom and the older children searched for her. There seemed to be many areas where she might have wandered off. The toilet was behind the house, the barn yard was in the west, and the garden was east of the house. Dad had used a plough to work some land south of the house. I remember the large furrows about 20 centimetres deep. Mom and the older kids ran frantically about in search of Laura. Laura was found asleep in one of the furrows that the plough had made. I guess Laura found a warm place to sleep, as she listened to her siblings play.

Mom was so thankful that she had dressed Laura in a red shirt that morning. That red shirt was easily seen when we walked toward the new field. What a relief to find her. Laura was picked up and taken into the house to sleep. Laura has never made any ripples unless it was to defend her twin. One day, as Laura and Lance went to feed the chickens and turkeys, Lance was attacked by the turkey tom. He was able to run away, but Laura grabbed that turkey around the neck and didn't let go until the turkey was limp. She had broken the Tom's neck. Lance called Mom, and she came with the axe and butchered the turkey on the spot. Gentle Laura got the nick name "Turkey Killer".

Laura was about six years old when Dad bought one of the country schools to make into our house. The old log house was torn down and the basement hole was dug right along side of the lumber house. One night the dog barked, and Laura went to check to see what "Smokey," the family dog, was barking at. Laura ran into the house and gasped, "The basement, the car, the Indians."

Dad went out outside and saw an old Indian car with six people inside. The front wheels of the car were hung over the basement hole. Everyone inside the car was very still, as they held their breath. The tractor pulled the car away from the hole.

Laura and Lance were always in the same grade. When Lance quit school so did Laura.

As Laura matured, she learned to sew. She worked at a sewing shop in Cold Lake for some time. She said, "I'm tired of hemming men's pants. Is there nobody who is able to make a hem on a pair of pants?" Laura made quilts for her family to display on their beds.

Laura also worked at Subway. He worked the early sift. Laura married Warren Somers. He is a soft-spoken man and never gets involved in other people's problems. He is a family man. His wavy hair, brown eyes, and broad shoulders made him a real "catch" for Laura.

Laura is a devoted wife and mother. Her family is put before most other things. She helps with the family business, keeping the books. Their children all drive trucks, Lindsey too. They haul logs and gravel and have built roads. Laura keeps all the books and tells her grown family, "Be good to me, or I'll cut your wages." I know that Laura is too kind to do it.

Laura and Warren have four children: Cameron, Russell, Andrew, and Lindsey. Cameron is not married. He lives with Laura and Warren.

Russell played hockey with the AAA team and three times he went to Minneapolis with the Northern Alberta Select team. He married Lindsay Krushelnitsky. This marriage didn't last. They had one daughter, Avery. Avery attends the Pierceland School. Russell met Donna, and they have a son named Hudson. They were married in 2014, Lindsay officiated at their wedding.

Andrew married Sabrina Gelowitz. They have three children: Hayden, Boyd and Gabriela.

Lindsey graduated and went to Grand Prairie for her horticultural studies. She has not worked in this field, as she is now a truck driver for the family business. Lindsey married Brian Smith. They have a son named Finlay.

Laura enjoys spending time with her grandchildren and is a built-in babysitter.

Josephine Elizabeth Burge was the last child born in this large family. Josie was welcomed into our family on February 23, 1961. Josie was an eight pound, twelve ounce baby. She is the last sibling and a cherished person. Josie had the advantage of older brothers and sisters to take her places and give her things that the other kids didn't have. Josie wanted to do everything that Laura did. She didn't understand that Laura was about three years older. Josie went everywhere with Mom and Dad because she was not in school yet. One day as Josie travelled with Mom and Dad, she said to Dad, "I'm thirsty and water won't do." I know that the majority of us didn't get pop to drink, but Dad rushed to buy her a pop. When Josie started school, Mom had to be careful not to tell of any plans about her and Dad going places because Josie was sure to be sick in the morning. How smart kids are! Josie may be the baby, but she will stand up and fight to have her say. She said, "Most of my life I was told to sit down and shut up because I didn't know anything because I was too young."

After Josie graduated from Pierceland Central High School, she met her rhinestone cowboy, Jerry L'Heureux.

Jerry is a short man with many stories. He can tell a tale with colourful words and hold your attention and keep you laughing the whole time. His eyes twinkle as he is engrossed in his story. Jerry has dark hair and a witty personality and can talk to everyone. Josie married Jerry in August 1979.

Nelson walked Josie down the aisle on her wedding day. Nelson didn't have a daughter, and Josie's dad was deceased. This was Nelson's big walk with his sister bride.

Josie has worked in the winter months for a caterer and as a short order cook at the ski hill. Jerry is blessed to have Josie's help in all his undertakings. Jerry isn't afraid to try new things. He has bees for honey, cattle for steak, and a gravel pit if you are in need of gravel.

Jerry likes to help others and will put his work on hold to support whoever needs him. Jerry likes to visit, and the coffee pot is always on. Sometimes Jerry forgets about his work and has an extended coffee break and needs to do his chores in the dark.

Jerry is an interesting person and Josie and Jerry have a lot of company, as their home is a fun place to visit. Josie and Jerry have three children: Clinton, Derek, and Mandy.

Clinton is their oldest son; he was born with a disability. He attended school in Cold Lake and now works at Tim Horton's coffee shop. His job is very important to him. Clinton is able to share a home with another boy. They have some help to get their meals and with the cleaning. Josie takes Clinton home for the weekends.

Derek graduated from high school and is now a heavy duty mechanic. He met Jennifer Hayward, and they have two sons, Riley and Landon. They live on acreage in Cold Lake and visit the home farm often.

Jennifer loves all animals. She drives school bus for the Cold Lake area. She is a tall, slim girl with a Barbie doll body. Her eyes are brown to accent her golden hair.

Mandy also graduated in Cold Lake. She went on to college and became a power engineer. She isn't married at this point. Mandy works in Cold Lake. Mandy is a farm girl and loves the outdoors. As a young girl, she enjoyed gymkhanas with her horse Pepper. It's a big outing to float down the river in late August, have a wiener roast, and relax along the riverbank. Mandy is a fun- loving girl and can entertain anybody who drops in for coffee or tea.

Mandy was bridesmaid for her cousin, Lindsey. She said, "The hardest part was to act like a lady and wear a fancy dress and high heels."

And Josie was my last sibling to write about.

Mom saw yesterday, and now she looks forward to tomorrow, as her life continues with blessings full of children, grandchildren, great and great great grandchildren. I dedicate this book to my mother who lived a hard, but satisfying life. The many sacrifices she made allowed her family to grow and find their place in this world. Thanks mom and all my siblings who helped me to find a life full of action, joy, love, and peace. I plan to continue to move ahead. And accept this wonderful life full of all the unseen changes. I am at peace with my awesome life, but I know , as I flip the page to another day, a new episode will begin. I want to hold onto each chapter with joy, and I ask God to continue to guide me until I meet him face to face in eternity.

Mom said, "All my children are good, efficient people and take responsibility in their families. I guess I must have done something right when I raised them." Yes Mom, you did well!

I wish to thank my sister Debbie Hemple, my friend Chris wild, and my daughter Angie, for the help and inspiration that they gave me as I put my words unto paper. My big family accepted the opportunity when they appeared; we kept our minds and hearts open, and we did not pull down the shades, but embraced all issues, as they appeared. Each of us has made our own mark, as we live in a wonderful life full of changes. I acknowledge and accept each of my siblings for who they have become.

The End

Previously published articles include:

"Jack's big Feet", *Grainews, 2013*

"House with a Heart", *Alberta Trappers,* 2013

"The Auction Sale", *The Story Teller,* 2013

"Prayer of Gratitude", *Seniors Paper,* 2013

"Light my Lamp," *Insight,* 2014

"My Grandson", Poetry Institute of Canada, 2014

"The shoe horn stood in grandma's kitchen", *Seniors Paper,* 2017

"A former teacher celebrates with her students on their 80th birthdays"

Printed in Canada